D0963582

Matthew Polly is an award-winning travel writer for *Slate*. A Princeton University graduate and Rhodes Scholar, his work has also appeared in *Esquire*, *Playboy*, and *The Nation*. He lives in New York City.

AMERICAN SHAOLIN

FLYING KICKS, BUDDHIST MONKS,
AND THE LEGEND OF IRON CROTCH:
AN ODYSSEY IN THE NEW CHINA

MATTHEW POLLY

GOTHAM
BOOKS

GOTHAM BOOKS
Published by Penguin Group (USA) Inc.
375 Hudson Street, New York, New York 10014, U.S.A.

Penguin Group (Canada), 90 Eglinton Avenue East, Suite 700, Toronto, Ontario, Canada M4P 2Y3 (a division of Pearson Penguin Canada Inc.); Penguin Books Ltd, 80 Strand, London WC2R 0RL, England; Penguin Ireland, 25 St Stephen's Green, Dublin 2, Ireland (a division of Penguin Books Ltd); Penguin Group (Australia), 250 Camberwell Road, Camberwell, Victoria 3124, Australia (a division of Pearson Australia Group Pty Ltd); Penguin Books India Pvt Ltd, 11 Community Centre, Panchsheel Park, New Delhi–110 017, India; Penguin Group (NZ), 67 Apollo Drive, Rosedale, North Shore 0632, Auckland, New Zealand (a division of Pearson New Zealand Ltd); Penguin Books (South Africa) (Pty) Ltd, 24 Sturdee Avenue, Rosebank, Johannesburg 2196, South Africa

Penguin Books Ltd, Registered Offices: 80 Strand, London WC2R 0RL, England

Published by Gotham Books, a member of Penguin Group (USA) Inc.

Previously published as a Gotham Books hardcover edition, February 2007

First trade paperback printing, January 2008

1   3   5   7   9   10   8   6   4   2

Gotham Books and the skyscraper logo are trademarks of Penguin Group (USA) Inc.

The Library of Congress has cataloged the hardcover edition as follows:
Polly, Matthew.
American Shaolin : flying kicks, buddhist monks, and the legend of iron crotch : an odyssey in the new China / Matthew Polly.
p.   cm.
ISBN: 978-1-592-40262-5 (hardcover)   ISBN: 978-1-592-40337-0 (paperback)
1. Martial arts—China. 2. Shao lin si (Dengfeng Xian, China) 3. Polly, Matthew. I. Title.
GV1100.7.A2P65   2006
796.815'5—dc22   2006025384

Printed in the United States of America
Set in ITC Caslon 224
Designed by Sabrina Bowers

For my teachers

CONTENTS

A NOTE ON SPELLING AND PRONUNCIATION

While there are several arguably superior systems for the romanization of the Chinese language, *pinyin* is the approved system of the People's Republic of China and most international publications. It is therefore used throughout this text with two exceptions. The first is popular English spellings of proper names and places like Confucius (*Kong fuzi*), Hong Kong (*Xianggang*), and Canton (*Guangdong*). Second, while most American dictionaries spell "kung fu" as two words, I reduced it to one, "kungfu," because I didn't want thousands of orphaned "fu"s populating the pages of my book with no "ck"s to keep them company.

Pinyin's system of spelling does not always correspond to standard English pronunciation. To help the Western reader, here are a few of the major differences. The letter "q" sounds like "ch," so Monk Deqing's name is pronounced De*ch*ing. The letter "x" sounds like "sh," so Deng Xiaoping's name is pronounced Deng *Sh*aoping. The letters "zh" sound like a "j" combined with a "ch," so the city of Zheng Zhou is pronounced *Jh*eng *Jh*oe.

AMERICAN
SHAOLIN

"Until a man is twenty-five, he still thinks, every so often, that under the right circumstances he could be the baddest motherfucker in the world. If I moved to a martial arts monastery in China and studied real hard for ten years. If I just dropped out and devoted my life to being bad."

—*NEAL STEPHENSON*, SNOW CRASH

吃亏学乖代价高，
笨汉非此学不到。

"To suffer and learn a lesson, one pays a high price, but a fool can't learn any other way."

—*TRADITIONAL CHINESE PROVERB*

PROLOGUE

July 1993

低棋也有神仙着。

"A poor chess player can still make a remarkable move."

—*WANG YINGGUI*, LIU NAN SUI BI

It had been a calm night at the Shaolin Temple before the fight started.

A French photojournalist named Pierre was throwing a small banquet at the Shaolin Wushu Center's restaurant for several of the martial monks and Shaolin's "expat community," which consisted of two Norwegians who were visiting for the week and Shaolin's two American students, John Lee and myself. Pierre had been assigned to take photos of the Shaolin monks for a French magazine, and I had arranged for my friends and instructors Monk Deqing, Monk Cheng Hao, and Coach Yan to pose for him. The session had gone so well that Pierre had invited us all to dinner.

We were seated around a large table in the middle of the restaurant, which was built by the government and reflected the Communist Party's taste in architecture: oversize, poorly constructed, and rectangular. Maoist aesthetics are a tyranny of straight lines. The restaurant had the dimensions of a high school basketball gymnasium and was only three years old, but already rundown. It was usually only filled at lunch when droves of tourists made day-trips to visit the Shaolin Temple, famous throughout the world as the birthplace of both Zen Buddhism and the martial arts. The only other guests that night were a group of six Chinese men sitting at a banquet table a hundred feet away. A dozen waitresses were lounging around arguing with each other about who had breakfast duty the next morning.

We had finished the toasting phase of the banquet, where much thanks is given and much *baijiu* is choked down. (*Baijiu* is Chinese rice liquor that tastes and affects the digestive system like a combination of sake, moonshine, and Liquid Drano.) We were just settling into the main course when the waitress who was serving the other table came over and whispered something to Deqing and Coach Yan.

Deqing's face immediately went red with rage. He and I had become close friends over the last nine months of my stay, so I was used to his mood swings. But I had never before seen him this angry.

"He really said he wants a *qie cuo*?" Deqing asked, gripping his glass so tightly I though he might shatter it. "Challenge match?"

"Which one is he?" Coach Yan asked.

The waitress pointed to the other table. One of the men raised his cup in a toast. He was big for a Chinese man, maybe six feet tall and 180 pounds. He was wearing thick spectacles, which was also unusual in rural China.

"His name is Master Wu," the waitress said. "He says he is a kungfu master from Tianjin. Those are his disciples with him."

"*Tai bu gei women mianzi*," Deqing said with disdain. "So not giving us face."

As Deqing continued to rant, Pierre, who did not speak Chinese, asked me in English, "What is happening?"

"The man at the other table, Master Wu, has requested a *qie cuo*—a challenge match," I said. "He wants to fight Shaolin's champion to see whose style and skill is superior."

"Why are the monks so angry?" Pierre asked. "They are kungfu masters. Isn't this what they do?"

"Almost never," I said. "Mostly they train, teach the occasional foreigner, and perform for tourists. Challenge matches are infrequent. I've only seen one. It is considered incredibly rude to walk into someone else's school and offer an open challenge. It's contemptuous."

"I will fight him," Deqing continued. "I will beat him to death!"

Coach Yan held up his hand. "Let me think for a moment."

Coach Yan was as calculating as Deqing was spontaneous. At age twenty-five, he was also older than the nineteen-year-old Deqing and his superior at the temple, so Deqing fell silent. Coach Yan had the perfect face for a kungfu movie villain, a kind of striking ugliness. His eyebrows slashed upward, his cheekbones punched out from his face, and his dark skin was pocked with acne scars. I liked him. But I was careful around him.

Or at least I was until that night.

Coach Yan was staring off into the near distance. He had Shaolin's honor to consider. This was further complicated by the presence of the French journalist. The Shaolin monks had been touring Europe off and on over the last three years and had become extremely popular there. Pierre's photo-essay would help them considerably, so Coach Yan had to consider Shaolin's international reputation.

Watching Deqing, my friend and teacher, stew in his rage made me feel like I had to say something.

"I will fight him," I offered.

I didn't mean it, of course. I was just being polite, the way you are supposed to be polite in Chinese, whether you are sincere or not. It was a gesture to show my fellowship, my team spirit. And I knew there was no way Coach Yan would take up my offer. Shaolin was crawling with expert fighters in their prime who had trained for a decade or longer. Even after nine months of training, I was a beginner at best. Besides, I was *laowai*—literally "old outsider"—a polite term for white foreigners.

After making my faux offer, I waved the waitress over to order another round of *baijiu*.

I turned to see Coach Yan looking at me with a slight smirk.

"*Bao Mosi,*" Coach Yan said, using my full Chinese name, *Mosi* (Matthew) and *Bao* (Polly), "will fight him first."

Deqing was incredulous.

"He cannot fight him first," he protested. "I am his teacher. I will fight first."

What he didn't say, but which was implicit, was that Deqing considered himself to be Shaolin's best martial artist (almost everyone else did as well). Coach Yan was asking the team's star player to step aside for a fourth-string benchwarmer.

The panic must have been obvious on my face, because Coach Yan's smirk widened ever so slightly as he responded. "No, the *laowai* will fight him first."

Deqing wasn't ready to give in yet.

"You cannot let him fight first. What if he loses? This is a matter of Shaolin's reputation, Shaolin's face."

Coach Yan finished another shot of *baijiu*.

"I am thinking of Shaolin's face. If the *laowai* loses, no face is lost, because everyone knows that *laowai* are no good at kungfu. And we will have had a chance to study this stupid egg's fighting style. Then you'll have an easier time beating him. But if the *laowai* wins, then Shaolin will gain much face. It will demonstrate that the Shaolin Temple is so great that even its *laowai* disciples can beat a Chinese master of another style."

As they continued the debate, I felt an overwhelming fear grip me in the gut and squeeze like a hunter field-dressing his kill. I stood up with every intention of fleeing, until I saw that the entire table was looking at me.

"I will be back in a moment. I need to use the restroom." I waved halfheartedly at my glass. "Too much booze."

Willing myself not to run, I sauntered as nonchalantly as possible to the outhouse in back, the concrete hole-in-the-ground cesspit standard in rural China. I crouched inside that box for several minutes, my mind racing through various possibilities for escaping the situation. *Fake an injury? Disappear?* Unfortunately, there were none that did not involve a tremendous personal loss of face. And then there was my teachers' loss of face to consider. Although I had been in China less than a year, their value system had already sunk in too deep for me to actually back down.

I walked back to the table holding on to the hope that maybe Coach Yan had changed his mind.

He had not.

"*Bao Mosi*, it is decided," Coach Yan said, an anticipatory glee in his eyes. "You will fight Master Wu in the training hall in fifteen minutes."

"Fifteen minutes?"

"Let's go," Coach Yan said.

Built by the Henan provincial government as a tourism center in 1989, the Shaolin Wushu Center consisted of the restaurant, a fleabag hotel for tourists, a two-story apartment building for staff, and the main complex, which contained some offices, two training halls for the students, and a performance hall where the tourists paid to see the Shaolin monks display their talents. In a daze, I walked alongside Deqing down the steps to the main complex. For moral support, he quoted his favorite martial arts maxim to me: "I do not fear the 10,000 kicks you have practiced once; I fear the one kick you have practiced 10,000 times."

Before I entered the training hall I could hear the crowd noise. I walked in to find that in a matter of minutes word had spread about the challenge match, and the hall was jammed with employees of the Wushu Center, Shaolin monks, and many of the peasants who worked in the village—a remarkably quick turnout for a community without phones. This was spectacle of a serious order: a foreigner in a *qie cuo* match with a northern master. The crowd was electric. They smelled blood.

Master Wu was conferring with his students in one corner of the training hall, which was dominated by a cracked wall mirror and a huge green performance mat. I noticed that the Norwegians had brought their extensive video equipment and were setting up a tripod. There was no way I was going to allow them to make a permanent record of my likely ass-whooping. I had visions of it making the rounds of Europe's martial arts community: *La Défaite de l'Américain*. So I explained to them in English that it was considered rude in China to film a challenge match, and they put their cameras away. I suppose it was a good sign that I still had enough of my wits about me to lie.

Handling Pierre was not nearly as easy. A violence junkie, he had come to Shaolin as a break from his previous assignment as a war photographer in Serbia and Kosovo. Wound several turns of the screw too tight, Pierre's favorite story was about how he had once shattered the glass showcase of a rude Hong Kong merchant with his steel-tipped army boots. He was pointing at these same boots now as he tried to convince me to persuade the monks to let him fight Master Wu in my place.

"Matt, I grab this guy by the neck and bring his face to my knee," Pierre said as he slapped his knee. "Then, I kick him with these boots. You see these boots. I kick him, right up the ass."

I tried to ignore him as I stretched my cramped legs.

"You tell them I fight him," he said. "I kick him with these boots. You see the tips. Up his ass."

"Pierre, you're not a student here," I said. "You are not a disciple of Shaolin. I am. They won't let you fight him."

Unfortunately, this was true. My level of panic was rising, and I was now feeling light-headed. There was a buzzing in my ears that wouldn't go away.

"But I kick him with this boot," he continued, "my boot right up his ass."

"Pierre, it's not possible, and I need to get ready."

"But I kick him—"

I turned to John Lee, looking for some American backup in dealing with this nutty Frenchman.

John was still built like the high school linebacker he had been a year earlier. He stuck his head with its baseball cap turned backward between Pierre's face and mine. Then he slid his muscled frame between us and said with his wide, easygoing, frat-boy smile, "Pierre, dude, chill, bro."

I looked over to the other end of the room to see Coach Yan negotiating with Master Wu. I couldn't hear what they were saying, but I could see Master Wu motioning to his eyeglasses and shaking his head.

Coach Yan walked over to me.

"Do you know what a challenge match is?" he asked.

I wobbled my head side-to-side with uncertainty.

"*Chabuduo*," I said. "More or less."

"A challenge match has rules," he said, tipping his head back at Master Wu and rolling his eyes in disgust.

Coach Yan's face was tight with rage, his body tense and ready to lash out. I tried not to look him straight in the eye. Of all the monks, Coach Yan was the most in touch with his inner monster— especially if less than totally sober—and was the most likely to crack a bottle over your head if you made the mistake of offending him. His mean streak wasn't wide, but it was deep.

He stepped closer and lowered his voice so only I could hear him.

"Fuck his mother," he snarled. "He came into our house and challenged us. *Tai bu gei women mianzi!* This fight has no rules! I want you to beat him to the ground. You hear me? To the ground."

Coach Yan stepped back, switching into the role of referee, and waved with both hands for the combatants to approach. Master Wu and I walked out into the center of the room, stopping about five feet from each other.

Master Wu shifted into a cat stance, his weight largely on his right foot, his left foot resting lightly in front, a strong defensive position. His hands slowly circled in front of his body like a water-wheel. His dark eyes locked onto me from behind his thick glasses.

I moved into the standard Chinese kickboxing opening stance— my body at a forty-five-degree angle to Master Wu with my left leg forward, my weight balanced about 40/60 between my front leg and my back, my left fist forward, my right fist up protecting my chin. I was trying to relax my body. It was an exercise in force of will to get myself to stop bouncing on my toes. Bouncing is seen as a sign of nervousness.

Wu was heavier and stronger than I was, with the kind of stocky frame common to farmers, but I was taller and had the longer reach. That was going to be crucial because by settling into a defensive stance he clearly had no intention of attacking first.

TALE OF THE TAPE

"White Hope" Polly		"Master of Tianjin" Wu
21	Age	30ish
6′ 3″	Height	5′ 10″
27.5″	Arm Length	25″
155	Weight	185 or so

I tried to clear my head. I had sparred extensively since arriving at Shaolin, but this was the first real fight—street clothes, no rules—that I had ever been in.

Coach Yan clapped his hands to indicate the start of the challenge match, then stepped away. He wasn't going to referee after all. We were on our own.

BOOK ONE

WANDERER

September 1992

人到难处才见心。

"It is only when a person gets into difficulty that
one can truly see his heart."

—*TRADITIONAL CHINESE PROVERB*

1

THE FIRST STEP

Some people have an inner voice. I have an inner to-do list. And since I'm a glass-half-empty type of guy, my list is entitled "Things That Are Wrong With Matt." Whenever I am in danger of feeling too good about myself, that list starts flashing in my head.

When I was fifteen the list read:

THINGS THAT ARE WRONG WITH MATT

1. Ignorant
2. Cowardly
3. Still a boy/not a man
4. Unattractive to the opposite sex
5. Spiritually confused

"Ignorant" was at the top of the list because that summer I had picked up a copy of *The New York Review of Books* at the local Borders in my hometown of Topeka, Kansas, and tried to read it. Even with a dictionary I couldn't make heads or tails of it. I didn't catch the references, comprehend the contexts, or understand the meaning of the foreign phrases like *fin de siècle*, which popped up constantly in almost every review. I'd discovered there was this entire intellectual world where people were talking to each other above my head, and it bothered me.

I examined the bios of the authors. They were mostly professors from elite universities. So I went back to Borders and bought all the books with titles like *How to Write a Winning College Essay*,

Applying to the Ivy League, How to Cram for the SAT. I did every-thing they advised. I crammed all summer. I read *War and Peace* and wrote an essay on it. When I went back to school that fall, I started the Spanish club at my high school so I could be president and demonstrate leadership potential.

It worked. They let me into Princeton.

During the fall of my junior year of college, I was in a Cornel West philosophy seminar and had just finished a little soliloquy expounding on the influence of Nietzsche on Heidegger when I re-alized I actually understood what I was saying. As I finished, I leaned back in my chair with pride, and the list flashed in my head.

THINGS THAT ARE WRONG WITH MATT

1. ~~Ignorant~~
2. Cowardly
3. Still a boy/not a man
4. Unattractive to the opposite sex
5. Spiritually confused

I was suffused with the sweet glow of success. I had eliminated number one and couldn't have been happier. I was only a junior, but in my head I was done with college. It had served its purpose.

The feeling lasted for a good couple of weeks or so, and then the list started flashing again.

THINGS THAT ARE WRONG WITH MATT

1. Cowardly
2. Still a boy/not a man
3. Unattractive to the opposite sex
4. Spiritually confused

I was back to my slightly depressed baseline. But now there was hope. I'd found a way to happiness. All I had to do was eliminate the rest of the items on the list, and I'd be blissful forever.

While my primary focus since starting college had been the elimination of "ignorance," I had also been working on "cowardly," which had been the original chart-topper on my list ever since grade school. I had been taking kungfu classes since freshman year, because when I was nine years old I had seen a rerun of David Carradine's *Kung Fu* and was never the same again. Carradine's character Caine, the half-Asian Shaolin martial monk who wandered the Old West righting wrongs, seemed to be as strange and helpless as I felt, but yet was a total badass. Whenever I'd reread my favorite fantasy novels—*The Lord of the Rings* and the *Dune* series—I would rewrite them in my head with myself as the hero's sidekick. And I always had super Shaolin kungfu powers.

My obsession with kungfu had led to an interest in Chinese culture. In my sophomore year, I took a course on the intellectual history of China and fell in love with the Taoist philosopher Chuang-tzu. He was the only religious thinker I'd read who had a sense of humor and took delight in the absurdity of the universe. His teachings later influenced the creation of Chan Buddhism (Zen in Japanese), and that soon became another passion of mine. I was so earnestly obsessed I even signed up for Chinese classes in order to read Chuang-tzu and other Zen texts in the original language.

But with all the reading and language study, I hadn't had much time to devote to kungfu, and by the spring of my junior year I felt no more able to defend myself after three years of study than when I began. My heart still trembled when I felt physically threatened. And my first instinct whenever I heard a voice raised in anger was to look for the exit. I was all flight and no fight.

So I decided to apply the same method to eliminating "cowardly" from my list as I had "ignorant." I had attended a venerable institution that specialized in educating ignorant young minds, and after several years of hard work, I no longer felt like an idiot. Now all I needed was to find a venerable institution that specialized in turning scrawny, ninety-eight-pound weaklings like me into badasses. And if it was also a religious institution, then maybe I'd be able to eliminate "spiritually confused" in the process.

It was around this point, through some fateful realignment of the cosmos, that I happened to read Mark Salzman's memoir *Iron and Silk*, which tells the story of a Yale graduate who studies martial arts with a kungfu master in China, and got a bright idea.

I went to Professor Gu, who was the only professor I knew from mainland China.

"I want to go to China and learn about kungfu and Zen Buddhism," I said in Chinese.

He looked at me seriously and asked, "Do you want to learn really real kungfu or just have some fun?"

"I want to learn really real kungfu, of course."

"Are you afraid to *chi ku*?" Professor Gu asked. "Eat bitter?"

It was Chinese slang for "suffer."

"No," I lied, unable to keep from smiling. The same question had been put to Salzman when he was studying kungfu in China, and he had given the same response.

"Then you must go to the Shaolin Temple," he said.

He continued to speak about how hard it was to study kungfu and how diligent I would have to be, but I wasn't listening anymore. As soon as he said "Shaolin" I was sold.

As the birthplace of Zen Buddhism and kungfu, Shaolin was, basically, the father and mother of both my obsessions. But I hadn't believed it was real. It had always seemed like something from the mythical past, the Camelot of martial arts. Hearing that the Shaolin Temple actually existed in the present day was like destiny tapping me on the shoulder. I was absolutely certain it was the right place to go for my training.

Unfortunately, no one but Professor Gu and I thought this adventure was a good idea. My friends assumed this was one of my flights of fancy, and that I'd change my mind at the last minute. My other professors suspected it was a covert cry for help. And when I returned to Kansas at the end of the school year and told my parents of my plans, they were beside themselves.

They had good reason to be worried. This was 1992, before China had become a cover story for *Time* and *Newsweek* as the next superpower, before China's wealth and development had advanced far enough to be obvious to the rest of the world. In 1992, the international image of China was that of an impoverished country run by Communists who had only three years earlier slaughtered hundreds of unarmed democracy protestors in Tiananmen Square. As far as the world was concerned, China was

North Korea with a larger population, food, and slightly better hairdos.

My mother, who puts the welfare of her children above all else, cried.

"What will happen to you?" she asked. "They kill boys just your age."

"They don't kill foreigners."

"What if they put you in prison, torture you, and make you sign confessions?"

"Mom, that was Vietnam."

"We don't know anyone in China to help get you out. You'd be stuck there, forever!"

At first my father tried to reason with me, because as a doctor he prides himself on being a rationalist. Given the woman he married, it's really his only option.

"I was talking to some of the Chinese surgeons at the hospital," he told me one day. "And they say China isn't safe."

"Of course they say that. They're Taiwanese. It's like asking Miami Cubans what they think of Fidel Castro."

"They say there is a lot of Buddhism and kungfu instruction in Taiwan."

"Yes," I said. "But it's not Shaolin."

"This is insanity. You don't even know where the Shaolin Temple is."

He had a point. Professor Gu did not know where it was. None of the travel books about China had its location. Officials at the Chinese embassy had hung up on me three times when I put the question to them. And since Al Gore had yet to invent the Internet, I couldn't search for "Shaolin." (Today it takes less than five seconds to find its location on Google.)

To be fair, I probably could have found the location if I had really applied myself to the problem, but for me the mystery of Shaolin's location was part of the excitement. I had decided to fly to China and ask around until I found someone who knew the answer. That's the way quest heroes did it in the fantasy novels I favored. Maybe I'd chance upon an old crone who'd give me a magical artifact to help me on my journey.

"I don't understand why you won't go to Taiwan," my father continued. "You could teach English."

"Anybody can go to Taiwan and teach English. That doesn't prove anything."

"But how are you going to make any money if you go to a country that is too poor to pay you to teach English?"

"I'm not going to teach. How would I get any good at kungfu if I taught English eight hours a day?"

His patience finally exhausted, he laid down the gauntlet.

"Then I don't see how you're going to pay for the trip," he said. "Because I won't."

"There's money in my college fund."

"That's my money."

"But it's in my name," I said, looking down at the floor.

I knew I was crossing the Rubicon with him.

My father didn't talk to me for a long time after that. Every once in a while over the next few days I'd catch him staring at me with that look of primal male suspicion: *Is this really my son?*

I can't say I blame him. My father is about as decent, honest, and hardworking as it's possible for a man to be. He had grown up poor and put himself through college and medical school so that his children could have a better life. And after all this expense and sacrifice, after sending off his Catholic, Ayn Rand–reading, science and math geek of a son to one of America's finest institutions of higher learning, what did he receive back three years later? A liberal, a religious studies major (not premed!), and a Buddhist. It was enough to break any God-fearing, Reagan-loving father's heart.

I wanted to explain it all to him, but I was too ashamed. How could I tell my father that I had been the boy that bullies loved to hate, that along with tetherball and four-square, "beating the shit out of Matt" had been an unofficial playground activity, that I had never once stood up for myself and fought back, that even years later when one would have expected any normal person to have grown out of it I still shook like some abused Pavlovian dog whenever a voice was raised in anger, that the playground still infected my dreams, that I was tired of running, that I couldn't live with myself as I was? No, it was better to let him think I was some spoiled, ungrateful little shit than a coward.

I requested a leave of absence from Princeton, ostensibly to re-search my senior thesis for a year, and began making preparations for my journey.

On the first day of September, my mother took me to the Kansas City airport by herself. She was crying as I stepped onto the plane.

I was smiling with eager anticipation.

2

LOST IN
TRANSPLANTATION

It was a shock to discover that after three years of studying Mandarin in college I could not actually speak Chinese. I had been pretty certain I could right up until the moment I landed in Beijing and caught a cab at the airport.

I'd handed the cabbie a little card that read GREAT WALL SHERATON in English and Chinese and said in what I thought was Chinese, "I go there." From that moment on, he talked to me nonstop in a language I did not recognize. I tried to interrupt him.

"I am sorry," I said. "My Chinese speaking level is not very high. Please, could you speak more slowly?"

But he didn't seem to hear me, so I tried to interrupt him again. And again he ignored me. He kept on rambling, and I kept on not understanding.

I panicked, suddenly losing all sense of the outside world. I didn't notice the brand-new, perfectly straight highway the government had recently built to connect the city with the airport. I barely noticed the tollbooth, another new installation. I no longer even heard my driver, who would not stop speaking. All I could hear was a voice inside my head quietly cursing, *you stupid shit*, over and over again.

It had been twenty-six hours since I stepped onto the plane in Kansas City. The jet lag was affecting me like extremely strong pot—my body felt dense and heavy, my mind was disoriented and paranoid. *Where was I? Was this China? Did I get on the wrong connecting flight in Narita?*

I rolled down the window. I felt like throwing up.

The cab pulled beneath an underpass. A wooden wagon driven by an oxen and filled with scrap metal pulled to a stop beside my cab as the light turned red. At the last moment a black Mercedes with tinted glass whipped around and in front of the wagon. (I would soon learn this was the sedan of choice for high-ranking government officials.) Angered by the car's exhaust, one of the oxen head-butted the back of the Mercedes. The driver of the Mercedes and the peasant driving the wagon were still shouting at each other when the light turned green and we pulled away.

After dodging the traffic, we turned into a street that took us through an outer wall and delivered me to the entrance of the Great Wall Sheraton. As I paid my fare and hopped out of the car, the red-coated, gold-buttoned doorman at the Great Wall Sheraton said to me in stilted English, "Wurcome."

"Do you speak Chinese?" I asked him in Mandarin.

"Your Chinese is very good," he said to me in Mandarin with a Beijing accent—heavy on the "r" sounds.

Overwhelmed, I hugged him. After an awkward moment, I let him loose.

As cover, I said, "My driver does not speak Chinese. Why?"

He glanced into the car.

"He is not from Beijing. Probably from the South. Everyone down there speaks a different dialect. I was in Shanghai and didn't understand a word people were saying. But what are we to do? People are now free to move around. It is *luan*," he said. "Chaos."

I had solved my first, unexpected problem. I was in fact in China, and I did know how to speak the language, albeit haltingly and at about a sixth-grade level. The sudden relief I felt was quickly displaced by the daunting task of finding the Shaolin Temple in such a vast country.

As the doorman carried my bags through the marbled lobby of the five-star Sheraton, I asked him, "Do you know where the Shaolin Temple is?"

"Where what is?" he asked.

"Shaolin Temple," I said again, trying to get the tones just right.

Chinese is a tonal language. Words spelled the same way mean different things when pronounced with one of the four different tones: the 1st stays level, the 2nd rises, the 3rd sinks and then rises, and the 4th falls. For example, the sentence "*ma* [1st] *ma* [4th] *ma* [3rd] *ma* [1st]?" means "Did mother curse the horse?" First-year Chinese students either use their heads or their index fingers to try to get the tones right: half the class looks like bobble-head dolls, the other like conductors of a Lilliputian orchestra.

"Where?" he asked again.

I broke down and used my index finger, making a Nike swoosh for the third tone *Shao* (literally "young") and a rising flick for the second tone *lin* (forest). "*Shao* . . . *lin*." Still no comprehension. I tried a different approach.

"You know, kungfu," I said, making some vague punching motions.

"Oh, the Shaolin Temple. You want to study kungfu?" he laughed. "The Shaolin Temple, I am not certain. I think it was destroyed."

My heart dropped.

"Destroyed? What do you mean?"

"It is no longer," he said. "Do you want to visit the Great Wall? I have a friend who is a tour guide."

I stopped in the middle of the lobby. My mind was flying through exit options. The fall semester at Princeton had already started; I'd have to wait until spring semester to reenroll. I'd have to go back to Topeka and live with my parents. And this after we'd had such a big fight over my decision to go. I'd need to find a job to pay the money back. What had I spent so far? $1,400 for the plane ticket. $50 for the visa, $10 for the cab. I'd have to stay at least a day or two, at $110 a night, before I could change my tickets . . .

There was no way I was going back yet. Even if there were nothing left but charred remains, I'd see the Shaolin Temple.

"No, I do not want to see the Great Wall," I told him.

I was still trying to convert my expenditures up until this point into minimum-wage hours when the doorman, who had carried my bags into my room, asked if I wanted to help him convert some of his local currency into dollars.

"My cousin, you understand, she is a very diligent student," he explained. "She has been accepted to a college in America. But all she has is RMB. She needs American dollars. Will you help a friend?"

Appropriately for the country that invented paper money, China had two currencies: the people's money (RMB) and foreign exchange currency (FEC), the only type of money the Bank of China would trade for dollars. While it served various functions, FEC was basically a fiscal prophylactic. It prevented the local populace from catching financial foreign diseases (dollars, yen, francs), which tended to result in a feverish desire to leave the country permanently. Because RMB was nonconvertible, a Chinese millionaire turned into a pauper the moment he stepped out of the country. But this contraceptive method was already breaking down due to the growing number of *laowai* and the size of the black market. To the Chinese, every foreigner was a walking currency exchange. After "Hallo," "Shanja mahnie?" would be the mangled English I'd hear most frequently.

I didn't understand much of this at the time. All I knew was FEC and RMB were supposed to be exchanged at a 1-to-1 rate. The government-run Bank of China was trading FEC for dollars at 5.7 to 1. The doorman, my new friend, was offering RMB for dollars at 6.5 to 1. A great deal. Would $200 be okay?

Certainly.

That afternoon, as I sat staring at CNN in a jet-lagged fog, too tired to fall asleep and too exhausted to move, I was visited by another doorman, a maid, and two midlevel managers, all of whom had similarly remarkable, overachieving relatives in need of dollars for their studies abroad. It was not until several weeks later, after growing suspicious and asking around, that I discovered the black market rate was in fact 8.2 to 1. After traveling China by train in 1986, Paul Theroux would write at length about the Chinese saying, "You can always trick a foreigner." Six years later the Chinese were too savvy to ever use that phrase in my presence, but the attitude hadn't changed. Theroux thought the phrase, as well as being insulting, was inaccurate, but it wasn't in my case. I was the sucker at the table, and I didn't know it yet.

Of course, to be fair to those hotel employees, they still gave me a better rate than the Bank of China. The Chinese have another saying, "A fish stinks from its head."

The next morning I went to Tiananmen Square, the largest public square in the world. It is like a gray, stone version of the National Mall in D.C.—an open center surrounded by the government's memorials to itself. It is bound to the north by Tiananmen Gate, which leads to the Forbidden City and bears a humongous two-story portrait of Mao Zedong as its only ornament—China's Lincoln Memorial. To the west is the Great Hall of the People, which houses the National People's Congress—the Capitol rotunda. To the east is the National History Museum—the Smithsonian.

The last media image I had of China was of that college kid, my age, standing in front of a People's Liberation Army (PLA) tank, a live test of Gandhi's thesis that nonviolent resistance can defeat machine guns, tanks, and army bayonets. Gandhi was wrong that day. I was visiting Tiananmen to pay my respects.

Today Tiananmen was filled with picture-taking mainland Chinese tourists, most of them with a small child in tow. (In 1979 Deng Xiaoping had established a fairly strictly enforced one-child-per-family policy to control population growth.) As I closed my eyes for a moment of silence, I heard a shotgun blast.

I hit the deck. I looked around with my hands covering my head. *Boom!* The shotgun fired again. I located the shooter. It was a Beijing taxi, backfiring.

As I pushed myself to my knees, I found myself face-to-face with a Chinese toddler wearing crotchless pants, which allowed him to tinkle and poop as freely as a pet, his uncircumcised boyhood swinging freely in the breeze. He was staring with concentration as if to determine what species of creature I was—*Biggus nosus*. I smiled. He picked his tiny nose. Scraping myself and what little dignity I had remaining off the stones, I stood up. The boy's parents, rural peasants visiting their capital, were smiling. Wrapped in an army surplus winter coat, the husband pointed his camera at me and raised his eyebrows. I nodded. Then he pointed to the ground, indicating that he wanted to re-create the shot of me on my stomach cowering in fear. I demurred.

I decided to get some directions. I had my *Fodor's China* book with me. I walked over to a police officer (or maybe it was an army officer—it's hard to tell in a police state) and opened the book to the map of China.

"Excuse me, could you tell me where the Shaolin Temple is?" I asked in Mandarin.

He ignored me, staring straight ahead.

"I am sorry. My Chinese is not very good," I said, trying to enunciate clearly. "Could you please tell me where the Shaolin Temple is?"

He didn't flicker. Thinking I was getting the tones wrong again, I pantomimed a few kungfu moves.

"You know kungfu?"

Still no reaction. But the sight of a tall, skinny *laowai* making kungfu strikes next to an army guard gathered a crowd of onlookers, mostly elderly men and women.

"What do you want?" one of the old women with gray streaks through her hair asked in a friendly manner.

They were all smiling at the potential discovery of an amusing anecdote they could tell their friends when they returned home.

I pointed to the map of China and asked, "Do you know where the Shaolin Temple is?"

"*Aiya*," she said. "Wow! The *laowai*'s Chinese is excellent."

"Oh, no, it is inadequate," I said, dropping my head. "Totally inadequate."

"Look, the foreigner is humble," she said, continuing to speak to the rest of the group about me as if I weren't there. They all nodded in agreement and approval.

One of the men agreed by saying, "His Chinese is better than *Dashan*'s."

This started an argument. A woman in the back disagreed, "This *laowai*'s Chinese is good but not quite to *Dashan*'s level."

And so it went for several minutes. I later learned that *Dashan* (big mountain) was the Chinese name of Mark Rowswell, a Canadian, who had come over to teach English in 1988. His Chinese was so perfect, in particular his skill at a traditional form of comedic dialogue rich in puns and allusions called *xiangsheng* (crosstalk), that Chinese television variety shows regularly booked him as a performer and emcee. After his first appearance, he became a national celebrity and his Chinese the gold standard against which every other *laowai*'s Chinese was compared, usually unfavorably. As such, I would soon come to realize *Dashan* was the bane of every expatriate's life.

Finally, I interrupted. "So where is the Shaolin Temple?"

"Oh, it is in Henan," the first woman said, pointing to the center of the map.

A sense of relief washed over me, "So, the Shaolin Temple is there?"

She looked at me pointedly. "In the past it was there. It has been destroyed."

"Are you sure?"

"During the war it was destroyed by the Japanese."

I felt like I'd been punched in the stomach. But before I could turn away another old woman in the crowd came to my rescue.

"What kind of words are you saying? The Shaolin Temple has been rebuilt. My nephew visited it last year."

"No, the Japanese destroyed it," the first woman insisted.

"That was the southern Shaolin Temple in Fujian Province. The northern Shaolin Temple in Henan was rebuilt by the government."

"Grandmother," I asked, showing her the map of China. "How do I get there?"

The woman drew an imaginary line on the map from Beijing to Zheng Zhou, Henan's capital, and said "huoche."

"I am sorry," I said. "I do not know the meaning of that word."

She smiled and made the universal steam-whistle "choo choo" noise, garnering laughter from the crowd.

I thanked her profusely and immediately hailed a cab.

Beijing's streets, the straight, wide avenues connected by a series of concentric ring roads, contained the entire history of human transportation: horses, donkeys, oxen, tractors, trucks, European luxury cars. But on that first visit it was the bicycles that caught my eye, mostly old 1950s paperboy models, gray with baskets in front, a migratory mass that flowed through the traffic in the hundreds, the thousands, swarming pedestrians and cars, moving like a flock of birds. As my cabdriver weaved in and out of the traffic toward my hotel, the groups were so dense that I held my breath every time one of the bicyclists made a sudden move, certain that this would cause a domino crash that would bring down the entire fleet of them, but it never did.

"How long have you been a cabdriver?" I asked when we stalled at a stoplight.

"Hey, your Chinese is excellent."

"No, it is not very good."

"No, no, you speak well. Do you know *Dashan*?"

"I have heard of him."

"He's Canadian. What country are you from?"

"America," I replied.

"America is a good country. Very strong."

"No, it's just average."

"Oh no, it is great. Not like China. China is inadequate. Too backward."

"But you are progressing rapidly," I said.

"Not enough. We'll need fifty years of progress to catch up with America."

"But on the economic front, China's progress is much faster than America's," I said, thinking of the double-digit GDP growth that China had enjoyed over the past decade since Deng's reforms took wing.

"You say the economic aspect," he said, having caught my other meaning. "You don't think the political aspect is progressing?"

"Not after June 4th."

That was the date of the Tiananmen Square massacre.

"Ah," he sighed and went silent.

For the first time, I noticed the laminated mini-portrait of Mao Zedong hanging from his rearview mirror. As it twisted around I saw that the other side had a portrait of Zhou Enlai—a hero of the Communist revolution and the driving figure behind China's rapprochement with the United States in the 1970s.

I waited for a moment, trying to decide whether to press forward. I couldn't get the image of that student standing in front of a tank out of my mind.

"What do you think of what happened?" I asked.

I was expecting him to be either evasive or ill-informed. The Chinese government had put out a lot of propaganda saying that the students had attacked the army first and the army was acting in self-defense. What he said surprised me.

"What I think is those college kids who are supposed to be so smart were really stupid. Fucking college kids."

"What do you mean?"

"What do they know about democracy? What do they know about running the government? In five thousand years of history China has never had democracy. These stupid college kids want a revolution? They want democracy? *Fangpi*!" he spat. "Fart!"

Less than 5 percent of Chinese students attended college in the early 1990s, so they were the elite of the elite, and not always well loved by the rest of the country.

I tried again, "But freedom is good—"

"Freedom? How do we get freedom? Revolution? Revolutions don't bring freedom. They bring *luan*. And what does chaos bring? Starvation. Who starves? Not college kids. The poor starve, that's who."

"But don't you think it would be better to have more political freedom?"

"The government gives us economic openness. The people get richer. In return, we don't bother the government about political openness."

I leaned back in the seat. This wasn't going the way I thought it would.

"Don't you want both?" I asked.

"China has a saying, 'Slowly, slowly go.' Look at Russia. It used to be China's big brother. They told us what to do. Then you Americans went over there and told them to have political and economic openness at the same time. How are they now? Now, Russian girls come to China to work as prostitutes. Now, we are big brother."

"But you don't think it's bad that the army killed its own people?"

"It is a pity," he said and was silent for a moment. Then he tried to explain himself again more slowly and deliberately.

"Look at it this way, China has more than one billion people," he said. "So we have a few less now."

He looked back in the rearview mirror at me. I must have had a look of horror on my face, because a wicked gleeful smile spread across his face. Freaking out the *laowai* was fun.

"You know what would be the best thing for China?" he asked.

"No, I don't," I said, knowing I was being set up.

"Get rid of half the people. That'd be about right. Just take half the people and kill them."

"That wouldn't be too easy," I said, playing along. "How would you choose?"

"I'm glad you asked. I will tell you, my friend," he said, enjoying himself. "China should go to war. Yes, China should go to war with America. And then China should send our soldiers into battle without any weapons."

"China already tried that."

"Really?"

"Yes, during the Korean War."

"Heh, that's right. Which side won?"

I remembered my grandfather telling me stories about how American soldiers on the backs of jeeps would fire into charging PLA units carrying broken broomsticks as their only weapons. The machine gunners would shoot until their barrels melted.

"Neither," I said.

We rode the rest of the way in silence.

Over the next two years I would ask a variety of Chinese people, including some Beijing college students, what they thought about the Tiananmen Square massacre and heard essentially the same response, although usually with less contempt for the protestors. The demonstrations were premature, they told me. China was not ready for democracy. A repressive government was preferable to *luan*.

Luan was the most terror-inducing word in the language, and given the country's history, particularly its twentieth-century history, it probably should be. So the people and the government had come to an implicit social contract: The government (i.e., the Communist Party) would help the people lift themselves out of poverty, and in return, the people would not protest the repressive political power of the government.

And after the people were rich? I would ask. Mostly the Chinese would just shrug, "Who knows?" But I met one businessman who said with a refreshing cynicism, "You can't buy love, but you can buy freedom."

3

SLEEPING BEAUTY

The North Beijing train station was a vivid example of the kind of pervasive poverty the Chinese people were willing to concede their political freedom to escape. It looked like a refugee camp after a war of ethnic cleansing. Actually, a refugee camp looks better, because at least it has Red Cross tents. The lines of waiting travelers spread out of the terminal into the surrounding area for hundreds of yards. Clearly some of the peasants had camped out for days waiting for tickets. Everywhere I looked there were old women, pregnant women, and little kids trying to nap with only a coat or a piece of cardboard between them and the damp stone ground.

I had packed a sleeping bag, in case I would have to camp outside the Shaolin Temple to gain admittance, like Caine did in *Kung Fu*. Faced with the possibility of having to sleep outside the Beijing train station, this entire adventure was beginning to feel nightmarish. I fiddled with the travel pouch holding my passport and return airplane ticket. I went to an old peasant woman, who looked to be at the back of the line, and asked, "Should I wait behind you?"

"No," she said and pointed to the other end of the hall. "*Laowai* over there."

I cut through tangled lines until I finally was able to squeeze inside the building. The station was a vast gothic structure with huge arched ceilings. There were several dozen ticketing booths, each of which had lines that stretched beyond the building. I asked a young man where I should go to buy a ticket to Zheng Zhou, thinking that maybe the lines were divided by geographical region.

He pointed across the hall. I glanced above him and saw for the first time that there were two ticket windows at the far end with only a few people standing in front of them. I bumped, jostled, and apologized my way through twenty-plus lines until I broke free to these windows at the end. I knew I was in the right place because the only people in these lines were foreign backpackers like me.

It turned out that the lines were divided by the three ways to travel by train in China. The peasants were in line for hard seats, the cheapest tickets. There was no assigned seating: They were crushed into train cars with wooden benches where they had to press for a seat. Many chose to sit on their bags in the aisles. Tickets in the next class were for hard beds, which were individually assigned. These were a series of open rooms with six beds, stacked three high on either wall. Tickets in the highest class were for soft beds, the very rough equivalent of sleeper cars in America or Europe: private rooms with only four beds. These booths at the end sold only soft-bed tickets, which were about ten times as expensive as hard-seat tickets and required FEC to buy. I paid about $30 for the eight-hour overnight ticket to Zheng Zhou with great relief. I would have paid almost anything not to have to wait for days in the hard-seat lines.

A night of fitful sleep on a rocky train further jostled my scrambled circadian clock. I walked out of the Zheng Zhou train station with newly intensified jet lag. It was six in the morning and I desperately wanted to find some place where I could go back to sleep.

Zheng Zhou is the capital of Henan Province, a landlocked agricultural state in the center of the country. It is a small city by Chinese standards, with a population of only two million. Being far from the ocean, it had not yet felt the deluge of foreign investment that was transforming China's coastal regions and bringing foreigners over in large numbers.

The locals were surprised to see a *laowai* in their midst. Little kids pointed at me and ran away. Women smiled before hiding their faces in embarrassment. Men shouted out "Hallo! Hallo!" It was as if a celebrity were in their midst. A man stopped me to take a picture with him. I grinned for the picture until I realized that the man next to me was standing stiffly with no expression on his face. The Chinese don't smile for pictures.

Zheng Zhou was gray and dirty. The sky was dark with pollution and the threat of rain. The concrete buildings surrounding the square were gritty with dirt. It was a city in desperate need of a bath. So was I. The train station was surrounded by hotels, most around ten stories high. I picked out the one whose Chinese neon-sign name was accompanied by an English translation, The Greenhouse Inn, assuming its bilingual facade indicated it was superior to the rest. I was disabused of this notion as soon as I walked inside. The Greenhouse Inn apparently got its name from the verdant color of its mold. Unlike the people outside, the hotel clerk was not delighted to discover a foreigner ringing the desk bell. He grumbled and cursed, while taking his own sweet time filling out the extra paperwork required for foreigners, the better to keep track of us. I paid in FEC.

He handed me a piece of paper with the number 804 scrawled on it.

"What about the key?" I asked.

He waved me away, "Ask upstairs."

When I arrived at the eighth floor and stepped off, I realized that each floor had its own key girl, a young woman whose job it was to open doors for guests. Two goals in a Maoist economy are to keep people working whether their job is necessary or not (idleness is the bourgeoisie's workshop) and to make sure everyone is keeping an eye on everyone else. The key girl was a perfect example of these two goals in action, a spy on every floor. Deng Xiaoping had set about changing all of this after rising to power following Mao's death in 1976, attempting to shift the economy slowly from communism to capitalism, a gradual privatization. His catchwords were *gaige* (change) and *kaifang* (openness). The presence of key girls or lack thereof was a good indication of where you were on the openness/change spectrum. The Beijing Sheraton, a foreign-Chinese joint venture, had given me my own key card.

My key girl looked in every way like an average twenty-something

Chinese urbanite. Her radiant black hair fell to her shoulders. Her slightly rounded face was pleasant but unexpressive. Over her slender body, she wore a white blouse of thin material and a medium-length skirt. I looked down at her name tag. It had her Chinese name and its English translation: Moon.

Finding herself suddenly in front of a foreign male had unnerved her. Her hands were shaking slightly. I smiled and told her my room number in Chinese.

"Aiya, you speak Chinese!" she cried clapping her hands to her mouth.

"Just a little."

"Your Chinese is so good!"

"Better than *Dashan*'s?"

She clapped her hands together. "Are you friends with *Dashan*? He's very famous!"

"No," I said.

She visibly deflated. I was really starting to hate the guy.

She opened my door and brought me a hot-water bottle for tea. I offered her a tip. She waved it off, "Tips are against regulations."

She hesitated for a moment before deciding to pour me a cup of tea. She hesitated another moment before deciding to pour herself a cup and join me.

I sat down in a chair, hoping for a short conversation. She sat on the bed.

"What country are you from?"

"America."

"America is a great country. Very powerful. Not like China."

"But China has advanced rapidly," I said.

"No, it is inadequate. It will take seventy years before it is acceptable."

"I have heard it will only take fifty years."

"Who told you that?"

"A cab driver in Beijing."

"Well, Beijing is different. It is rich. Not like here. We are very poor."

I yawned. Moon froze, caught between her professional obligation to leave and her desire to continue this welcome relief from the boredom of her job. She decided to stay.

"Why are you in Zheng Zhou?" she asked.

"I'm going to the Shaolin Temple to study kungfu."

"Really? My little brother is in Shaolin studying kungfu."

This woke me up. Finally, I had confirmation that the Shaolin Temple still trained students.

"I need to go there tomorrow," I said. "What is the best way to get there?"

"You need to go tomorrow? Why not stay in Zheng Zhou for a couple of days and see the sights?"

"What sights?"

"There is the Yellow River."

"I need to get to Shaolin. Can you tell me what is the best way?"

"There is a tourist bus that leaves for Shaolin at eight o'clock in the morning," she sighed, disappointed. We sipped our tea without looking at each other for a couple of minutes. "Did you know that China invented kungfu?"

"Yes, I did."

"Chinese culture is very deep."

"Yes, it is."

We fell into silence again.

"Do you know the history of Shaolin?"

"Not really."

So Moon taught me the history of the Shaolin Temple.

Shaolin was founded in 492 A.D. The Chinese emperor had noticed that one of his favorite Buddhist monks, an Indian named Batuo, preferred meditating in isolated areas away from the imperial court, located at the time in Luoyang—a city about 200 miles west of present-day Zheng Zhou. So the emperor built Batuo a temple in a forested valley inside the Song Mountains, halfway between Luoyang and Zheng Zhou. Batuo became Shaolin's first abbot and was soon joined by a small community of monks.

Shaolin might have remained just another nameless monastic community if not for the arrival, circa 525 A.D., of another Indian Buddhist missionary named Damo—Bodhidharma in Sanskrit. According to certain versions of the story, Shaolin's abbot refused

Damo admittance. The exact reason is unknown, but Damo had a tendency to rub people the wrong way. He had had to leave the Southern imperial court—China was split into two polities at the time—after upsetting the devout Emperor Liang Wudi by dismissing his good works (building temples, publishing scriptures, supporting monastic communities) and his personal dedication (the emperor was a vegetarian, prayed frequently, attended Buddhist rituals, and wore monk's robes) as having no spiritual merit.

After the abbot's rejection, Damo climbed Mt. Song, which rises about 2,000 feet above Shaolin, and entered a cave barely big enough for two men to sit in. He vowed not to leave until he achieved enlightenment. In the religious texts written half a millennium later, he is said to have remained there for nine years before he achieved his goal, meditating with such intensity that his image was burned onto a rock in the cave. A stone with his visage painted on it sits in Shaolin today. He is pictured as a hairy man with round, bulging eyes—one legend has it that he cut off his eyelids so he wouldn't fall asleep while meditating. In keeping with the self-mutilation theme, his first disciple, Huike, is believed to have cut off his right arm to prove his dedication.

When he came down, Damo was made abbot of Shaolin and taught the other monks that meditation was the key to achieving enlightenment. As he had with the emperor, he rejected the idea that religious ritual and good deeds helped the seeker. In fact, they could be a hindrance, because they tended to increase the ego and spiritual pride of the practitioner. A complete negation of self could be achieved only through morning-to-evening sessions of sitting meditation in which the monks sought to keep their minds completely blank. His teaching became the basis of the Zen sect of Buddhism.

But Damo soon discovered a problem. Days of doing nothing but sitting turned the monks' muscles to mush (a problem familiar to many modern-day office workers). His answer was to introduce a set of eighteen calisthenic exercises. These exercises ultimately developed into kungfu, or so it is believed in China.

Whether the Chinese invented kungfu or it was previously developed elsewhere (India, possibly Greece) and brought to China, it is clear that the martial arts captured the imagination of the Shaolin monks, and they in turn captured the imagination of China.

Shaolin was the first known Buddhist monastery to develop its own fighting system—quite unusual for a religion whose pacifism rivals that of the Quakers.

The most common explanation for this anomaly is self-defense. China's political landscape was in turmoil at the time; an isolated mountain monastery was a tempting target for roving bands of marauders. The tradition of martial monks probably began with guards who were responsible for defending the temple. Their individual fighting techniques were strung together into series of movements, or forms, for teaching purposes. Over time the interaction between the guards and the monks ritualized these fighting forms into a kind of moving meditation, commingling the practical with the spiritual, the martial with the art.

In the sixth century, several factions were vying for control of the empire. One was led by the evil warlord Wang Shichong. To help his cause, he kidnapped the Tang prince, Li Shimin. That was his first mistake. His second was to ransack the Shaolin Temple. According to the legend, thirteen Shaolin monks (there were probably more) entered his camp, defeated his guards with their superior martial skill, killed Wang Shichong, and rescued the prince, who later became the first Tang emperor. One of Li Shimin's first acts was to grant the Shaolin Temple extra land and the monks a special imperial dispensation to eat meat and drink alcohol, making Shaolin the only Buddhist monastery in China that is not vegetarian and dry. (Today the monks have a joke that goes: What do you get for extending the life of an emperor? He shortens yours.) The emperor had set up for himself a military academy of celibate men, a force loyal to him and unencumbered by the worry and entanglements that affect warriors with wives and children. The monks who focused on kungfu became known as martial monks (*wu seng*), while those who remained exclusively devoted to Buddhist practice were called cultural monks (*wen seng*).

Over the next thousand-plus years, the Shaolin monks became the heroes of the Chinese people. They battled against Mongol invaders and Japanese pirates. Shaolin was a rebel base against occupying foreign rulers, particularly the Manchus of the Qing dynasty. Shaolin was a center for the development of the martial arts across China, with fighters coming to Shaolin to train, and Shaolin monks evangelizing in other areas. It was also the first martial arts franchise. A second Shaolin Temple was built in Fujian Province. There is some evidence there were others. Japanese monks studied at Shaolin in the twelfth century, taking back its Zen teachings and its martial arts. The impact of the combination of the two on Japanese life was so dramatic that one could argue the entire country was one big Shaolin Temple until the Meiji period. Shaolin even inspired a rivalry with the Taoist Wu Tang Temple, which developed its own style of fighting to challenge Shaolin's. Wu Tang disciples were famous for their skill with the sword (Chow Yun-Fat's character in *Crouching Tiger, Hidden Dragon* was a Wu Tang disciple), while Shaolin's monks were famous for their skill with the staff, a less bloody weapon . . .

Actually, Moon's history lesson didn't take place at quite this level of sophistication. Her formal education had ended in the eighth grade, and I was at best a precocious child in Chinese. It took a couple years of research to piece together Shaolin's early years—a mixture of fact and fiction written many centuries after the events by acolytes.

Our conversation went more like this:

"The Shaolin monks fought Japanese [something]."

"I am sorry, What does [something] mean?"

"Do you know the word for [something else]?"

"So sorry, what does [something else] mean?"

"Men who steal."

"Oh, right, right, thieves."

"So [something] are thieves who ride in boats."

"Oh, pirates. Okay."

The extent of her Shaolin knowledge eventually exceeded the limits of my Chinese vocabulary, and our discussion trailed into silence. She seemed forlorn. My head ached from always being about two sentences behind in the discussion. I stretched my arms into the air to show I was tired and maybe we should end the conversation. She sighed, glancing off at the floor, her neck at a chopping-block angle.

"What's the matter?" I asked.

"Nothing," she said, sighing again as she leaned her head back and exposed her throat.

Wanting to change the topic, I asked, "How do you like your job?"

Her response: another sigh.

I offered, "Just so-so?"

"Oh, you understand my heart," she said touching her chest.

I hadn't up until that moment. She was watching a romantic comedy where the international man of mystery meets the cute working-class girl with a heart of gold. He's supposed to sweep her off her feet, not fall asleep. The problem was we were genre incompatible. I was starring in a quest movie: young man travels to exotic land, overcomes obstacles, acquires cool skills, learns important life lessons, comes of age. She was looking for love; I was looking for Yoda. She needed rescue; I needed my rest.

I cleared my throat, "Ah, well, yes, I probably should get some sleep. When is the bus to Shaolin tomorrow?"

Another sigh. "Eight in the morning."

"Right, yes, well, I should get up around seven. Best for me to get some rest. How do I arrange for a wake-up call?"

"I will take care of it," she said as she dragged herself from the room.

"Thank you, thank you, thank you," I said.

In Chinese, you never say something once when you're trying to be polite—it sounds curt. You have to say it at least three times.

As I undressed, I had a chance to contemplate the irony of my situation. For the last three years I had been reading Zen and other mystical texts with an ever increasing fervor. I had started to believe I might be called to a religious life. To test this possibility I had decided as soon as I landed in China that I would take a personal vow of celibacy. My goal was total personal transformation. It was simple spiritual physics. Personal change was a matter of applying enough pressure over a long enough period of time: $C = pt^2$. And here I was less than a week into my trip being sorely tested. Maybe the vow didn't take the effect of law until I reached the Shaolin Temple.

The phone rang. Over the line I heard the song, "I Love a Man

Who Never Comes Home." It was one of thousands of saccharine East Asian pop tunes, which made Air Supply sound like Metallica. As I was trying to figure out if this was some glitch in the telephone system or if someone was pranking me, I heard Moon's giggle.

"Do you like the song?"

"Right, right, right, yes, okay. It is not bad."

"I love this song."

"Good, good, good," I said. "Okay then, so you have arranged for my wake-up call, right?"

Sigh. "Yes."

"Thank you, thank you, thank you."

That night I dreamt I was sitting outside the gates of the Shaolin Temple, an isolated monastery on a windswept mountain. Each time I knocked on the massive doors, I was told to go away. After many months had passed, the gates finally opened from the inside. I stepped through to find myself standing above a void. I could hear myself scream as I fell.

I jolted awake to find a woman leaning over me. A nurse? Was I in a hospital? My body clock still haywire, it took me several moments to realize it was Moon. I stared around the room, trying to remember where I was. The early morning light was shining through the crack in the curtains.

"Good morning," I said.

"Good morning," she giggled.

"It's you."

I looked down. The sheet was covering my lower half. My clothes were on the chair in the corner. I was trapped.

"Yes, it's me. I told my coworker to take the night off. I worked all night to make certain you woke up."

Now I felt trapped and guilty.

I tried to smile at her, "You are very hardworking. Your boss should give you a raise."

She giggled and leaned closer to my chest, "Your skin is so white."

"I spent too much time in the library."

"So white, so beautiful," she said, leaning even closer.

At six foot three, 156 pounds of pale skin and bone, women had used a number of phrases to describe my body—"Skeletor," "bird legs," "Ethiopian albino." *Beautiful* was not one I'd ever heard before. Was she mocking me? I didn't know yet that in China pale skin was considered more beautiful than tanned, because it showed you were rich enough not to have to labor outside under the sun like a peasant.

"You like white skin?"

"It is so beautiful," she said, her face now within inches of mine. It was rapturous, a young woman about to have all her prayers answered.

What could I say to her? *It's not you, it's me . . . and my vow of celibacy?*

No longer able to stall, I ran for it. I flipped out of bed and hustled my tightie-whitie covered buns to the chair in the corner. I hopped into my jeans and slipped on my shirt before turning around again.

"I am so late," I said, throwing on the rest of my clothes.

I made it out of that room in record time with Moon trailing behind me. I kept hitting the button for the elevator. Moon was crestfallen.

"Look, when I come back to visit Zheng Zhou, I'll stay here and then we can see each other again," I said.

She smiled.

I stepped into the elevator and turned back to wave good-bye.

Her face fell as she realized I was lying.

"You are not coming back," she said.

The elevator doors shut.

I didn't go back.

4

KUNGFU WORLD

The intended purpose of the highway that linked Zheng Zhou to Luoyang, and thus Shaolin, may have been to transport goods and people across Henan's interior, but its actual function was to serve as an arena for elaborate games of chicken. It had four lanes, but none of the drivers used the exterior two. So when they wanted to pass—which they did frequently because the assorted vehicles, spanning the continuum of motorized conveyances from tractor to semi, varied so greatly in speed—they used the opposing traffic's lane, especially if they were, say, rounding a corner or heading up a hill.

As our bus approached one particularly high hill, our driver decided to pass a three-wheeled tractor being steered by a wooden pole connected to the back wheels like a rudder. At the same moment, a Volkswagen behind us decided this was a propitious moment to pass our bus. Our bus took the opposite interior lane; the sedan sweeping left took the opposite exterior lane. It was the Cornhuskers' option play. All three drivers honked their horns as a safety precaution, but then again everyone on the road in China honks his horn with metronomic regularity, so it only added to the cacophony. As we approached the top of the hill, an open coal truck appeared, heading straight for us. Its driver's only option was our exterior lane, which he swerved at the last moment to take, escaping a painful death but losing that particular round of chicken.

"*Ni bu yau ming!*" the coal-truck driver shouted at us. "You don't want life!"

It was the most common driving curse in China and pretty much summed up the driving conditions.

Halfway through the three-hour trip on Henan's highway of death—multi-vehicle pileups were a weekly occurrence—my right thigh started aching. I had been furiously pressing on an imaginary brake pedal in the floor, the same as my father always did when I was driving and he was in the passenger seat.

The Chinese often used the term *luohou* (backward) both to describe certain ways of thinking as well as certain parts of their country's economy. As we moved into the interior of Henan, I observed *luohou*'s literal meaning: Every step forward was an economic step backward from the more wealthy and advanced coastal regions. Concrete gave way to brick and white-tiled buildings. Business-casual clothing of the city became the rough cotton of farmers and peasants, who squatted along the side of the highway smoking cigarettes as they breathed in the exhaust of the trucks passing by. At regular intervals of about thirty minutes we drove through little towns, each one poorer than the last.

The final town before Shaolin was Deng Feng, where the bus stopped for lunch. It was hard to decide exactly what its most depressing aspect was. Was it the charcoal grime that blanketed the town? The dejected expressions on the faces of its citizens? The trash strewn across the streets? I came to think of Deng Feng as the irredeemable armpit of China, quiet desperation made manifest, a justification for mass suicide. It was so awful that I nicknamed the town Darn Fun.

Deng Feng sat at the base of the Song Mountains, the Chinese Appalachians—it featured short peaks covered with trees and extreme poverty. From here it was a thirty-minute winding journey on two lanes to reach Shaolin. As we rounded the final curve to my destination, there was a fifty-foot cast-iron statue of a Shaolin martial monk guarding the entrance to the Shaolin village, a one-road cul-de-sac running west into a valley surrounded by five mountain peaks.

I had expected a windswept, isolated monastery. This is not what I discovered. Cars and tourist buses were backed up before the entrance to a parking lot. Packed along the sides of the road were dozens of lean-to restaurants made of cracked plaster and chipped concrete to feed the tourists, and several dozen corrugated-tin-roof shacks sold kungfu tchotchkes. Donkey-drawn wagons waited at the entrance of the parking lot to carry the tourists the half-mile to the temple. And then there were the more inventive attractions dreamt up by local entrepreneurs: a World War II cargo plane with a sign claiming it was Mao's first plane, the ski lift that took tourists up to the top of one of the mountain peaks where they could fire machine guns, or the 2,000-year-old mummy that was actually a dead monkey. The isolated monastery had been turned into Kungfu World, a low-rent version of an Epcot Center pavilion.

The one exception to all the tourist trappiness was the six or seven private kungfu schools with similar names—Shaolin Kungfu University, Shaolin Wushu Academy, Shaolin Wushu and Kungfu School. Together they trained more than 10,000 teenage Chinese boys—and a smattering of girls—who paid tuition of around $100 a year to study kungfu all day long, six days a week for ten months out of the year. School uniforms were jogging suits made in the school's colors—just like *Enter the Dragon*—so, scattered among the thousands of tourists clogging the road were gaggles of students in red or yellow or blue suits, skinny and dusty and clutching various kungfu weapons: wooden staffs, tin swords, dull-pointed spears. On the southern side of the road, where the valley stretched out for half a mile, color-coordinated blocks of several hundred students practiced traditional Shaolin forms on the hard-packed dirt. A coach barked out the cadence through a bullhorn as the students moved as one performing the next move.

I bought a *laowai* ticket (ten times the Chinese price) to enter the village proper, demarcated by a gate manned by smug police officers wearing comically oversize sunglasses. I was in utter shock. *The Shaolin monks live here?*

Intermingling with the Chinese tourists, I walked the half-mile from the gates of the village to the entrance to the Shaolin Temple. The courtyard and the gates to the temple itself—with the Chinese characters for "Shaolin" above—looked as I expected. I had seen them before in kungfu movies. It turned out that countless Hong Kong film crews would come to the temple for a day or two to film a scene in front of those gates, below the Shaolin sign, for the requisite element of vérité. There was a TV crew filming the gate as I approached; production assistants were trying gallantly to keep the tourists at bay while an attractive Taiwanese reporter said something about Shaolin's history into her microphone.

I followed a tour group through the temple, which was fairly modest by contemporary Chinese standards. It was the size of several football fields, consisting of a dozen or so courtyards, a few larger-than-life Buddha statues, prayer rooms, and wooden statues of martial monks in various kungfu poses. Almost all of it was a reconstruction of recent vintage, part of the government's effort to increase tourist revenue after the devastation of the Cultural Revolution. The most impressive part of the temple was the the stone floor in the old training hall. Traditional Shaolin forms have various stomping techniques. Over the centuries, generations of Shaolin monks have pounded the stone block floor, creating two paired rows of giant footprints, indentations the size of large watermelons—the negative space a visible testament to the monks' devoted pursuit of martial perfection for a millennium and a half.

But I was worried about another negative space. Where were the monks? I searched the monastery. There were plenty of tourists and tour guides. There were peasants selling refreshments. There were even money changers in the temple (*"Laowai*, shanjah mahnie?"). But there were no monks. I retraced my steps, growing more and more anxious. I had traveled halfway around the globe only to discover that the temple was empty of the very people I'd come to find. After two hours of fruitless searching, I started to hyperventilate. If I'd failed, I'd have to go back home with my tail between my legs.

I wandered out of the temple, despondent. Immediately to the west is Shaolin's other famous attraction, the Pagoda Forest. Dating back a thousand years, it is the temple's graveyard. The ash remains of various abbots and Shaolin heroes are buried in pagodas (or *stupas*), tall, narrow, vertical structures of elaborate brick and stonework. The height and size of the pagodas varies depending on when they were built and the importance of the monk. I wandered around trying to read the names on the plaques. Frequently in Shaolin movies, the monks are portrayed battling their enemies by jumping around the tops of these pagodas. It seemed that all that remained of the real Shaolin monks were these ashes.

Amituofo (May the Buddha bless you) is what the monks—while pressing both palms together and bowing—said in the movies when introduced and when departing. It was also a phrase of hope. As I wandered down the street, I repeated it over and over again. *Amituofo. Amituofo.* Maybe the monks had left the temple for one of the private schools? Maybe they were on vacation? The Pagoda Forest marks the western end of the village, where the concrete road turns to dirt and trickles off into a field surrounded by mountain peaks. I turned east to retrace the village's single road.

I approached the Shaolin Wushu University (*wu* means "martial," *shu* means "arts"), a cracked-concrete compound just east of the temple. As soon as I entered the gate—the Chinese love walled structures with gates, mini–Forbidden Cities—I was immediately surround by red-jogging-suited teenage Chinese boys. "Hallo! Hallo! *Laowai*, hallo!"

I went over to an older man, assuming he was one of the instructors, and asked if he knew where the Shaolin monks were. Chinese words exiting a *laowai*'s mouth created a sensation. A larger crowd soon gathered. I repeated my question. He kind of laughed in a mirthless way and pointed east, away from the temple. So I repeated my efforts farther down the road at the next school with the same results. I was working my way one by one down the street toward the highway. Finally, I hit Taguo, the last school before Shaolin's one road meets the highway. It was a series of red-brick buildings without an outer wall or gate. It was also the first school where the students who surrounded me seemed less intrigued and more hostile to my presence. I finally found an instructor, a twentysomething man wearing only kickboxing shorts.

"Excuse me," I said.

"Tourists are supposed to stay back on the road," he said dismissively.

"I am not a tourist. I want to study kungfu with the Shaolin monks."

"Why?" he said with a slight sneer. "*Laowai* are no good at kungfu."

As youngsters with kungfu weapons in their hands pressed

closer, I began to feel like Piggy in *Lord of the Flies*. My courage collapsed. I nearly fell as I backed out of Taguo.

As I reached the cracked-concrete stone, I started to think that this had to be the single lowest moment of my life. I had left everything I knew behind, journeyed thousands of miles, and spent thousands of dollars in pursuit of a dream that had seemed absurd to my friends, my teachers, and my parents. And now it looked like they had been right.

Then, as I stood there wallowing in my own private pity party, a vision appeared before me: a young boy with a shaved head, wearing the orange robes of a Buddhist monk. Short of being a card-carrying member of NAMBLA, I couldn't have been more excited to see him.

Amituofo.

He was dodging through the crowd of tourists, local salespeople, and teenage kungfu students from the various academies. I followed him. He turned into an alleyway between two restaurants. The dirt path had wooden shacks on each side, each emitting the sounds of kungfu fighting. Inside, students from the schools were watching pirated Hong Kong chop-socky movies playing on VCRs and small TV sets—Shaolin's multiplex. Past the huts, an area opened to several outdoor pool tables where boys played on the uneven felt with chipped, hand-carved pool balls. At the end of the alley, the young boy in monk's robes turned into a hut.

I ducked to avoid banging my head while entering the hut and discovered Shaolin's video arcade, which consisted of two standup games: *Asteroids* and *Street Fighter II*. The young monk put a coin into *Street Fighter II,* the classic martial arts game. I watched him play a couple of games before I asked if I could challenge him. It would be too sad to try to calculate how many hours of my life I had spent playing *Street Fighter II,* so I'll just say it was clearly more than my Shaolin opponent. His Blanka was good; my M. Bison was much better. After two quick games, he turned to me and said, "You are very good."

"No, no, no, I'm not," I said and paused. "My name is *Bao Mosi*."

"I'm called Little Tiger," the boy said. "*Amituofo*."

"*Amituofo*."

Uncertain what else to say, I let Little Tiger leave and wander ahead of me, before I started trailing him again. He went up the stairs and entered the Shaolin Temple Wushu Center, the one compound I had not entered previously because I had assumed it was a tourism center rather than a school. It was the best-built structure in the village. The steps leading to the entrance were stone; the rest of the schools had dirt paths. There were two large statues of Shaolin monks. The signage was machine-carved instead of hand-whittled. The concrete walls weren't cracked. The creamy yellow paint looked new.

I hustled up the stairs, but by the time I had entered Little Tiger was nowhere to be found.

The central building of the Shaolin Temple Wushu Center was shaped like a horseshoe. An oval hallway encircled the large, circular performance hall. I peeked through one of the windows where the raggedy curtains were ripped. Inside, 500 wooden auditorium seats surrounded a large red mat of Olympic proportions. I followed the hallway to my left, but the doors to the performance hall were secured with flexible bicycle locks.

At the end of the left side of the horseshoe was a counter selling Chinese paintings. A bucktoothed man in a purple jacket smiled at me and pointed at his paintings. From the black paint staining his fingers I guessed they were his own work. I shook my head.

Behind him was another glass door secured by a bicycle lock. Through the glass I could see a green mat. It was a square, two-story practice room. A dirty mirror covered the far wall. As I stood next to the painter, he asked, "Shanja mahnie?"

"I want to study kungfu with the Shaolin monks," I said in Chinese.

"Really?" he asked, surprised.

"Yes."

"Wait here," he said, walking off to his right.

There were a series of wooden doors along the back wall. He knocked on the door with the sign INTERNATIONAL AFFAIRS OFFICE and entered. He returned a couple of minutes later with a slight man, wearing a rumpled, polyester-blend brown suit and tie.

The man asked me in faltering English, "American?"

I answered in English, "Yes."

He pointed to himself, "Ling."

"Hello, my name is Matthew."

He pointed at me, "Kungfu?"

"Yes."

He ushered me into the room he had just exited. It was a concrete box with nothing in it but a desk and three chairs—the walls were unadorned, the paint peeling. It looked like some Soviet Bloc interrogation room—a place where no one could hear you scream. Mr. Ling pointed to a chair for me to sit in, mumbled something in English, and left.

He came back with a man dressed identically in the same brown suit, gray silk socks, plastic dress shoes—the only difference was where Mr. Ling had about six keys attached to an outer belt loop, the other man had a dozen. In a country where every building had a gate and every door a lock, the number of keys was a signifier of rank. The man's nickname, I'd later learn, was Comrade Fish, not only because he had a lazy eye but also because his handshake—a Western custom the Chinese were adopting with various levels of success—was limp and clammy.

Comrade Fish's smile didn't rise to his eyes. He left his sweaty palm against mine. I tried not to shudder.

Dropping my hand, he turned in Mr. Ling's general direction and said in Chinese, "Ask him if he wants to study kungfu here."

Mr. Ling, who was apparently the school's translator, said to me in English with an extremely embarrassed smile, "[Mumble, mumble] kungfu?"

I said in English, "Yes."

"Yes," Mr. Ling relayed to Comrade Fish in Chinese.

"How long does he want to study here for?"

Mr. Ling asked me in English, "How [mumble, mumble, unintelligible] time?"

I said in English, "A year, maybe two."

He translated to Comrade Fish in Chinese, "He is not certain."

I decided this charade was not helping my cause, so I said in Chinese, "I want to study kungfu with the Shaolin monks for one year, maybe two."

Both Comrade Fish and Mr. Ling were surprised, but not because I had spoken Chinese. They were shocked by the length of time I proposed to stay. Their eyes lit up like cash registers. It hit

me. I wasn't in an interrogation room. I was in a far scarier place—
the back sales office of a used car lot. Comrade Fish excused himself, returning after a couple of minutes with yet another stale brown
suit, a tall, thin man with a weak mustache. I'd later learn his name
was Deputy Leader Jiao, the second in command at the Wushu Center. Of all three men, he had the greatest number of keys hanging
from his belt loop.

Deputy Leader Jiao asked me to repeat how long I wanted to
stay.

"I'd like to study here for a year, maybe two," I said again.

Deputy Leader Jiao said, "The price for room, board, and private training is thirteen hundred American dollars per month."

I exhaled. That was almost all the money I had on me.

It had never occurred to me to worry about cost. In the kungfu
movies, disciples pay their teachers in sweat and tears, not American Express traveler's checks. I tried to weigh the decision as they
watched me like vultures. It was not like I could go home without
having tried to study with the monks. But these men dripped with
deceit. They were the first party apparatchiks I had met, and I was
still new enough to the country to find it ideologically disconcerting to discover that Communists were greedy bastards. Bastards, I
had expected, but greedy was a surprise.

It felt like a scam, so I said, "I will have to think about it a day
or two. Is there somewhere in town where I can stay?"

Their disappointment was obvious. Comrade Fish said without
looking at me, "Mr. Ling can take you to the hotel. We should be
good friends. If you need any help with anything come find me."

I turned to Deputy Leader Jiao, but he left without saying good-
bye. Clearly, I had wasted his precious time.

I picked up my huge backpack that I had left in the hallway.
Comrade Fish was whispering something to Mr. Ling. As I was waiting I heard the sound of someone practicing kungfu to the right of
the office. I walked in its direction and found another practice room
exactly the same as the one to its left. The difference was that the
door was open and inside there were people training.

It was a sight I had been dreaming of: two Shaolin monks with
shaved heads, maybe twenty years old, wearing orange robes with
black sashes and teaching a class. Well, they weren't exactly teach-

ing; they were actually posing with their older, late fifties–early sixties, prosperous-looking Chinese students, who were taking pictures with state-of-the-art cameras. After a series of still shots, the monks demonstrated a traditional Shaolin form for the mini–video cameras.

I found myself standing inside the room, not conscious of walking in without asking. One of the older Chinese ladies came over to me. "Where are you from?"

"America. And you? You don't dress like you're from the mainland."

She laughed as if I'd just said the funniest thing in the world.

"We're from Singapore. We are all students in the same kungfu school. Our master brought us here for a week of training. Today is our last day. The monks are marvelous, don't you think?"

As I talked to the woman I couldn't keep my eyes off the monks. She told me their names: Cheng Hao (Shi Xing Hao was his Buddhist name) looked like a Chinese James Dean, cool and handsome; Deqing (Shi Xing Hong) was the one with the charismatic personality and explosive techniques.

The first part of their Buddhist name, *shi*, means "monk." The second part denotes their generation—in this case, *xing* is the thirty-second generation. The generation is always one higher than the monk's master. The third part of the name is unique and is often taken from the monk's Chinese name. Buddhist monks are supposed to use only their Buddhist name. But at Shaolin, this rule, like many others, was at best loosely observed.

Deqing and Cheng Hao's poses were precise, their techniques were blindingly fast and their kicks snapped like their legs were made of rubber bands. They were faster than Bruce Lee. They were better than the wire-enhanced kungfu actors in the movies. I had never seen such a display of martial art skill.

I was particularly riveted by Deqing. As he moved through the forms for the video cameras, he could barely contain his energy. After finishing, he could barely contain his joy. The old ladies were fussing over his tremendous talent and he was trying to "aw-shucks" them, but he couldn't help from laughing with pleasure. Unlike the Communist Party officials in the office I had just escaped, his face was a kaleidoscope of emotions. There was none of the calculation or delay between feeling something and expressing it that I had noticed in almost everyone else I had met in China. Deqing's emotions were spontaneous and vivid. Cheng Hao had a Hollywood cool about him, but Deqing was clearly the star.

The pleasure of performing in front of the cameras had pumped Deqing up. After running through the beginner Shaolin forms that the monks had taught the Singaporean students, he decided to put on a show. For the next two minutes, he punched, kicked, jumped, backflipped, front-flipped, back-handspringed, 360-barrel-rolled through the most complicated and exquisite form I'd ever seen. He finished with a series of spinning, jumping kicks. His leaps were so high, his hang time so long that for just a moment I had the feeling that he had defied the law of gravity and would never fall back to earth. My breath caught in my throat. For a moment, I believed that maybe man could fly.

I was sold.

I walked out of the training room and went over to the office. I told Mr. Ling and Comrade Fish that I was staying for at least a year. Their grins were salacious. I continued, "But I only have enough for the first month. I'll pay you month by month."

I handed over thirteen Benjamins. With that I became a student of the Shaolin Temple.

5

LIGHTS, CAMERA, ACTION

Waking up after my first night at Shaolin, I finally took notice of my room, one of twenty in the two-story structure. It wasn't quite the Bates Motel, but it was close. It was three years old, built in the eighties style of non–joint venture accommodations: peeling wallpaper, exposed wires, broken bulbs, a stained carpet, a bathroom with loose tiles, no shower curtain, and a toilet you didn't want to touch. At least the water worked. The cold water, that is—hot water was piped in only once every three days for thirty minutes, unless a VIP was staying the night or I yelled and screamed loud enough to qualify as a VIP for the evening.

But none of this bothered me. I had found the Shaolin monks and as soon as I saw how they lived, I felt immensely fortunate and guilty. After all, I had carpet, two beds with a mattress, a desk and chair, a private sit-down toilet, a bathtub, a TV that worked, a door that locked, and no roommates. The monks lived on the second floor of the circular performance hall and looked down on where they worked every day—the equivalent of actors boarding in the rafters above a theater. Their floors were concrete, and their bath was a washbasin, which they filled with boiled water at night to wash their hands, feet, and faces. Their beds were straw padding over wooden boards, and, except for the most senior monks, they slept two to a bed, head to foot. Their toilet was a hole-in-the-ground outhouse.

It was nearly a month before I had the courage to ask one of my teachers to show me where he lived, and when he finally agreed, after much embarrassed hemming and hawing, I immediately asked Mr. Ling if I could live with the monks. I wanted to be part of the community, but it was illegal for foreigners to live or train anywhere else in Shaolin. Mr. Ling said that this was for my health and safety, but the increased revenue was also pretty convenient for the government-run Shaolin Wushu Center, a synergy that was a perfect example of Deng Xiaoping's description of the Chinese economy: "Socialism with Chinese characteristics."

I had wanted to start my training immediately, but Mr. Ling informed me, without explaining why, that the monks would be busy for the next three days. It took me half a day to discover that I had wandered into Shaolin on its 1,500th birthday. A weeklong festival was in progress. If I were a superstitious guy (which I am), I would have taken this unlikely coincidence as a fortuitous portent, as destiny at work (which I did).

It turns out, however, that there is some debate about Shaolin's exact year of birth. Because 495 A.D. is also often cited, Shaolin would throw itself another 1,500th birthday in 1995. So much for superstition. At any rate, the monks were busy performing for the increased number of tourists and various East Asian media outlets that had descended on the village to celebrate the event.

Shaolin was right to celebrate. Fifteen hundred years, more or less, of continued existence is almost unprecedented in the history of religious orders and it is even more impressive given the extreme ups and downs of Shaolin's past. The twentieth century was arguably its roughest patch. The problem, to simplify, was the introduction of firearms into China during the late nineteenth century. Immediately, the self-defense efficacy of being a twenty-year master in, say, the double sword, the rope dart, or the three-section staff dropped off the cliff. (God made man, but Sam Colt made him equal.) In 1900, the Boxers—members of a Chinese secret society who believed they could harden their bodies through iron kungfu practice to the point where they were impervious to bullets—attacked British soldiers stationed in Beijing. Rarely has the historical conflict between magic and science, mysticism and technology, been so dramatically put to the test with such lopsided results. When the smoke cleared, only the British soldiers remained standing.

One moment the kungfu masters, and the Shaolin martial monks in particular, were at the top of the warrior food chain, and the next they were helpless. Shaolin would be occupied and partially burnt down by a local warlord in the civil wars of the 1920s. In the early 1940s, it was occupied again and further destroyed, this time by the Japanese. Mao Zedong, who wanted a clean break with China's feudal past and also feared Shaolin's historical role as a sanctuary for revolutionaries, banned the practice of kungfu in the 1950s. During the Cultural Revolution (1966–76), his Red Guards sought to finish the job, dragging the few remaining Shaolin monks who had not already fled through the streets for public "criticism" and private floggings.

The Shaolin Temple was an abandoned wreck when Jet Li, an eighteen-year-old actor and martial arts expert, visited in 1981. He was making a movie called *Shaolin Temple*, the brainchild of Deng Xiaoping's pragmatic reformers. Having inherited a devastated, impoverished nation from Mao, they needed to generate revenue. The easiest method for a poor country with a rich cultural history is tourism. So the Chinese tourism board invited a Hong Kong production company to make a movie celebrating the famous Shaolin legend of the thirteen monks who rescued the Tang prince.

The effect of the movie, mainland China's first Asian blockbuster, was dramatic. Life started to imitate art. Thousands of young boys ran away from home to become Shaolin monks like Jet Li's character—so many, in fact, that the government had to build special trains to send most of them back. In addition, tens of thousands of East Asian tourists, for whom Shaolin is one of the most cherished cultural sites, began arriving annually.

Shaolin was reborn. Tuition from private kungfu students and tourism formed the basis of the village's new economy. Peasants from the surrounding areas gave up their hardscrabble farms to cater to the tourists. Only three Shaolin monks had survived through the purges of the Cultural Revolution, but they had many students in the area, some of whom opened the private schools to cater to the young, tuition-paying Chinese students, the best of whom became new Shaolin monks, slowly rebuilding the community.

It didn't take the East Asian media, starved for some fresh angles, long to ferret me out. An aggressive Taiwanese TV producer had heard there was a Chinese-speaking American who intended to study at the temple for a year or more. Comrade Fish in tow, he approached at lunch on my second day and began his flattery routine.

"It is so wonderful that an American has such a deep and profound interest in Chinese culture," the producer said in Chinese. "Your presence in Shaolin demonstrates you are a fascinating person of great insight. Your participation in our insignificant little television show would help show the mutual friendship between our two cultures."

I smiled as he continued to needlessly waste his breath. He had me at "hallo." No red-blooded American can resist the siren song of TV exposure. It's our God-given right.

The producer, the cameraman, and I went up to the hotel where I was staying after lunch. They wanted to film me walking down the hall, opening the unlocked door, and entering my room. I was confident I knew how to walk, open doors, and enter rooms. Apparently I did not. It took me five takes to get it right. Next they wanted a shot of me reading in my room. Despite many years of practice, I wasn't very good at this, either. It took eight takes before I was able to turn the pages properly. I had seen countless of these background segments on TV shows without ever realizing that they were so elaborately staged.

There are few things more nerve-racking than trying to act normal with a camera in your face and someone shouting at you to "act normal." By the time we arrived in the training hall I was already a wreck. It didn't help that all thirty of the Shaolin monks—who I had not met yet—were lined up waiting for me. Nor did I feel much better when the producer explained that I was supposed to sit for an interview in Chinese while the monks practiced behind me. Here I was in the same room with my heroes and they were serving as extras in my first TV appearance.

The interviewer, a stunning Taiwanese woman with a perfect porcelain complexion whom I'd seen at the temple gates my first day in Shaolin, arrived with a flourish. We sat down facing each other on the green mat. The microphones were attached. The cameraman got into position. The interviewer smiled her lovely smile at me. She was no doubt reviewing the questions in her mind. In my mind we were in a far more romantic locale.

"I'm sorry," I said in Chinese. "Could you repeat?"

"Why did you come to Shaolin?" she asked again.

I was aware that I was no longer on a beach. I was in the training hall of the Shaolin Wushu Center. I had found the monks. A beautiful woman was speaking Chinese. I had studied Chinese. There was a camera on and a light in my face. Everyone around me was expecting me to say something. I had no idea what.

"Why did you come to Shaolin?" she repeated again, her tone still mellifluous but the corner of her eyes narrowing in frustration.

"Right, right, right," I stuttered back in Chinese. "Because Shaolin . . . good." I had regressed back to first-year classes. I was even conducting the tones with my right index finger.

"Did you come to study Shaolin kungfu?"

"Right, right, right, kungfu good, very good, very, very good, incredibly good."

I tried to smile.

Hers was frozen. "How did you learn about the Shaolin Temple?"

"I'm sorry, could you repeat slowly?"

"How . . . did . . . you . . . learn . . . about . . . Shaolin . . . Temple?"

"Right, yes, right, ah, movies, watching movies."

"Which movies?"

"Movies."

She hissed, "Do you want to become a Shaolin monk?"

"The monks are very good. Their kungfu is very, very good."

She slammed the microphone down.

"I thought you said he spoke Chinese. He's a *bendan*!" she shouted at her producer. "Stupid egg."

For some reason, the Chinese are not very fond of eggs. "Stupid egg," "bad egg," and, worst of all, "turtle's egg" are common insults.

There are a number of boxers of whom it is said need to be hit hard before they wake up and start fighting. I was like that. Suddenly I remembered all my Chinese, knew exactly what was happening, and understood everything she had said. I replied in fluent Chinese, "I'm sorry, I know compared to you I must seem very stupid. Maybe you want to ask the questions in English? How's your English?"

She blanched.

The cameraman tried not to laugh. Clearly, he thought she was a bitch, too.

Furious, she stalked off, ending the interview. I was relieved until it occurred to me that I was unlikely to displace *Dashan* as China's most fluent Mandarin-speaking foreigner with my "Shaolin . . . good" performance. Even worse, the filming wasn't over. They wanted me to perform one of the Shaolin forms I had learned. The problem was that I hadn't learned any Shaolin forms in the last thirty hours.

This did not dissuade the producer.

He had the monks stand in a semicircle as if they were examining their American disciple's skill. As they lined up I pleaded with the producer not to make me do this. I tried to explain that the only forms I knew were from a Southern style of kungfu. These were not Shaolin forms. It would be inappropriate for me to pretend they were, like making the sign of the cross in a synagogue.

Like any good television producer, he couldn't have cared less.

As I stood there panic-stricken, waiting for the cameraman to set up, waiting to humiliate myself, I looked back at the monks. Deqing caught my eye. He smiled, shrugged his shoulders, and winked at me conspiratorially. From that moment, I knew he would be my best friend.

It took several takes before they let me and the monks go. I vowed that day to never do TV again. It was a vow I'd end up breaking repeatedly. The world media loves Shaolin. Before I left I would be filmed by Hong Kong, Japanese, Thai, Polish, British, and American TV crews. But most often, it was the state-run Chinese TV station that came to Shaolin to film a segment on Shaolin's American disciple. I was the poster boy for Western appreciation of China's profound cultural traditions. When I traveled through China, I would occasionally meet someone who had seen me on TV.

Invariably, they would say, "Your Chinese is quite good. It is almost as good as *Dashan's*."

6

A COKE AND A SMILE

I walked over to the Wushu Center restaurant, fifty feet away from my hotel, for breakfast. Inside the restaurant a dozen waitresses, who represented about a quarter of the entire female population of the village, lazed around. Only guests at the hotel ate breakfast at the restaurant, and most days I was the only guest. Lunch was their busy meal, when the day-tripping tourists and businessmen came to eat. The woman in charge of the restaurant, Fangfang, came over to try to assess what her primary customer for the next year-plus liked to eat.

"Meat," I said, like any good Midwesterner.

She wanted to know what else I wanted to eat besides meat, suggesting several vegetarian dishes. I told her I didn't care what the vegetable was as long as there was a meat dish at every meal.

I didn't understand why she was having so much trouble with this request. We went back and forth for several minutes. What I didn't know was that Fangfang had been given the restaurant as a kind of franchise, part of the recent experiments in controlled capitalism. She paid the leaders a certain fee every year for the right to run the restaurant. Any profits she made above that fee and her operational costs she could keep for herself. But I was paying my fee to the leaders, who were giving her a small percentage of my $1,300 each month. Meat dishes are the most expensive part of any meal. As Fangfang was suggesting the delightful varieties of nonmeat dishes, and I was insisting on beef, chicken, or pork, her mental cash register was calculating the cost differentials.

We settled on meat for every meal but breakfast. I agreed to enough vegetable dishes to make my mother proud. And then I spent the next ten minutes trying to explain the concept of french fries. Fangfang eventually called out the cook. I knew the Chinese word for "potato," but my vocabulary lessons had not included the adjective for "deep fried." We ended up in the kitchen, which I immediately wished I had never seen given the rusted utensils and festering puddles of water. Trying to pantomime the process of making french fries, I explained how the oil had to be poured in high enough to completely cover the sliced potatoes.

The chef stared at me for a moment before saying, "Why would you want to use so much oil?"

"Because they are delicious."

"It is a waste."

Fangfang and I went back to my table to continue our discussion. She turned her attention to beverages.

"What would you like to drink? Tea?" she asked.

"No, it's too hot to drink tea when training."

"Beer?"

"For breakfast?"

"Water?"

When I had been trying to find the monks the day before, I had seen Shaolin's creek, a tiny bed of fetid water on the south side of the road. It was where all of the town's trash and human waste seemed to end up. It was also where little peasant boys took empty water bottles down to refill, recap, and then sell to the vendors, who resold them to a new batch of tourists. I was not going to drink any water at Shaolin that wasn't boiled first.

"Do you have Coca-Cola?" I asked.

"You want to drink Coca-Cola at breakfast?"

I momentarily thought about explaining but realized I didn't know the Chinese term for "hick."

"Yes," I said.

"We don't have it. How about Jianlibao instead?"

I agreed and soon found out that Jianlibao, China's national soft drink, tastes a lot like Sunkist minus the sugar and carbonation. After breakfast, I decided to search for a supplier of Coke.

Just outside the temple's courtyard was a row of fifteen or so stalls, tin-roofed wooden shacks selling identical convenience store goods like boiled eggs, packaged Spam, bottled water, soda, beer, peanuts, cigarettes, etc. I went down the line trying to find someone who sold Coke. They all had Jianlibao but no Coke until I arrived at the very last stall, which was run by an ancient man and his young granddaughter.

Grandfather had the weathered face and hands of someone who had spent a lifetime working the land. He also moved with the deliberate pace of the peasants of China: Subsistence farming is hard but slow work. It took him a minute to stand from his stool and offer me a seat on another stool, then another minute for him to sit back down. He pointed at his granddaughter. She went into the back of the stall to look for the Coke. While she searched, he spent a good deal of time getting comfortable on his stool. Finally settled, he pulled out a pack of Chinese cigarettes and offered me a smoke.

"Thank you, but no, Grandfather. I don't smoke."

"I have foreign cigarettes." He searched his pockets until he found a pack of 555, a popular British brand.

"No, really, I don't smoke."

"You prefer Marlboro?" he asked, reaching over to the wooden case where the cigarettes were kept. "They are American."

"No, really, I don't smoke," I said.

He looked slightly hurt, and I was once again confused. I'd soon learn that the offering of a cigarette was the equivalent of saying, "Let's be friends and do business together." The Exchange of Cigarettes was the opening act of all banquets. Accepting someone's cigarette meant you were willing to enter into a relationship. Rejecting a cigarette meant you didn't want to be friends and didn't want to do business. Or, if it were a cheaper Chinese brand, it might also mean you were a snob who felt the proffered cigarette wasn't good enough for you. A cigarette was the first thing offered when a cop stopped you for some infraction. If the cop took the cigarette, it meant you were getting off with a warning; if he turned it down, you were getting a ticket. Because 99 percent of Chinese males smoked, saying you didn't smoke was understood as a snub. (Women weren't supposed to smoke and so were exempt from the ritual. They did smoke, of course, just in much smaller numbers, although it was increasing rapidly in the coastal cities, where the younger generation saw it as cool, Western, and empowering.)

Who offered and who accepted a cigarette was a sign of social status, the petitioner of a favor versus the granter. At banquets, the low-ranking males jumped over each other to offer the most powerful man at the table a cigarette. Whose he accepted and whose he rejected set the pattern for the entire evening. But if you were of equal status you had to give a cigarette to the person who offered it to you. Chinese cigarette etiquette was complex enough to be worthy of a book by Emily Post and bizarre enough for a P. J. O'Rourke parody.

Grandfather was chewing over what had just happened in the methodical way old people do until he finally reached a common Chinese conclusion that saved me from a lot of awkward situations: *Laowai* were ignorant and rude, but it was not our fault. We were like the giant panda, a slow but charming endangered species that must be forgiven and protected lest it go extinct. Stupidity was our shield. The most perilous thing for a *laowai* was to demonstrate a deep understanding of the Chinese way, to achieve the status of *Zhongguo tong* (China expert). Once they knew that you actually knew better, they treated you like they treat each other, which was not so forgiving. But there was no danger of that happening to me yet.

"Would you like some peanuts?" he asked. "Maybe an egg?"

"No thanks. Just the Coke." He stared at me and smiled like I was a long-lost friend. I smiled back. About the time I didn't think I could smile anymore I hit upon a question: "Which cigarettes do you prefer, Chinese or foreign?"

"Foreign cigarettes are too expensive. And they don't last as long. But they taste better."

"How much are foreign cigarettes?"

"10RMB. Chinese are around 2RMB."

His granddaughter brought back a can of Coke. It had been back there for so long that it had acquired a thick film of dust. Grandfather wiped it clean slowly and methodically.

"How much is it?"

"4RMB" (fifty cents). I was surprised that it was as expensive as in America. But I had given up every other vice. I needed my carbonated-caffeine fix.

"I'll take ten cans."

This caused a flurry at the nearby stalls, where the other peasant-entrepreneurs had been leaning in to eavesdrop on our conversation. Word of my request raced down the line.

"What did the foreigner say?"

"He asked for ten cans."

"*Aiya!*" Several of the female merchants shouted.

Grandfather ignored the chatter and sent his granddaughter back to look for more cans of Coke. She could find only five more. He told me he could get the rest in a couple of days and to come back then.

I was the big spender that day. And Grandfather was the pleased salesman. The sellers jokingly heckled me as I walked past them.

"Hey, want to buy ten things from me?" one asked.

"What things?" I shot back.

"Anything you want!" was the reply.

Just as I passed the last stall the woman there called out, "Foreigner, where are you from?"

"America."

"Coke is American."

"Right, right, right."

She turned to the woman in the stall next to her. "See, Americans like American things."

The merchants were researching the international market.

As I walked back to the Wushu Center the waves of Chinese tourists for the day were coming the other way. They pointed and stared and giggled and said to each other, "*Ni kan, laowai*" (Look, a foreigner) and shouted "Hallo *laowai*!" to me and waved. Some even stopped to take pictures. But all of them pointed and shouted "Hallo!" Some of the young women would continue to stare until they realized this annoyed their boyfriends and then would say in Chinese to appease them, "He's tall, too tall," or "His nose is so big."

This was sort of charming the first four or five hundred times, but within weeks the excessive attention began to make me seethe like Sean Penn in his Madonna period. When tourists would point at me and shout, "Look, a foreigner," I'd find myself, more frequently than I care to admit, pointing back and shouting, "Look, a Chinese person." By the end of the first month, I was going to great lengths to hide out from the tourists during the day, just like the monks in the temple had been doing the day I'd arrived.

7

DEFECTION

On my second night at Shaolin, I went down to the performance hall to explore. Hanging from the wall was a banner that read in Chinese and English: CULTURAL EXCHANGE MUTUAL BENEFIT. The Chinese loved banners with slogans—they decorated many offices and were a common departing gift.

Cheng Hao, Deqing, and some of the other monks were doing what they did most evenings: hanging out in the performance hall, talking, laughing, and practicing kungfu. I've never lived in a community more obsessed with a single activity. Life here was a year-round kungfu camp.

Even after a long day of performances, the young monks were working on their techniques. Deqing was helping Little Tiger, the boy from the first day, with his spear form. Several of the monks were practicing their back handsprings in the "bouncy" corner of the performance hall. In the modern equivalent of the indented stone floor inside the Shaolin Temple training hall, the monks had jumped and landed so often and so hard on the wooden floorboards in the southwest corner of the Wushu Center hall that they were as loose and springy as a trampoline.

My presence quickly stopped the training. Within minutes I had a dozen monks and about thirty of the young Chinese boys who trained at the Wushu Center (there were about 300 tuition-paying students) sitting around and peppering me with questions. Because I was an American, the topic they all wanted to ask about was the big scandal that had recently rocked Shaolin. Two Shaolin monks,

Monk Yanming and Monk Guolin, had defected during the temple's first tour of the United States. Four months earlier, while I was calling the Chinese Embassy to ask if it had any information about the Shaolin Temple and despairing that I would never find Shaolin, the monks were, unbeknownst to me, on a ten-city tour of the country. They closed in San Francisco. Afterward, when the plane was sitting on the tarmac waiting to leave, party officials discovered to their great surprise and anger that they were short two monks.

"All of you were touring America this summer?" I asked, feeling like an idiot.

"Not us." Deqing said. "Another group of monks living in the temple."

"There are two groups of monks?"

Deqing was visibly uncomfortable at the question. "Well, we are all Shaolin monks, but some of us moved to the Wushu Center when the Henan government opened it as a tourism center and kungfu school in 1989. Those who were older or less interested in kungfu remained at the temple."

"Why did you move?"

"The training facilities are better," Deqing explained.

"And the government pays us a salary to teach kungfu and perform for tourists," Little Tiger added. "The temple monks have to beg for money from their disciples."

"Life is better here," Cheng Hao said. "But the government didn't give us much of a choice."

Deqing changed the topic. "Do you know what the situation is for Guolin and Yanming?"

"I didn't hear anything about any monks defecting."

This set off rumbles through the group. How could I not have heard of it? Two Shaolin monks defected! It was an international scandal! Had I heard the rumor that the Chinese government had sent out secret agents to try to capture the two monks and bring them home? Had I heard the rumor that Yanming and Guolin were hiding in a Buddhist monastery in upstate New York? I thought, but did not say, that if this were the case the Chinese government wouldn't have much trouble narrowing down their location. Maybe they had fled to California, one of the younger monks speculated.

Wherever they were, life was very tough for them, the monks decided. They had no money and no face—having embarrassed all of China and hurt Shaolin's reputation. Now it would be next to impossible for the Wushu Center to get visas to America. Hadn't they just proven what the American visa officers suspected?

Clearly feeling the other monks had aired too much dirt, Deqing changed the topic again. "Have you met Michael Jordan?"

"No."

There were some grumbles. How could I have not met Michael Jordan? He was the most famous American in China. The NBA had been cleverly marketing its property in the mainland for the last several years. Every week Chinese TV aired an NBA package that consisted of a carefully edited game of the week with all the boring parts like free throws, passing, and teamwork removed. It was the NBA distilled to its essence: one big slam-dunk contest. Come to think of it, that pretty much describes NBA play even without the editing.

"Have you met Mike Tyson?" Little Tiger asked.

In 1992, the Shaolin monks considered Mike Tyson the fiercest fighter on earth, a high compliment. Several of the monks popped to their feet to imitate Tyson's style, the way he ducked his head down to get into his opponent's chest and then pawed with a left hook to set up his doomed rival for a devastating right uppercut. Their impressions were uncanny.

"No, I haven't met Mike Tyson," I admitted.

The grumblings were more pointed. I hadn't heard about the defection, hadn't met Jordan or Tyson. Maybe I wasn't really an American. Could I be a Canadian parading as an American? An Australian?

They knew how to hurt a guy.

What followed was a test of my Americanness. They wanted to know what life was like in America, and they wanted the answers in terms of dollars and cents. How much could a kungfu instructor make in America? They wanted to know what other jobs they could do besides teach kungfu and how much money they could make. They wanted to know about the earning potential of delivery boys, waiters, cabdrivers, cooks, and policemen. They were particularly interested in the salaries for kungfu movie stars, although we did spend some time discussing the salaries of stuntmen and fight choreographers. I spent the rest of the evening pretending I knew exactly what each occupation made. It didn't really matter—the sums were so extreme to these boys that the difference in income for the various professions was irrelevant. All were far beyond anything they could imagine.

For the entire evening I was a first-person witness to what life was like on the opposite side of the globe, a walking economic report of American wages. I was the center of attention.

It was the last night that they would openly ask me about America in a large group with witnesses. For the next two months, they would largely ignore me. At the time, I assumed it was because I had answered all their questions.

I was wrong.

BOOK TWO

NOVICE

October–December 1992

吃得苦中苦，方为人上人。

"Only those who have tasted the bitterest of the bitter can become people who stand out among others."

—*GUANCHANG XIANXING JI*

1

EATING BITTER

On my first morning of training, my wake-up call was a Communist Party propaganda song blaring out of speakers placed on top of wooden poles throughout the village.

> *Socialism is Good*
> *Socialism is Good*
> *In a Socialist Country*
> *The People's status is High*
> *The Communist Party*
> *The Communist Party . . .*

The second verse of this cheery marching tune with its bouncy beat took up the importance of overthrowing the capitalist reactionaries and running off the imperialist dogs, which if I'm not mistaken meant me. I dressed in a certain state of disquiet. It's not every day you wake up in a village where 10,000 armed Chinese kungfu masters are being urged by a Communist anthem to rise up and throw down your colonialist-capitalist ass. As national welcomes go, it's not exactly, "Give me your tired, your poor, your huddled masses . . ."

The song itself was one of those odd reminders of China's recent ideological past that was becoming increasingly anachronistic, like the appellation *tongzhi* (comrade), which was no longer used by the general populace. Other than the leaders of the Wushu Center and the police officers who collected the ticket revenue for the government, the town's population now consisted almost entirely of private tuition-paying students, kungfu entrepreneurs, and peasant merchants—in short, a bunch of capitalist running dogs. Whenever I wanted to get an embarrassed rise out of younger, hipper Chinese, I'd start singing the "Socialism is good" song or call them *tongzhi*.

For several months, I tried to find out whose job it was to turn on the song's recording every morning, because it was played at such irregular intervals. Some weeks I woke up to it every day. Other weeks it was not played at all. (I imagined some *baijiu*-soaked apparatchik, sleeping fitfully as his liver converted the low-grade alcohol into sugar, deciding whether it was worth fighting back the hangover that morning to play the song.) No one seemed to know or care. It was background noise, something they'd rather ignore. And about six months into my stay, I noticed it hadn't been played in weeks, and without any fanfare I was never awakened by it again. The sputtering, inconsistent wake-up anthem falling silent forever was about as good a metaphor for the final death rattle of Communist ideological fervor as I encountered during my stay. But at the time this was far from clear, so as I dressed myself in the sweatpants, T-shirt, and tennis shoes that would be my uniform for the next two years, I felt a bit like the Manchurian Candidate.

When I walked outside the hotel, the dawn sun was rising over the mountains in a brilliant display of reddish hues, the Shaolin valley lighting up all at once. The last time I had been up at this hour, I had been pulling an all-nighter to finish a term paper.

I looked for the monks. It was now around six A.M., and I was signed up for four hours of private tutorial in two sessions, nine to eleven A.M. and three to five P.M. Pre-breakfast practice was optional, and everyone at the Wushu Center worked on what they wanted, usually something calisthenic.

The Wushu Center was built along the base of the Song Mountain. The motel and restaurant were on a plateau about fifty feet above the main building and the courtyard surrounding it. A half-dozen monks were frog-jumping—arms behind their backs, hopping up from the squat position—up the fifty stone stairs that connected the upper area with the courtyard below. Some of the older monks (mid-twenties) were running to the top of Song

Mountain, where they went to meditate and practice *qigong*, breathing exercises that are believed to increase internal power.

The courtyard below was a kungfu playground. Kicking bags filled with sand hung from wooden overhangs. Two monks were practicing a form on top of twelve leveled tree trunks planted in rows (a test of balance and control). Rainwater had collected in a giant, uneven concrete bowl. A monk walked along the edge of the bowl, trying to keep his balance as it tipped back and forth, sloshing the water around. There were a couple of loose tree trunks lying around. Deqing was doing squats with one of the trunks on his shoulders. His roommate Cheng Hao was bench-pressing another. The scene looked like the backlot of a kungfu movie studio. In a way it was. Asian film crews would regularly show up to shoot the monks exercising on the traditional equipment for an insert into one of their period chop-socky flicks.

But the main action that morning, as it would be most mornings, was on the concrete parking lot behind the restaurant, where the tourist buses parked each day at lunch. Someone had put up two rusty basketball hoops, and the teenage monks were working on their Michael Jordan moves. Christian missionaries had first brought over the YMCA version of the game shortly after its invention at the turn of the twentieth century, and it was still played across the Chinese countryside with great passion, if not much skill or knowledge of the rules. Dribbling was optional, passing a foreign concept, their shooting touch pure brick. I'd played on my high school's varsity basketball team (okay, warmed the bench, but there's no need to get technical). The monks were about as good at basketball as I was at kungfu—a perfect opportunity for me to employ Ricardo's theory of comparative advantage in the sporting sphere. I offered to demonstrate how the game was played.

I started with the dribbling drills, moved to passes, and finished with the jump shot with special attention paid to the proper wrist flick to get just the right amount of backspin. I was not unmindful of the fact that they seemed, if I was reading them correctly, more interested in scrimmaging with each other than attending my mini-seminar. "Hey, *laowai*, why don't you give us the ball back so we can play?" was my first clue. But what is basketball without a proper grasp of the fundamentals? Sure, some of my three-pointers may have rimmed out—the goal was slanted—but it was the principle that mattered. I had no intention of ending the lessons prematurely, because frog-jumping looked like my only other option.

Finally, they stopped passing my missed shots back to me and offered as a consolation that I be allowed to join one of the teams. Little Tiger wanted to be on my side. All eight of the other monks wanted to be against me. The Chinese are not the world's tallest people—the Houston Rockets' Yao Ming does not count, because (not many people know this) he is a cyborg—and the Shaolin monks were even shorter than the average mainlander, because the ideal height for their very acrobatic performance style of kungfu was about five foot five or five foot six. So the game consisted of me driving to the basket with the ball above my head while the monks tried to slap it away from me. Did I mention the monks had no real understanding of the concept of fouls, personal or otherwise? It was my first game of street ball against professional kungfu masters, and I've suffered from post-traumatic stress flashbacks ever since.

It was while I was trying to convince one of the sixteen-year-olds that the Leopard Claw Kidney Strike was not a legal technique, even in the NBA, that Deqing and Cheng Hao came over. Deqing, the monk who could fly, must have noticed a certain deficiency in my leaping ability, my white man's disease, because he called me over and asked me if I could dunk. I could, of course, under perfect conditions . . . like having a trampoline under the basket. But this was a challenge match.

"Sure," I lied. "Can you?"

"Pretty much."

It was a kungfu version of the final "bet" scene from *White Men Can't Jump*. I charged the basket, barely cleared it with my finger-tips, and rattled the ball around the rim before it popped out. So I tried again and again, and finally concluded that the basket was clearly taller than the regulation ten feet.

Then it was Deqing's turn. He sent a two-handed tomahawk crashing through the rim. And if this weren't humiliating enough, all the other shorter-than–Spud Webb monks proceeded to put on an NBA-worthy slam-dunk contest. I'd stumbled upon the Shaolin Globetrotters. I asked Deqing with incredulity how they did it. He pointed over to the monks frog-jumping up the staircase.

I spent the rest of the morning—and many more to come— hopping up and down those damn stairs.

After breakfast I met Cheng Hao in the training hall where I'd first seen him with the Singaporeans. He was to be my private tutor.

In the movies and the picture books sold to tourists, the myth is that the monks spent every moment of every day in exotic training practices. They would hang themselves from trees. They would eat their meals while balancing bowls on their heads. They would take naps hanging upside down. They would pour tea from hundred-pound teakettles. They would study ancient Buddhist texts while their masters broke bricks over their heads.

The pictures were real, not faked or staged. The monks could do all these things, because they were fantastic athletes. But this was not how they spent most of their training days. Instead, their regimen would be familiar to any professional athlete, which was why the visiting TV producers, always paragons of "truthiness," never filmed their normal practice schedule. The fantasy made for much more compelling TV.

A normal session went like this:

9:00–9:10—Run around the practice hall to warm up.
9:10–9:20—Perform a series of basic calisthenics across the mat: slide-steps, knee-raised runs, leaps of all types, more of those damned frog-leaps, tumbles, rolls.
9:20–9:25—Switch to basic kungfu moves—punches, kicks, and throws—and more gymnastic moves: leaping kicks, flips, back handsprings, barrel rolls, aerials.
9:25–9:40—Break for individual stretching with a particular focus on splits, full and side.
9:40–9:50—Kicking stretches.
9:50–10:00—Rest.

10:00–10:20—Practice individual movements in the particular
  form they are working on, or a specialized type of iron kungfu.
10:20–10:50—Take turns doing the entire form they are trying to
  perfect.
10:50–11:00—Warm down.

After lunch, the monks repeated the same schedule in the afternoon session. And this remained unchanged—day after day, for six
days a week—from preadolescence to the end of their fighting careers in their mid-twenties. Repetition was the key. For those four
hours they almost never altered the schedule. The prebreakfast
and post-dinner slots were the only times they could train individually. The only time they'd adjust their routine was if they had a
performance for a group of tourists during one of their normal training sessions, usually in the afternoon.

I made it all the way to the 9:40 kicking stretches before my in-
adequacies became obvious. I couldn't get my legs higher than my
chest and even that height required me to bow my head, arms, and
back forward like I'd just been punched in the gut. Cheng Hao tried
to keep an even temper. But I was so bad, he finally couldn't help
himself.

"Have you practiced kungfu before?" he asked.

"For three years."

"Seems more like three weeks."

The monks didn't have joints and ligaments. They had rubber
bands in their legs. Without the proper flexibility, it is impossible to
make Shaolin forms look right. It was one of the reasons the Chinese believe you have to start kungfu at a young age when the body
is limber and can be kept that way throughout the aging process. I
was starting at the stiff end of adolescence and trying to work my
way backward.

After stetching we moved on to the eighteen basic movements,
which were believed to be the same eighteen calisthenic exercises
the Bodhidharma disciples practiced, but probably weren't. These
movements cropped up with the greatest frequency in various
Shaolin forms, like Small Red Boxing and Luohan Boxing, which
consisted of fifty to sixty sets of techniques. One basic movement involved stepping forward while your right hand blocked and trapped

an imaginary opponent's punch as your left hand struck his face. Another basic movement required you to spin 360 degrees and use your foot to hook your imaginary opponent's leg while your left hand blocked his imaginary punch and your right struck him in the chest, knocking him over.

I spent a lot of time falling down during that first class.

The first thing I noticed about Chinese kungfu was its complexity. Both karate and tae kwon do were simplified and modernized at the turn of the century, in order to be taught more easily. Almost every movement in those styles has a very clear and obvious self-defense purpose. Traditional Shaolin kungfu is the opposite. It is complicated and obscure. I couldn't make heads or tails of at least half of the basic movements. They were so odd that they looked like interpretive dance moves. They were so complex it is impossible to describe them in words. I would later try to help an administrator at another Shaolin school clean up his English translation of a Shaolin forms book. It went something like: "Right hand is placed at forty-five-degree angle with fingers straight, palm pointed at the sky. Left hand is palm up at right elbow. Rotate 180 degrees with back leg moving perpendicular, while bending at the knee. At the same time, both hands sweep counterclockwise and . . ."

That first morning, Cheng Hao explained that there was a method to this apparent madness. Before the gun, kungfu masters had the most valuable and dangerous skills around. How was an older master to prevent some young hothead from picking up his best techniques in a year or so and then using it for evil ends—or worse, against the older master? How was he to keep the younger students long enough for them to feel proper loyalty to him and learn enough self-control not to bring the master into disrepute? Simple—he hid his best techniques in these complex movements, which contained a number of superfluous moves. After enough years of loyal training, the master would reveal the uses of certain techniques, which the student—having practiced them over and over again—had mastered without knowing it. I immediately recognized this technique from the "wax on, wax off" pedagogic philosophy of *The Karate Kid*.

But that was before the gun. Cheng Hao was more than happy to explain each self-defense application of the basic movements as he taught them to me. Even with the explanations the moves still seemed impractical. The angles of attack were odd. The combinations seemed needlessly complex. One technique involved hooking the back of an opponent's left ankle with the right foot and then trapping his leg with the right knee. At that same moment, I was supposed to lean forward to straighten the opponent's leg and punch at his chest to knock him over. The technique seemed useless to my untrained eyes.

"Master," I said after a few tries. "This spinning dog-hook technique seems too difficult to be effective."

Cheng Hao was quiet for a moment before he responded.

"Interesting you would say that. Last year there was a German karate instructor here who was very rude. Every day he insulted Shaolin kungfu and said it was not as good as karate. Finally, I said to him, 'Okay, you use any karate attack you want and I'll defend against it with a traditional Shaolin technique.' He faked a punch and then kicked a roundhouse. I used the same technique you just asked me about. I caught him under the knee and leaned until he collapsed. He had to use crutches to walk for the rest of the time he was here, but he never insulted Shaolin kungfu again."

Cheng Hao smiled and shrugged in embarrassment as he finished the story. "It was probably excessive, a violation of *wude*," he said. "Martial arts ethics."

"I hope you don't think I was being rude," I said.

"No, no, no, you were just asking a question."

"Because if you ever think I'm being rude, just tell me and I'll stop."

"Don't worry," he said. "I will."

Amituofo.

After thirty minutes of working on basic movements, Cheng Hao started to teach me Shaolin's beginner form, *Xiao Hong Quan*— Small Red Boxing. Most of Shaolin's beginning Chinese students study the basic movements for six months to a year before moving to forms. But, Cheng Hao explained, the monks sped the process up for us *laowai* who have less time, less patience for basics, and a greater need for external markers of our accomplishments. The monks knew that even before we were good at one form, we wanted to start learning the next. They had studied us closely.

Small Red Boxing had about fifty-five movements, more or less, depending on who was teaching it. Each master tended to teach Shaolin forms with small variations. It was, Cheng Hao said, why there were so many different kungfu styles in China. Over time, the variations on individual Shaolin forms became larger and larger until something new was created.

There are thousands, if not tens of thousands, of distinct styles of kungfu. There are styles devoted to every conceivable animal. There are "drunken" styles, regional styles, styles exclusively dedicated to one weapon. There are family styles, which are never taught to anyone outside a bloodline. There are external and internal styles, styles for ground fighting, joint manipulation (*qin na*), and even one focused on head-butting. Chinese kungfu is one of the most glorious examples of obsessive-compulsive behavior in the history of human culture.

Each style of kungfu is marked by distinct qualities. While most martial arts forms take advantage of the entire plane of a performance mat, Shaolin forms always stay on a single straight line. You attack to your right, stepping forward, and then at some point, you turn 180 degrees and attack to the left. This is because the fundamental principle of Shaolin kungfu is that it could be, if necessary, practiced "under the shadow of an ox." Cheng Hao demonstrated. Instead of stepping to the left or the right along a straight line as he did each technique, he would jump straight up into the air, complete the technique while aloft, and then land in the same spot as before. Then he would jump straight up in the air again, complete the next technique while aloft, and land in the same spot, etc. The line was reduced to a single point. I asked him why.

"I don't know. Maybe because the early monks lived in really small rooms," he said. Then he laughed. "I guess we still do."

Watching Cheng Hao teach Small Red Boxing was like watching a master mathematician teach high school algebra. It had been so long since he had thought about Small Red Boxing that it took him a few moments to walk through the moves for himself. And then, once he pulled the first part of the form from his long-term muscle memory, he soared through the first ten movements, his technique flawless, as perfect as I had ever seen a form performed. And then he stopped, scratching his head. He wasn't sure how to transition from move ten to move eleven. Was it duck, turn, and snap kick? Or did he turn, then duck, and snap kick?

He grinned sheepishly, "It's been a while since I taught this form. Usually one of the older monks teaches it." I asked him what he usually taught. "More advanced forms. My specialty is eagle. So if some foreigner wants to learn that, they call me in. But the monks who usually teach *laowai* are on vacation, so here I am."

Cheng Hao was a gracious, kind, and enthusiastic coach. It wasn't until nearly a year later that I learned he hadn't wanted to teach me. In fact, none of the monks did when they heard I would be staying for a year. Teaching took time away from their own training, and they didn't get paid anything extra for doing it. They didn't mind teaching for a short stay. It was a nice break from their monotonous training schedule and a good way to make foreign friends and contacts, which was useful for any monk who might be thinking about emigrating (or defecting). Teaching for a year, on the other hand, was a surefire way to limit a monk's personal kungfu progress. This was particularly painful for the monks in their performing prime, usually from sixteen to twenty-six years of age. Cheng Hao had drawn the short straw with me. To his credit, I never would have guessed it.

In thirty minutes I barely managed to approximate five of the movements. My technique was poor, my movements were awkward, my stances were unbalanced, and my strikes lacked any power. If I had been a Chinese student, Cheng Hao would have shouted all these failings at me, while occasionally whacking me with a wooden staff to emphasize his criticisms. Shaolin's pedagogical style was profoundly corporal. China has a saying parents often use with their children when they punish them, *da shi teng, ma shi ai* (smacking is fondness; scolding is love). But I was a foreigner. More important, because he was only nineteen, I was two years older than he was. So he only said, "Good . . . very good . . . better . . . you're getting better" as I stumbled through the morning.

After class I asked him about Shaolin's training methods and why they were so different than in the movies.

"Those are just movies," he said.

"Did the monks in the past train like in the movies?"

"Who knows? It is hard to separate life from fiction," he replied. "But they may have. The monks of the past were much tougher than us. Their lives were much more bitter."

"Your lives now don't seem easy to me."

"Oh, it is much better than in the past, much better than even when I came here nine years ago. At the Wushu Center we train indoors on mats, not outside on the dirt, as we did when I was a boy."

Like all truly civilized societies, Shaolin had a siesta culture. After lunch all the monks took their *xiuxi* (rest) until the three P.M. afternoon workout. The only exception was when a big tour arrived later than expected and the monks were roused to give a performance. That first day I was too excited about my first lesson with an honest-to-God Shaolin monk to fall asleep. That would be the last day I skipped a chance to recover before another class.

The two-hour afternoon session was identical to the morning workout, as every workout would be for the next three months. I ran. I jumped. I reluctantly frog-jumped. I rolled. I tumbled. I sweated. I stretched. I kick-stretched. I learned more basic movements. I fumbled through more of Small Red Boxing. And as I did everything, Cheng Hao said, "Okay . . . good . . . better . . . not bad . . . faster . . . with power . . . very good."

I went to bed that night as happy as I'm capable of being. I had found the monks, and I had trained with them. All was right with my world. I had trouble falling asleep. It had been a thrilling, incredible day.

It would be the last one without pain.

The second day is always the worst one for new students at Shaolin. My body hurt so badly it felt like a barracks of marines had given me a code-red blanket party, with particular attention paid to my legs. It took me ten minutes to get out of bed. I had to lift my legs with my hands to swing them over the edge. To stand, I had to rock back and forth. As soon as I was up on my feet, I fell forward into the chair next to the wall. I looked at the clock: 8:30 A.M. I had missed the early morning workout and breakfast. Even "Socialism is Good" had failed to wake me.

I limped down the staircase like a cripple. Right foot down one step, left foot dragged to meet the right, right foot down one more step, while I grasped the hand railing for dear life. I was a wreck. While I had been nobody's all-American before coming to Shaolin, I had been an active high school athlete, playing on the basketball, soccer, and tennis teams. I had studied tae kwon do, aikido, and kungfu in college. I had never felt this shattered before.

As I shuffled like a highly medicated mental patient into the main building, I bumped into the painter I had met my first day at the Wushu Center.

"Started your training yesterday, right?" he asked, smiling.

I didn't say anything as I limped past.

The monks were gathered outside the performance hall, waiting for someone to bring the key to open the bike lock holding the doors closed. Deqing took one look at me and laughed, "Having fun?"

"Too much fun," I whispered back.

All the monks cracked up.

Cheng Hao did his best not to smile when I finally made it to the practice hall. "You hurt?"

"No problem."

"Studying kungfu is very bitter."

"So it would seem."

It took everything I had that morning to run around the room and then try to jump, tumble, and spin across the mat. I nearly cried when it came time for the frog-jumping. I couldn't bend more than a couple of inches at the knees as I hopped across the mat.

"Your frog is very tall," Cheng Hao called out to me.

By stretch time, I was a quivering mess. The practice room was two stories high. Where the second floor would normally be, there was an internal balcony surrounding the room on two sides. Two staircases led up to it on either side, so people could go up and watch the practice below. The initial stretching was done with the aid of one of the staircases. The first stretch required me to place one leg up as high as possible, keep it straight, and then bend my nose to my knee. The problem was that the tendons behind my knee felt like frayed string about to snap. The pain was extraordinary, and my foot was two steps lower than it had been the day before.

I tried to bend toward my knee, but I couldn't get more than a couple of inches forward. Cheng Hao got behind me and started pushing on my back. I tried breathing through the pain. I tried placing my mind somewhere else, somewhere pleasant, on a beach in Acapulco, in the Playboy Mansion, at a Pizza Hut in Topeka. But there was no escaping this room or this unbearable pain. I grew frantic, certain that one of the tendons would actually tear.

"Master, I'm very sorry," I said. "But maybe I should skip to-day's practice until my leg heals."

"It won't help," Cheng Hao said. "If you rest until you feel bet-ter, then you practice, your leg will hurt just as much the day after. Better to get it over with now."

"How long will that take?"

"Six to seven days."

I was unable to imagine surviving a week of this.

"Put your nose to your knee," he said, pushing harder.

I started to beg, "Master, please, let me rest for one day."

"No, it won't help."

"My leg is going to break," I mewled.

"No, it won't."

When I was younger I loved reading war memoirs. I often won-dered if I could withstand being tortured. Now I had my answer. At that point I'd have given Cheng Hao anything—money, state se-crets, sexual favors—for a reprieve from kungfu training.

Somehow, he got me through that practice and the rest of the week with a combination of cajolery, shame, and song. He wanted me to teach and translate for him Ace of Base's "All That She Wants"—the most popular Western song in China at the time. We spent a great deal of time running around the room and debating whether the singer wanted another baby as in child or baby as in boyfriend. Cheng Hao insisted it was another child.

"If she already has a boyfriend, why would she want another one?" he asked.

I decided not to explain.

Cheng Hao turned out to be right. It took six days before my legs recovered, and afterward I was far more flexible. But it wasn't the last time at Shaolin I'd be pushed to the point where I would beg for mercy.

2

THE SHOW MUST GO ON

I had defied my father to come to Shaolin, because I wanted to go to the most isolated, cutoff, far-flung, off-the-map place in the Mandarin-speaking world. And like most people who are not careful of what they wish for, my dream was granted. And, after the initial thrill of success passed, I was completely miserable.

No friends, no family, not even any English-speaking strangers—Shaolin was total immersion. At some point within the first month I started talking to myself, which wouldn't have been so bad if it weren't for the fact that I was also answering myself. I'd never imagined how crucial English was to my sense of a unified self—part good and part bad, but all of a whole. I started to experience two versions of me: one English-speaking and one Chinese-speaking. Matt was a clever, thoughtful boy. *Bao Mosi* was a verbally impaired dunce, always nodding his head and smiling and saying "right, right, right" when he had no idea what had just been said to him and was desperately hoping his brain would be able to translate that last comment before the speaker veered off onto another track. *Bao Mosi* was constantly working under a ten-second delay.

"Are you [something]?" one of the monks would ask. "All of us are going to [something] [something]. Interested?"

"Right, right, right . . . okay," I would respond.

The Wushu Center had the only phone in the entire village capable of making international calls. It worked in about one out of every ten tries. The price was $8 per minute. The Wushu Center also had the village's only international fax machine. The price was

$20 per page. After failing several times to reach home by phone, I sent a short fax message per my mother's demand that I reassure her of my continued survival.

> Mother, your son lives still. But the natives grow restless. Please send more wampum. And some Peter Pan peanut butter. Food here is terrible. Will call when possible. Love, Little Lord Fauntleroy

Any letter or package from home took about thirty days to arrive: five days from America to Beijing, seven days from Beijing to Zheng Zhou, fourteen days from Zheng Zhou to Shaolin, then about a week for the Faulknerian drunks in the Shaolin post office to get around to telling me, the only American in the village, that a package had arrived from the United States. That is, if they hadn't developed a hankering for Peter Pan peanut butter. All my packages and letters were opened, some never made it, and if they did, the stamps were gone, because foreign stamps were collectibles.

I was so lonely that for the first and last time in my life, when not under threat of being grounded, I wrote letters. And not little notes, I wrote twenty-, twenty-five-, thirty-page, single-spaced treatises. I sent them to everyone—my parents, my friends, my ex-girlfriend—mostly, it pains me to say, my ex. Inspired by the example of all those married convicted felons, I had hopes of rekindling her affections with the power of my words. Fortunately, I have managed to repress all of those words, because they were most likely of the desperate, heartbroken variety, which are never particularly attractive. Nor, in general, is a college dropout who joins a Buddhist monastery. She sent a single Dear John letter back. Unfortunately, I remember every single one of its I-love-you-but-I'm-not-in-love-with-you words.

I was so completely cut off from any news that it wasn't until late December that I first heard the results of the 1992 U.S. presidential election. The painter, who had helped me when I first came to the Wushu Center, said to me one day, "America has a new president."

"Who won?"

"I am not sure, but I do know one thing," he continued, "*Bushi Bushi.*"

The Chinese phrase for "is not" is *bu* (2nd tone) *shi* (4th tone). The Chinese transliteration of George Bush's surname is *bu* (4th tone) *shi* (2nd tone). But I couldn't hear the tonal differences, because the painter's rural Henan accent was thick and my Chinese was still poor, so I misinterpreted him as saying that the president of the United States *bushi bushi* (is not, is not.)

I was momentarily confused. Why would he repeat "is not"? Was it for emphasis? Did something dramatic happen? The president "is not, is not"? Did he mean, "there is no president"? There was an assassination?

My heart started racing.

It is an indication of how deep my sense of isolation was that my first reaction was America had slipped into anarchy and the federal government had collapsed.

Sensing my distress, the painter repeated nervously, *"Bushi Bushi."*

"What did you say?" I demanded.

"Bushi Bushi."

Finally, I heard the tonal shifts and understood he was saying, "It is not Bush."

It was not until several weeks later that I discovered it was Clinton, not Perot, who was our forty-second president.

Shaolin kungfu has eighteen different official weapons, but there are forms for more. Shaolin has five main animal styles—tiger, leopard, eagle, snake, and praying mantis—but there are more. It is estimated that Shaolin has more than 200 open-hand forms, but no one has been able to record them all. Historians of martial arts explain the creation of all of these styles either for self-defense (Shaolin was an isolated monastery often attacked by bandits) or religious reasons (kungfu forms are a type of moving meditation), but that doesn't explain the complexity. It took me all of a week to come up with my own theory: boredom. Put a bunch of sexually repressed young men on a mountaintop with nothing to do but meditate and practice kungfu and the myriad of Shaolin styles is the result.

Unlike previous generations of Shaolin students, I had access to a TV, kungfu movies, pool tables, and *Street Fighter II* to occupy my free time. But even with all that, except when I was studying kungfu, I was like a jonesing addict in detox. I missed Western food, the English language, my friends and family. But I felt the aching loss of visual stimuli at least as much. Nights at Shaolin felt as tedious as extended car rides across the Kansas plains. Many evenings during that first month, the loneliness and isolation would grip me so hard around the chest I'd have trouble breathing. The worst of these panic attacks came on Saturday nights, because I had to face the prospect of Sunday without any kungfu training while all the time imagining all the fun my friends were having that I was not.

Shaolin's only truly interesting entertainment option was the monks' spectacular kungfu performances. There was no set schedule for them. They might not perform for several days, and then suddenly have three afternoon performances with an evening blowout. Tour operators would call at the last minute, hoping to get a better deal on the ticket prices. Or some government officials would appear with some foreign dignitaries they wanted to impress with a Chinese cultural event. Or a group would just show up at the door with a person in tow owed a favor by someone at the Wushu Center, and the monks had to drop what they were doing and put on a show.

The performances were designed like a superior version of the regular workout. The monks began with some jumping, leaping, and other gymnastic flips and falls across the mat. The youngest and least talented would start with basic leaping kicks. The difficulty of the techniques would ratchet up with each succeeding monk until the most talented concluded the warm-up: most often either Deqing with a series of whirling high kicks or Lipeng, a taciturn loner who could do twenty back handsprings on a space the size of a dinner table.

After limbering up the monks would execute the stretching kicks with military precision. Each back ramrod straight, every knee and elbow locked, every foot touching the top of every forehead, every leg snapping up and down almost faster than the eye could follow. Once this group warm-up was complete, the monks left the room to return one by one to perform their individual specialties.

These broke down into two groups: forms and *qigong* skills. Most of the *qigong* skills were iron kungfu feats. The Chinese believe in a concept called *qi*, which roughly translates as "vitality" or "breath" or "energy." They believe that *qi* courses through the human body like the Force in *Star Wars*, and this *qi* can be strengthened through breathing exercises and then focused to various parts of the body. Iron kungfu involves directing the *qi* to a part of the body to protect it from a blow. One monk was an expert in iron arm and leg kungfu. During the performance, various wooden staffs were broken over his limbs. A monk who specialized in iron stomach kungfu invited members of the audience to punch him as hard as they could. The blows had no observable effect. His facial expression never changed. Another monk broke bricks over his head.

Did *qi* protect them? In my experience, focusing the mind on a certain part of the body and imagining you were focusing energy there was helpful and necessary but not sufficient. Advanced practitioners of a particular iron kungfu had hardened that particular part of the body for so long and with such force that the physical alteration of their bodies bordered on deformity. Deqing, who practiced iron fist, had fists that were so thick they looked like pincushions—the fingers serving as the pins. Another monk, who practiced iron spear, had driven his fingers into hard dirt for so long that the four fingers of his right hand when held together were exactly the same length, his middle as short as his pinkie. And all the iron head practitioners had knots on their heads and spoke with stutters. So there are obvious limits to the power of *qi*: It can't stop bullets.

The iron kungfu performances were interspersed with expert form demonstrations. Except for one routine, none of the forms performed were traditional Shaolin-style forms. They were all variations of modern *wushu* competition forms.

When Mao Zedong banned kungfu in the 1950s, it was part of his overall ideological program to create a "New China" free from its feudal past and religious traditions. But banning kungfu was the equivalent of trying to outlaw high school football in west Texas. The Chinese are obsessed with kungfu; you can find septuagenarians practicing martial arts forms every morning in parks across the country. So Mao knew he needed to rechannel that passion. Because international sporting competitions were one of the fronts where the Cold War could be fought relatively safely, Mao and his cadre created two sports out of traditional kungfu: modern *wushu* and *sanda* (Chinese-style kickboxing).

Modern *wushu* was the kungfu equivalent of figure skating. Competitions, both with weapons and without, are held before judges who assign points based on the beauty and the technical difficulty of each participant's performance. The self-defense efficacy of the movements—the whole point of traditional kungfu—is irrelevant. Modern *wushu* is martial arts without the "martial." The emphasis is on speed, grace, beauty, and acrobatic ability. The highly stylized forms are peppered with the kind of flips and leaps you find in Olympic gymnastic competitions.

To support these new sports, the government made modern *wushu* and *sanda* part of the curriculum at the various *tiyu xiuyuan* (sports universities) across the country. It pushed for the acceptance of the two sports in international competitions. And it scoured the land for talented boys to be placed in intensive *wushu* training programs. The most famous product of the Chinese *wushu* machine is Jet Li, who was discovered during citywide sports testing in Beijing, enrolled in Beijing Sports University's *wushu* program— still considered the best in the country—and became a five-time national champion before making the movie *Shaolin Temple*, which launched his acting career.

Traditional kungfu masters from Taiwan and Hong Kong absolutely hate modern *wushu* because they (rightly) see it as a political assault on their art form with the intent of stripping away its martial and religious aspects. But the public loves *wushu*, because it is fast, beautiful, and the style most often seen in Hong Kong movies. Handsprings and back flips have zero usefulness in a fight, but they sure look cool. So that's what the monks gave the crowds. In fact, they had modified the competition *wushu* forms, which are highly regulated, to jazz them up even further. The goal was to excite, to maximize the "ooh"s and "ah"s. And they did, especially Deqing and Lipeng.

Lipeng was an expert in *Ditang Quan* (Floor Boxing), which

involved leaping into the air with various flying kicks and falling flat onto the mat. After entering with twenty back handsprings, he proceeded to do a series of front flips without using his hands, followed by several high-flying kicks, the last of which he finished by landing flat on his back. And so forth. As a pure example of acrobatic ability and physical toughness, it was breathtaking.

His only competition was Deqing, whose entire body was basically one fast twitch muscle. His endurance was lacking, but for the minute or so he was in front of the crowd he was an explosion of kinetic motion. He was so fast and so strong that he couldn't be bothered with the niceties of *wushu* forms, which require the feet, the hands, the head, and the body to be exactly a certain way at exactly a certain moment. He was too busy blowing through the form, leaping higher, spinning faster, charging harder. Deqing was the only monk that the other monks would make a point to watch. Part of it was his skill and part of it was the joy he exuded, but the major reason was that he was the only monk who consistently improvised new moves for his forms, sometimes on the spot. As great as the other monks were, once you had seen them do the same form exactly the same way a couple dozen times, you started to get a little jaded. Not with Deqing.

Deqing was once doing his version of Shaolin Drunken Style (created by a monk with a weakness for the bottle). In the middle of the form, he was supposed to jump into the air, complete a flying kick while rotating in a large parabola before landing flat on the left side of his body. But he had leaped too high and his body wasn't rotating over fast enough. He was going to crash flat on his back. So what he did was straighten his legs to stop his body's rotation, and then, in the middle of the air—six feet above the ground, laid out flat as a board—he rotated his hips, which flipped his body like a pancake. When he finally landed (it seemed like it took a minute), he was in a push-up position, his hands bracing his fall. A monk sitting next to me shook his head with awe and envy and exhaled under his breath, "Fucking Deqing."

I watched every performance I could. But even more entertaining were the monks' interactions before the show started. The monks were like a theater troupe. They bitched about aches and injuries. They complained about having to perform for small crowds. They were pumped when the house was packed or there were VIPs present. The less expert monks studied the performances of their betters, looking for techniques to appropriate. The stars were difficult to track down moments before their performances, usually arriving with a flourish at the last moment after one of the younger monks had been sent to fetch them. There was also endless backbiting about who was over-the-hill, who wasn't improving fast enough, who was shirking the performances by faking an injury, who was not as good as he thought he was, who never gave a good performance unless the crowd was large enough, who needed to learn something new instead of doing the same old form over and over again, who needed to spend less time instructing others and more time looking after his own deteriorating kungfu skills.

As the monks switched from the jogging pants and T-shirts they wore for practice to their orange monk robes, the banter would go something like this:

"Where's Lipeng?"

"I don't know."

"Go get him."

"Why should I go?"

"Because I told you to."

"Hey, who has a sash?"

"Where's your sash?"

"It's in the wash."

"That's why you have two."

"They are both in the wash."

"You're a stupid egg."

"You need to shave your head again."

"But it's so cold."

"When you bring the staff down on my arm, snap it. Be fast. Last time, you nearly broke my shoulder."

"If you don't like how I do it, get someone else."

"Where's Lipeng?"

"He's never here."

"Who's in the crowd?"

"A group of *laowai*."

"How many?"

"Maybe twenty."

"Where are they from?"

"America."

"How can you tell?"

"Everyone give full effort today. I don't want to see any laziness out there."

"Their clothes. And they're fat."

"I want you to do praying mantis form."

"I can't."

"Why?"

"My back. You know my back is hurt."

"It's been more than a month."

"But I already did praying mantis this morning."

"So you can't do it again?"

"My back. It really hurts."

"Okay, then do iron stomach."

"I can't."

"Aiya! Why not?"

"I have diarrhea."

"Then practice your iron asshole kungfu at the same time. Okay, the music has started. Everyone get ready. Will someone get Lipeng? Damn! Everyone ready? Let's go."

3

CHINESE MEDICINE

The Shaolin monks were my hosts, and I was their guest. The problem was I didn't want to be a guest. I wanted to be part of the family. But I was the ultimate outsider, a pampered foreigner who ate at the fancy restaurant and lived in the fancy hotel. I had a passport that allowed me to leave anytime I wanted. I had credit cards that could fund my departure. And I was an American: a citizen of the country the Chinese most envied, admired, and feared. After being an object of curiosity the first few nights, I was separated by a wall of polite distance. I had made it inside the Shaolin gates, but I wasn't a member of the community.

My only hope for acceptance was to earn their respect. Status among the monks was based on kungfu skill and/or willingness to suffer, "to eat bitter." There was not much chance I was going to impress any of them with my kungfu skills any time soon, so eating bitter was my only option.

Including the early morning workout, the average Wushu Center student trained five hours a day. I decided to try for eight. After the initial physical shock, I started adding hours. In week three, I added an extra session after dinner. In week four, I cut down on my siesta and added an extra hour before my afternoon session. I was up to seven hours a day before I got stuck. Each time I tried to add another hour, I slipped back a couple of hours the next day. My body just couldn't take it. But seven was more than anyone else and I soon became aware that others were taking notice.

My only companion during my 2:00–3:00 P.M. session was a button-cute ten-year-old girl. She was a student of Monk Lipeng's father, a wiry little man with a hard gaze and a scruffy Fu Manchu mustache. A descendant of a long line of martial arts masters, Lipeng's father brought his wife, daughter, and son, whom he had personally trained, to Shaolin because it provided the best opportunities for his family's particular skills. As a young boy Lipeng earned money for his family as a street performer, dazzling the tourists who came to Shaolin with his kungfu skills. When the Wushu Center opened, his talents secured a place, albeit a tenuous one, for his family. His father was given a job as janitor. And the family was given housing in the broom closet under the staircase next to my training room. Slats of plywood had been attached together and leaned against the staircase to provide what little privacy could be had in thirty square feet of the busiest corner in the Wushu Center. The first time I was invited inside I tried hard to seem unfazed by the space restrictions, which made an airline bathroom seem roomy. Lipeng's father finally asked me what I thought. I told him his home was very nice.

He smiled at my white lie. "No, it is inadequate, but it is better than where we lived before."

"Where was that?" I asked.

"A cave."

"Ah, a cave, right . . ." I said, as my brain frantically searched for an appropriate response. "Well, this is definitely better than a cave in so many ways."

"We have a floor now," Lipeng's father said.

"True, true, true, no dirt, that's one."

"And less bugs," his wife added, smiling.

"Right, right, right, that's another," I said. "I hate bugs."

"And there's electricity," Lipeng's father concluded.

"So much better," I said. "Yes, yes, yes."

Like many of the young children at Shaolin, the little girl I trained with in the afternoon was an economic orphan. Her parents were so poor they couldn't afford to raise her. Lipeng's father was a distant relative, so he agreed to take her on as a disciple, proving that there were still lower rungs on China's economic ladder than living under a staircase. In return for her training, room, and board, the little girl did all the chores asked of her. After seeing her sweeping the floor outside their home, I nicknamed her Cinderella.

We were both beginning students, training alone with private teachers. We were both Shaolin outsiders: she an orphan girl, me a *laowai*. We were both a long way from home, and we were both miserable. So we became fast friends. She had it tougher than me, because Lipeng's father was from the cruelty-is-kindness school of kungfu instruction. If she didn't do everything perfectly, Lipeng's father would shake her and shout, "If you don't work hard, I'll send you away and then you will have no one left who can afford to feed you!"

One day Lipeng's father ran her through a series of exercises so brutal and extreme that I came dangerously close to intervening. He was training her to do back handsprings. After making her do a handstand for ten minutes, he had her bending backward like a pretzel for a hundred repetitions until she could barely stand up anymore. After that class, Lipeng's father said to me, "I know you think my teaching method is severe, but you will see it will be the best for her. In this world, she only has one chance and that is to be excellent at kungfu."

Because Cinderella was so often on the verge of tears, I decided to make it my mission to cheer her up. So during that hour when we were training alone each day, I did what you do with kids to make them laugh: pratfalls, airplane lifts, pretend to be a monster chasing her around the room. And then as soon as Lipeng's father entered the training hall we'd act like we didn't know each other. He was smart enough to know that as a teacher he was in need of a good cop.

Those early afternoon sessions and my acquaintance with Lipeng's father probably saved my martial arts career at Shaolin. After about a month, I developed this aching tenderness in the area right below my kneecaps. When I tried to snap a kick, a jolt of excruciating pain shot up and down my body. None of the monks knew what to do. Even Cheng Hao said it was bad enough that I should rest until it healed, which meant it must have been really serious. The only thing more bitter than training at Shaolin was living in Shaolin without being able to train. After several days of watching me forlornly wander the halls, Lipeng's father told Cheng Hao to have me visit him at home the next night.

It turned out the Wushu Center's janitor was the only person in

Shaolin skilled in traditional Chinese medicine. As I walked into their home under the staircase, I found Lipeng's mother cooking a meal over an electric burner and Lipeng's father cooking a strange brackish yellow stew over another burner.

"Have you eaten?" Lipeng's mother, an unfailingly pleasant woman, asked me.

It was a common greeting in Shaolin. In a nation where millions of people went hungry every day, "Have you eaten?" was the equivalent of "How are you doing?" If you had eaten, you were doing well. If you hadn't, you weren't. The expected response was "Yes, I've eaten," even if you hadn't, or "I am about to," even if you weren't, but the possibility was left open to say, "No, I haven't" if you were really starving and had no prospects for food anytime soon. In such cases, the questioner was obliged to invite you to dinner.

"Yes, I have eaten," I said.

By leaning over and sliding carefully, I was able to make it to their bed, where Lipeng's father directed me to sit down for my examination. To all outward appearances, he looked like any other commoner in Henan. He was short and scrawny, maybe five foot five and 125 pounds, and wore a baggy white T-shirt, sweatpants, and a local brand of tennis shoes. The only exceptions were the preternatural fierceness of his eyes and his right hand, which was at least 50 percent larger than his left. It looked like a transplant from a giant, and it had a callus the size of a silver dollar along the fleshy part of the palm. He was obviously an advanced practitioner of iron palm kungfu.

As he looked me over, he was intermittently soaking his right hand in a yellow stew, which on closer examination contained what looked like a collection of samples from a nature trail walk: bark, weeds, leaves.

"Chinese medicine," he said.

"You practice iron palm kungfu, yes?"

"Yes," he said. He went on to explain that hardening the body was only half of iron kungfu practice; Chinese medicine was the other half. It was needed to heal that part of the body so one could continue practicing just as hard the next day, otherwise you'd have to wait for it to heal on its own. "Without medicine, your iron kungfu can only improve so much."

He went over to grab two smooth, palm-size river rocks and presented them to me. I knew this was the point where I was supposed to strike them with my palm. Nothing makes an iron kungfu practitioner happier than seeing the look on an inexperienced student's face when he attempts what the master has perfected. I struck the stones as hard as I could. The reverberation ran up my arm and rattled my teeth. His grin was wide. Then he set one stone on top of the other and brought his hand down once and then twice, before the top rock split in two. I'd seen wood, brick, and concrete blocks broken, but never something as hard as river rocks. This was the equivalent of having a Harvard Medical School diploma above the door.

"Will you fix my knees?" I asked.

"I don't normally treat people. It is too much trouble. But I like how hard you are training. You are not afraid to eat bitter. And you are kind to my student. So I will treat you," he said. "But I will have to travel to many different places to buy the ingredients for your medicine."

"How much will that cost?"

We worked out a price, which I felt had a slight but not egregious foreigner surcharge added to it, and I left. If it worked, it'd be worth every penny because if my knees didn't heal, I'd have to return to America for treatment. From that point forward, I nicknamed him Doc.

Five days later Doc returned from his trip, and my Chinese medical treatment began. Twice a day, I went to him for a thirty-minute session. Like his iron palm kungfu medicine, my mixture was boiled in stew but with a browner result. It looked like wet mulch. A washcloth was placed over each knee and a bowl underneath each leg. Then Doc poured the no-longer-quite-boiling medicinal stew slowly over the washcloths, watching to see just how much I squirmed.

"Oh! Ah! Ow!"

"Hot?" he'd ask, smiling.

"Yes."

"Too hot?" he'd ask, smiling more.

There was only one appropriate answer to that question: "No."

"Good."

On the fifth afternoon of treating my knees, which still hurt as much as before, Doc posed the question he'd been waiting to ask, "What do you think of the Wushu Center leaders?"

His eyes were bright, expectant. How I answered the question would either secure or destroy our *guanxi* (relationship). My assumption was that no janitor living under a staircase could have any great affection for the bosses, so I went with the honest answer: "I hate them to death."

He grinned at the fervor in my voice. "Yes, they are awful. Bad people."

I grinned back. Nothing cements a friendship like agreement on whom to hate.

Doc and I discussed the leaders and their individual flaws. The head of the Wushu Center was Leader Liu. He was your typical political appointment: tall, broad shouldered, executive hair. He wore a suit well, but it was as empty as his head. It was clear that his striking wife was the brains behind Leader Liu's ascent up the Henan Communist Party ladder. The Wushu Center was a plum position. Besides the extra money he could pocket, foreign tours offered one of the best opportunities for junkets. On every tour, the Wushu Center leaders secured a number of extra places for important local politicians, who could not otherwise afford a foreign trip, trading these spots for political favors.

The brains of the Wushu Center, as so often is the case, rested with the number two, Jiao Hongpo, or Deputy Leader Jiao. He was the final leader I had met the first time I arrived at the Wushu Center, the one with the most keys. Extremely tall and thin, Deputy Leader Jiao was the only former Shaolin monk who was also a member of the party, no small feat and a testament to his operational skills. (Less than 5 percent of China's population belongs to the Communist Party, and you need references from at least two current members to join.) In Deputy Leader Jiao's universe there were no straight lines, only angles, and everyone was working one. He took a kind of Machiavellian delight in this worldview, and he often wore a slightly cynical smirk when he was in a negotiation. Asking a favor of Deputy Leader Jiao was a fool's errand; no one came out ahead of him in an encounter. It was obvious to all that he was biding his time until Leader Liu moved on to something more prestigious. Deputy Leader Jiao had grown up in the area. Shaolin was his life. And in his own supremely self-interested way, he was quite devoted to it.

Vice Deputy Leader Me was the number three, and he was widely considered to be the most honest, straightforward, and reliable one of the bunch, which is why he was rarely seen and never allowed in on any big decisions. I only once had any dealings with him in the time I was in Shaolin.

As Doc and I discussed the leaders, he let slip, "They wanted me to teach students for them and demonstrate my iron hand kungfu for the tourists. But I refused. I'd rather pick up trash than work for them."

I felt a wave of admiration wash over me. In a country that often seemed like all the independence had been clubbed out of it, here was a man who chose to live in a broom closet rather than kowtow to the Wushu Center emperors. He was the first person I'd ever met with more stiff-necked pride than my mother.

"How did you learn kungfu?" I asked him.

"My father taught me. His father taught him. We have our own family style of kungfu. It is not Shaolin."

"Then why did you come to Shaolin?"

"Because the best martial artists in the world are here. I wanted Lipeng to have the best training. I taught him when he was a boy, then I hired other masters to teach him their styles."

"Does he study Chinese medicine?"

"Not yet."

"Will you teach it to me?"

"I'm sorry. I can't."

"I can pay for lessons."

"Money doesn't matter. I will only train my son . . ." Doc paused, "when he wants to learn. It is our family tradition. My father taught me. You understand?"

"Okay," I said. "But can you tell me what's in the bowl?"

"It's also a secret. But I will tell you one of the ingredients." He held up what looked like a piece of hard beef jerky. "This is rat's skin."

It was some pretty magical rat's skin. My knees healed in ten days and never bothered me again.

While Doc was treating me for my knees, he urged me to keep practicing despite my injury.

"But I can't kick."

"Your arms still work."

"What should I do with my arms?"

"I can teach you an iron kungfu," he said.

"Would you?"

"You are a hardworking student. You should learn as much as possible while you are here."

Lipeng had mastered the greatest number of iron kungfus of any monk in Shaolin, which was why I was excited to have his father teach me. Lipeng's most popular trick was iron stomach kungfu. His stomach muscles were so strong he could vacuum seal a large serving bowl to his stomach that was impossible for anyone to pull off. This was a big crowd pleaser during the monk's performances. Lipeng would distend his stomach with air, place the bowl over his belly, then contract his muscles, sealing it to his torso. Members of the audience were invited down to try and pull the bowl off his belly. They never could.

I told Doc I didn't want to study any iron kungfu that caused permanent or visible damage. I didn't want deformed hands or a stutter.

"I can teach you iron forearm kungfu," he said. "You won't notice any difference."

I hadn't heard of that particular kungfu.

"What usefulness does iron forearm kungfu have?" I asked.

"Your arms become so hard that when you block your opponent's punch or kick, his arm or leg is hurt instead of you."

The practice started with thirty minutes of *qigong* exercises. Doc had me standing outdoors breathing heavily in and out of my nose while rubbing my forearms over and over again. It took a long time before I stopped feeling like a weirdo.

After the *qigong* warm-up, Doc would pick out a thick tree trunk, and I would spend the next thirty minutes banging away at it full force with my forearms. Actually, I'd spend five minutes banging away at it full force and the next twenty-five minutes asking

Doc if it had been thirty minutes yet. The pain was extraordinary and cumulative, like taking a hammer to a bruise and trying to make it bigger.

After banging the tree, Doc would cook up a special iron kungfu herbal stew, and I'd soak my arm in the concoction. The stew did seem to relieve some of the pain, but it had the side effect of staining my arms a sickly yellow. For months I walked around with forearms that were black and blue and yellow.

After six weeks of practice, I started to get a little cocky. During their iron kungfu demonstrations, the monks used these special wooden staffs, which are hard but brittle so when they break they snap cleanly and loudly. One night I was in the performance hall with some of the monks, bragging about my iron forearm training.

"Sure it was bitter at first," I said. "But I am getting used to it."

"Do you think you could break a staff?" Cheng Hao asked me.

"Of course."

Cheng Hao grabbed a staff. I stuck out my arm. He brought it down sharply, cracking my right forearm. The staff snapped in two. My arm was sore but, goddamn, that staff was no match for Iron Forearm Boy.

"Let's try the left one," I said, puffed out with pride.

I didn't notice that Doc was watching me through the window.

The next day he called me into his apartment under the staircase. I was surprised to find Lipeng inside waiting for me. He rarely talked to me, or anyone else for that matter.

"*Bao Mosi*, I saw you demonstrating your iron forearm kungfu last night," Doc said. "You have improved quickly."

I expected him to be pleased, but Doc didn't look happy with me, and he was not the kind of man you wanted to upset. He could crack a skull with that iron palm.

I pulled out my most ingratiating smile, "It is only because your teaching is so excellent, master."

"Right, right, right. Here, let's you and I hit our forearms together."

I suspected a trap but could see no way out of it. Doc and I gently started banging our forearms against each other. I was surprised to discover that his were less hard than mine. We picked up speed and strength: right inside, right outside, left inside, left outside.

Over and over again. Finally, Doc stopped. He rubbed his forearms. "Good, very good. Your forearms are much tougher than before."

"You do not practice iron forearm kungfu, master?"

"No, never. See, after only six weeks your forearms are harder than mine," he said, setting me up. "Why don't you try with Lipeng?"

Lipeng rolled up his sleeve. Full of myself, I swung my right forearm at Lipeng's right forearm as hard as I could. It was like hitting a steel post. A jolt of pain ran straight up into my skull, popping my eardrums. My hand went into spasms. For several moments, I tried but was unable to close my fist.

"His arms are harder than stone!" I said.

"I started training him when he was six." Doc said.

"I didn't know he trained iron forearm kungfu."

"No, you didn't," he said with a stern look. "No one does, because he doesn't go around showing off all of his skills. Do you understand?"

"Yes, I understand, master."

"Good," Doc said. "I will see you tomorrow."

And with that, my lesson was over.

4

ROOMMATES

It took two months before any of the monks visited my room. Cheng Hao and Deqing were the first. When I opened the door one Sunday evening, they were dressed in the team's finest Western clothes: dress shirts, jeans, and black boots. The monks only owned a few outfits between them, so their wardrobe was a socialist collective. Any item bought while on foreign tours was freely borrowed based on need.

After entering my room, Deqing pulled out two samurai daggers.

"These are gifts for you," he said.

I invited them to sit down and poured tea for all of us.

"We are very sorry we haven't come to visit you earlier," Cheng Hao said. "We know how lonely you must be."

"No problem, no problem, no problem," I said, not meaning it.

Deqing continued, "It is embarrassing, but the leaders told us all it would be a bad idea to be seen spending too much time around you."

"Why?"

"You remember we told you that after Shaolin's last trip to America two monks defected?"

"Right."

"The leaders are afraid that some of us may want to defect also, and you might help us."

"Do some of you want to defect?"

"Possibly," Deqing said with a smile.

"Then I guess I will have to help you. What do you need?"

"The trip to America is planned for the spring," Cheng Hao said. "But we are touring Japan first."

Deqing said, "I need you to tell me how much you think a Japanese would pay for various martial arts equipment. For example, I can buy a Shaolin sword for $10. Do you think they'd pay $100?"

The idea of a Shaolin monk hawking kungfu equipment to the Japanese disturbed me.

"Why would you do something like that?" I asked.

"For the money," Deqing said, confused by my confusion.

"But you're a Buddhist monk," I said with an unmistakable tone of disapproval in my voice. "You're not supposed to make lots of money."

His emotions always on vivid display, Deqing's eyes narrowed, his mouth tightened, and his face turned bright red. I'd shamed and insulted him and for a moment he looked like he might hit me. Cheng Hao intervened.

"*Bao Mosi*, it is true that Buddhist monks are not supposed to concern themselves with money. But the leaders have seized all our passports to prevent us from leaving China. To get a second passport, we have to *zhao homen*," Cheng Hao said. "Find a back door."

It was slang for finding the right government official and bribing him.

"Oh, I see. I'm sorry, sorry, sorry," I apologized, desperately backtracking. "Yes, I believe the Japanese will pay $100 for a Shaolin sword. What else do you have to sell?"

Cheng Hao went through the list—nine-section whips, Shaolin T-shirts, Shaolin daggers. Deqing stayed quiet the rest of the time. He was still chewing over what I had said to him.

As I chewed over what I had said as well, it took me several days to realize I was suffering from a minor case of Orientalism. I felt like I had grown up in a shallow, materialistic society and wanted the Chinese to be wise and profound—in short, bracingly poor—so I could get my deepness fix before returning home. It had bothered me that while I was trying to become more like my romantic fantasy of the Chinese, they were trying to become more like their avaricious fantasy of Americans. We were two ships passing in the night.

It took Deqing, who quite rightly wondered where I got off criticizing his desire for a better life, much longer to forgive me.

Weeks later at the end of a practice session with Cheng Hao and Deqing, a scrum of younger Shaolin monks came bursting through the door to the training room. They were shouting, laughing, stomping, and smacking the ground with wooden staffs. A rat the size of two fists was zigzagging between their feet. The monks were trying to kill it before it reached the back door of the training hall that led into the mountains.

The rat was too quick for them to strike it with their staffs, but with the help of Cheng Hao, Deqing, and myself, we were able to encircle it. Realizing it was trapped, the rat stopped in the center, out of staff reach, and coolly surveyed its situation. Deqing stepped toward the rat and stomped his foot to frighten it. The rat didn't move. Deqing stomped his foot again. This time the rat leaped at Deqing and landed on his right thigh, a distance of at least five feet.

Surprised, Deqing kicked his leg, but the rat had its claws dug into his cotton pants. Deqing hopped on his left and kicked with full force with his right. It took five or six kicks before the rat was thrown off (or perhaps it decided to let go). The rat landed outside the circle next to the back door. Before anyone could react, it darted under the door and out to safety.

Deqing let out an awkward, embarrassed laugh. "Damn, even the rats at Shaolin know kungfu!"

This comment set off peals of laughter from the younger monks.

"Looks like he won the first round, Deqing."

"You afraid to fight the rat again?"

"You might want to learn rat kungfu."

Deqing let it go on for a couple of minutes, before saying, "Enough, enough, enough, already."

As the young monks were leaving the room, one turned to another and said, "What the matter, Little Zhang? Are you sad you won't be eating rat meat tonight?"

"I don't eat rat meat," Little Zhang replied defensively.

"Yes, you do. I've seen you."

"It wasn't rat meat."

"It was rat. You're a rat-meat-eater, rat-meat-eater, rat-meat-eater."

Deqing joined me for dinner that night. I had started inviting the monks to eat with me when I realized the restaurant served me more food than I could finish and the quality of the restaurant food was much better than the kitchen at the back of the Wushu Center where the monks, the Wushu Center students, and coaches ate. Most declined because they didn't want to be criticized by the leaders for fraternizing with the *laowai*. Deqing was secure enough in his position at the Wushu Center not to care.

Halfway through dinner I asked Deqing the question that had been on my mind since the afternoon. "The monks don't really eat rat meat, do they?"

"Not anymore. Times are better now."

"You're saying you used to eat rat?" I asked in disbelief.

"Five, ten years ago, sure. We never had any meat, and sometimes we'd get so hungry for it that if we caught a rat we'd eat it. But it almost wasn't worth it, because rat meat is so tough, it takes more energy to chew than it provides. And rats taste terrible," he said, shaking his shoulders in disgust at the memory.

"How old were you when you came to Shaolin?"

"I was eleven."

Deqing looked out the window with his brow furrowed as if trying to make up his mind about something. Finally, he turned back to me and started to speak.

"My father killed a man," Deqing said. "He was a truck driver. One night his brakes failed and he ran over an old peasant crossing the road. He was convicted and sentenced to ten years in jail."

"That's so unfair," I said.

Given the dilapidated state of most vehicles, most roads, and all traffic safety regulation in China, it was a wonder every truck driver in the country hadn't run over somebody.

"True, it wasn't his fault, but a man was dead. We lived in one of the nicer houses in my hometown in Zhejiang Province. Have you been to Zhejiang?"

"I haven't had the honor yet."

"I should take you. It is beautiful. My mother sold the house and all the furniture to help pay down the fine. But she only had enough money to reduce the sentence to seven years."

In China, most criminal punishment is either/or. You do the time, or you pay the fine. Or some combination of both.

"We had to move into a tiny hovel. The neighbors had always been envious of us. We were considered a wealthy family. But the crime and the move made us lose face. The boys at school started picking on my younger brother."

In China, the one-child-per-family policy was less strictly enforced in the countryside than in the cities, especially if the children were boys. There was a traditional Chinese proverb that was still repeated: "The more sons, the more happiness."

"You never told me you had a younger brother." I said. "What's he like?"

"He's an intellectual like you. Good in school. Likes to read. Not very good in a fight. So I started getting in fights at school to defend him. The teacher complained to my mother. She was desperate. Without my father's salary, she didn't have enough money to feed us both. So one day, she packed my bag and told me we were going on a trip. When we arrived at Shaolin, she dropped me off and said, 'You like to fight. Maybe the monks can teach you something.' Then she left me here."

As I listened to Deqing I was watching for some sign of emotional reaction to this terrible Sophie's Choice his mother had made. But he told the story like a trauma victim, like it had happened to someone else. And given how expressive Deqing usually was, this was almost as horrifying as the story itself.

"I knew I had to work hard to impress the monks. I didn't have any money for classes, so I watched them and practiced by myself. One day, one of the Shaolin monks noticed how hard I trained and took me into the temple to teach me.

"But I still didn't have any money for food. When I got too hungry, I'd linger outside a restaurant with my chopsticks. I'd wait until the customers had finished their meal and were walking away, and then I'd run to their table and eat what they had left before the waitress had a chance to clear the table. Imagine this little boy eating strangers' leftovers."

As he said this last sentence, the emotion finally returned to his voice and face. His eyes narrowed with anger and his face flushed red with the shame of the memory.

This was the boyhood wound that created the man who sat before me, whose kungfu contained such fury.

Deqing kept staring at me, and I knew he had told me his story only because I had questioned his right to make money. I wanted to crawl under the table to escape his gaze.

"I'm sorry, I'm sorry, I'm sorry," I said, my voice trembling.

"Why? It wasn't your fault," Deqing said, but kept his hard stare on me.

"I'm still sorry."

One of the first things I noticed at Shaolin was that Chinese men were much more physically affectionate than *laowai*. I noticed because after I started to hang out with the monks in their barracks, I found my back slapped, shoulder or thigh squeezed, hand held. And I found myself telling myself, "Don't pull away. Hold steady. Breathe through your nose."

I knew it was perfectly innocent, because in my daily walks to get my supply of Coke, I'd see boys walking arm in arm. Eventually, I started to notice that young women would do the same with each other. Finally, I realized that the male and female couples who came to Shaolin as tourists never touched each other in public. They walked side by side and talked to each other like intimates, but their bodies never touched. And so I drew the conclusion that physical affection was channeled into same-sex relations, because public displays of affection between the sexes was taboo.

The most exuberant public displayer of affection, because he was the most exuberant at everything, was Deqing. The first time I was walking down the street with him to visit the temple, he put his arm around my shoulder, squeezed, and said, "I like you."

"I like you, too," I replied. And because I couldn't help myself I added, "as a friend."

Deqing pulled his hand away from my shoulder, dropped it down, and clasped mine. As we walked down the road, I kept repeating in my head, *Breathe through your nose.* And my eyes darted at the people who passed us in the other direction to make certain no one was looking at us with suspicion.

But then Deqing interlaced his fingers with mine, and I literally jumped into the air. When I landed, my knees were locked, and my sphincter had tightened like I'd stepped on a nail.

Deqing looked at me funny, "Is there something wrong?"

"No, no, no, nothing is the matter," I said as I walked down the street like Frankenstein, all the while reminding myself that Deqing was interested in someone far fairer than me.

Of the 300 or so Chinese students at the Wushu Center, five were female. But there was only one who drew the attention of all the boys. Lotus was sixteen and in her first bloom of beauty. She had this impossible figure, like a Chinese version of Lara Croft. When she went out onto the street, she stopped traffic. Men rooted themselves to the ground and craned their necks to watch her pass. She was a triple take. Bite-your-knuckles beautiful. And Lotus knew and enjoyed it.

One day when I was practicing the nine-section whip—a chain made of nine two-inch-long metal spikes linked by metal hoops— she walked past. As I turned my head to stare, the whip caught on the wrong part of my arm, twisted around and smacked me hard on the head.

I couldn't stop myself from crying out in pain.

Seeing what had happened out of the corner of her eye, she giggled. Afterward, whenever she'd spy me in the courtyard practicing the nine-section whip, she'd find a reason to saunter past.

I'd have broken my vow of celibacy right then and there if Lotus had been interested in anything more than teasing me. But she was Deqing's girl.

Every night after practice, Deqing and Lotus would meet in the training hall, ostensibly so he could help her perfect her straight-sword form. But it was really an excuse to be together without anyone being able to openly accuse them of dating.

He'd shout in the harsh voice of Shaolin instruction, "What's the matter with you? Straighten your elbow, and drop your shoulder!"

She'd just giggle. And after a while, he'd start showing off his prowess at kungfu. An expert in lightness kungfu, he'd run up and across the wall like Spider-Man—four, five, six steps before gravity finally reclaimed him. It was like watching the captain of the football team and the head cheerleader flirt after practice.

No one said anything to him about it. All of us boys were too busy staring at Lotus with our tongues hanging out. But behind Deqing's back, tongues wagged with speculation about whether they'd end up married.

Because the Chinese tend to hit puberty later (at fourteen to sixteen) and because it is a sexually conservative country, especially in the rural regions, the Chinese don't usually start dating before they are eighteen. Deqing was nineteen and, more importantly, at the height of his mastery.

It was common for Wushu Center monks who had reached the peak of their power to find a special female friend to focus the extra energy they no longer needed to improve their kungfu skills. It would start innocently enough and over a two- to three-year period, if things worked out, gradually become less innocent, so that by his mid-twenties, when a monk was ready to retire from performing and leave the monastery for the wider world, he could give up the robes and marry.

But it didn't work out.

Suddenly, about two months after my arrival, Deqing had free time during the nightly practice sessions, and Lotus was nowhere to be found. If she walked past him during the day, she turned her face away from him. In response, Deqing started to pay attention to one of Shaolin's skankier groupies.

Yes, groupies. The Shaolin monks were fantastic athletes and the most famous young men in all of Henan Province. As is always the way with such situations, they had an ardent female fan base. Young women from Deng Feng, and occasionally as far as Zheng Zhou, found excuses to travel to Shaolin and linger. The monks were supposed to be celibate, which gave them the added attraction of being both safe and a challenge. The groupies would stay long enough to make a concerted effort to crack one of the eighteen- to twenty-two-year-old monks' vow of celibacy. And when they more often than not failed, they would stop returning to Shaolin. The monks preferred the girls from the village who studied kungfu, but there was always a steady supply of new young women willing to test their luck and feminine charms.

A couple weeks after the split, Deqing, Cheng Hao, and I were at dinner in a local restaurant, a five-table, concrete-floor affair, when Lotus showed up, drunk. Deqing led her outside. Cheng Hao and I couldn't make out her words through her tears. When Deqing returned, his face was red. Cheng Hao and I pretended like nothing was wrong.

Three days later, Lotus left Shaolin.

Deqing came to my room that night for counsel. Early on, one of the monks had asked me how many girlfriends I'd had, because it was assumed Americans were as sexually libertine as the characters in our movies and TV shows. I'd told him three, which made me forever after—word spread fast at Shaolin—the resident expert on the subject of male-female relations. I suppose they could have done worse, but it's hard to imagine how. O. J. Simpson, perhaps.

"*Bao Mosi*, I feel terrible," Deqing said. "I ran Lotus off."

"Did you tell her to leave?"

"No, but I paid attention to that Zheng Zhou girl."

"Why did you?"

"Because after I ended things with Lotus, she kept begging me to take her back. But I couldn't."

"Why? You two seemed happy together. And she is so beautiful it would kill a man to leave her."

"Yes, she's beautiful to the point of death. But I'm a monk."

"So nothing happened between you two?"

"No, no, no," Deqing said, dropping his eyes, hunching his shoulders, covering his reddened cheeks with his pincushion hands. Incapable of hiding his feelings, he was the worst liar I ever met in China.

"Deqing, why would Lotus want you to take her back, if nothing was going on?"

"Okay, okay, okay, maybe I kissed her once."

He looked up, but his eyes wouldn't meet mine and his face was still red.

"Deqing . . ."

"Okay, it was twice. What does it matter? Once was wrong," he said, finally looking up at me.

"It doesn't," I laughed. "I just wanted details. I'm jealous.

Besides, it was your first time, right? So you needed once to practice. And twice to get it right."

His faced turned red again, but he laughed and grabbed my knee. "You're naughty," he said. And then he thought for a moment. "Do you think I'm a bad monk?"

"No, I think you're nineteen. I doubt Siddhartha Gautama himself could have turned Lotus away when he was your age. The Buddha had already had his fill of women before he became a celibate."

"This is true. This is true. This is true." Deqing said, the tension in his shoulders releasing slightly. "But still I wish she hadn't left. What will become of her kungfu training?"

"Heaven gave Lotus all the talent she'll ever need to succeed in this world."

"*Aiya.* She'll probably end up as some Hong Kong businessman's *mishu*," Deqing said, aghast. "Secretary."

It was slang for "mistress."

"I doubt it."

"Why?"

"She's not tall enough," I said.

There was nothing a five-foot-five or five-foot-six Hong Kong, Taiwanese, or Singaporean businessman seemed to love more than a mainland mistress who was significantly taller than he was. She didn't even have to be particularly beautiful. In the luxurious Japanese- and Western-built shopping malls in Beijing and Shanghai, you'd see these young women, usually on platform shoes to add an extra couple of inches, towering over their middle-aged sugar daddies—always with bags filled with Prada and Gucci dangling from their lanky arms. Any village girl who made it to five-eight or better had hit the genetic lottery and moved rather quickly to the big cities to cash in her ticket. I often wondered if China would have received as much direct foreign investment from the Chinese diaspora if it hadn't possessed these long-limbed natural resources.

Deqing laughed his big laugh, leaned over, and pinched my cheek. "You're a good friend."

"But one thing I don't understand," I said. "Why did you break it off with her? Most of Shaolin's young monks eventually leave the temple to marry."

"If I hadn't ended it now, more things would have happened,

and then I would have had to marry her. And then I'd be stuck here for the rest of my life. And I want to spread Shaolin kungfu and Shaolin's fame to the rest of the world."

I suddenly understood what motivated Deqing.

"You mean you want to be a movie star," I said.

"What better way to spread it?"

When Hong Kong, Taiwan, and mainland China film crews visited the temple, they usually wanted background or training sequences of the monks to splice into their films. The producers would pay the leaders, and the monks would be rounded up to perform. They'd film wide shots of dozens of monks running through forms, kicking bags, and balancing on tree stumps for a day or two, then leave.

But one day as I entered the performance hall, I found a man I didn't recognize sitting in front of the monks. They were lined up in military parade formation.

"Who is that guy?" I asked Little Tiger.

"He is a movie director from Taiwan," Little Tiger said, excitedly. "He is filming a martial arts picture. One of the major roles is a Shaolin monk, and he wants to cast a real Shaolin monk for the part. Imagine, a lead role! I wish I was older."

One by one, the monks performed their specialty: drunken staff, eagle, double sword. Deqing gave, as always, the signature performance. But Lipeng and Cheng Hao were also very good.

After the demonstrations were finished, the monks were each required to read a line of dialogue. Because most of them had received little if any formal education, the director resorted to feeding them the line and asking them to repeat it.

That night Deqing was high-spirited. He had a bounce in his step, although he studiously avoided mentioning the audition.

The next day the director announced his choice. It was Cheng Hao. Deqing was crushed, and Cheng Hao pleased, but both pretended otherwise.

Little Tiger summed up the collective sentiment of the monks. "In movies, good looks are more important than skill."

I stayed neutral. Deqing had his mother and his family's lost honor to worry him. But Cheng Hao also had family concerns. His father and mother had moved from the northern city where they used to live to Shaolin after his father had lost his factory job, leaving Cheng Hao as the sole family provider on a salary of less than $40 a month.

After Cheng Hao's departure to Taiwan, Deqing disappeared for a couple of days. When he came back he was wearing a retainer. I'd known he was self-conscious about his buckteeth, because every time he'd let out a wide-mouth laugh, he'd lower his lip to cover his front teeth a fraction of a second later.

"Where did you find a tooth doctor in Henan?" I asked.

"A friend told me about one in Zheng Zhou who could fix my two front teeth. I've hated them ever since the injury."

"I didn't know you injured them."

"Yes, we were doing a four-man form. Two of us had to jump onto the other two monks' shoulders and fight with swords. My foot caught in the folds of my partner's robes. As I fell my two front teeth dug straight into his head."

"What happened to him?"

"Oh, he was an expert in iron head kungfu, so he wasn't injured."

Six weeks later, word spread that Cheng Hao was back. I ran up to his and Deqing's room. A rapt crowd was listening to Cheng Hao recount his experience, most especially Little Tiger, who kept interrupting.

"The director was very helpful. He'd sit with me at lunch every day and give me acting tips."

"What was the lead actress like?" Little Tiger asked. "Was she pretty?"

"Pretty is as pretty does," Cheng Hao said. "She was very arrogant. She would talk to no one but the director."

"What about the actor? How was his kungfu?"

"He was terrible with a sword. He kept dropping it."

"Was he worse than *Bao Mosi*?" Little Tiger asked.

"Hey!" I said. But Little Tiger had ducked behind several other monks and was out of reach.

"During the movie, the director told me he wanted to work with me again. And at the end of the shoot, he said, 'You will be *hong*.'" Cheng Hao said. "Red."

"Why would he say you'd be the color red?" I asked.

"*Hong* is slang for famous," Little Tiger laughed. "Stupid egg."

Deqing had had enough. "All right, that's it. Everyone out of my room."

Cheng Hao was too blissed out to notice Deqing's mood. Wanting to share the moment, I remained.

"Can you believe it? 'You will be *hong*.'" Cheng Hao said, imitating the director's deeper voice. "'I want to work with you again. You will be *hong*.'"

Deqing valiantly tried to ignore Cheng Hao, but around the tenth time Cheng Hao said the word *hong*, Deqing lost it.

"Of course he said those things to you. He's a director. That's the kind of flattery they use on actors."

"I don't know," Cheng Hao said, surprised by Deqing's vehemence. "He told me several times."

Deqing threw his arms into the air. "He was lying to you. Directors are all liars. That's how they get country bumpkins like you to kill yourself for them for a fraction of what they pay the Taiwanese actors."

Because he was a peacemaker by nature, Cheng Hao said, "Maybe you're right." But he didn't believe it in his heart.

"How much did they pay you? 1,000RMB? For six weeks! You couldn't get a Hong Kong actor for six minutes for 1,000RMB. Directors are all liars."

"Maybe you're right."

Deqing turned away. He clearly felt guilty for raining on his friend's parade but wasn't able to admit it to himself yet.

For months afterward, I'd greet Cheng Hao with, "You're going to be *hong*." He'd laugh and shake his head, but his eyes would light up.

Then one day, I repeated the line and his laugh was weak and his eyes were dead. That's how I learned that he finally knew Deqing had been correct.

The director never contacted Cheng Hao again.

5

SHAOLIN'S CHAMPION

I didn't think much of Coach Cheng when I first saw him, because I failed to look at his hands. All I saw when he shuffled into the practice hall that afternoon while a bunch of us were horsing around was a man in his late twenties, head down, shoulders slumped, paunch protruding. It was not until I saw the reaction of the monks, who slapped him on the back and welcomed him home like a returning hero, that I looked at his hands. They were two ham hocks, twice as large as they should be for a man his size, the telltale sign of a Chinese kickboxer.

Deqing introduced us. "This is Coach Cheng. He is a national champion in *sanda*. You should see his kicks. They are amazing."

With the faintest of smiles, Coach Cheng modestly demurred, "They're nothing, nothing, nothing."

"It's an honor to meet a national champion," I said.

"No, no, no, it is nothing special."

Little Tiger had run off to find a kicking shield. He came back and gave it to Cheng Hao. "Here, hold this. Let Coach Cheng show *Bao Mosi* his kicks."

"I'm not holding it." Cheng Hao said, throwing the kicking shield to another monk, who didn't want it either. The shield was passed around like a hot potato before Deqing finally said, "All right, I'll hold it."

Deqing walked to the center of the room and braced himself behind the shield. Coach Cheng shuffled over. He stood lazily in the center of the room with his left leg in front of his right and his arms raised slightly. He looked so sleepy, it was like he was dozing. And then without warning, he woke up, lunging toward the bag, kicking it with a bone-shattering left side kick that knocked Deqing back ten feet. The man had jackhammers for legs.

Encouraged by the monks, Coach Cheng proceeded to put on the most amazing kicking display I have ever seen. His kicks were as supple as a professional boxer's punches: They snapped like whips but struck with the force of a baseball bat.

Filled with the joy of his genius, Coach Cheng finished his display with a couple of flying kicks and backflips. When he stopped in the center of the floor to applause, he dropped his head again, slightly abashed, and slowly withdrew back into himself. It was obvious that he was the type of man who is truly alive only when practicing his art. By the time he left, he was shuffling along like a sleepwalker.

Coach Cheng was living in Deng Feng at the time, and I didn't see him again until a month later. A Japanese man who claimed to be a karate master had come to Shaolin and caused quite a stir. Through a translator, he told the leaders of the Wushu Center that he wanted to challenge Shaolin's champion to a fight. It was the first challenge match I had heard about, and the fact that the challenger was Japanese only increased the stakes. Unlike the Japanese, the Chinese had not forgotten or forgiven the Japanese invasion and occupation of the country during World War II. The Chinese Communist Party (CCP), which had lost the unifying force of Maoist ideology after it started to tentatively embrace capitalist reforms, had fallen back on the old fail-safe: nationalism. Chinese popular culture was filled with reminders of the Communists' role in ejecting the Japanese and other colonialists after the Great War. It was their strongest claim to legitimacy. The Wushu Center was filled with dark mutterings about revenging Japanese aggression.

(Ironically, the Chinese Communist Party played only a minor role in battling the Japanese. It was the Chinese Nationalist Party [KMT] that bore the brunt of the heavy fighting and was significantly weakened in the process. Without the Japanese invasion, it seems improbable that the CCP could have won the "Nationalist-Communist" Civil War in 1950. But historical memory is rarely gracious, self-deprecating, or forgiving, especially in a police state.)

The next day a crowd gathered in the practice hall to see the match. The Japanese man, wearing a karate *gi*, stood in the center of the room, waiting. After a few minutes Shaolin's champion shuffled into the room, head hung low, shoulders slumped, paunch protruding. Coach Cheng took his position in front of the Japanese fighter, looking for all intents and purposes like he was about to fall asleep standing up.

Deputy Leader Jiao, who as a former Shaolin monk and a current Communist Party member had two official reasons to want to see the Japanese man crushed, stepped between the fighters in the role of referee.

"Ready?" he asked, looking at both fighters. Then he clapped his hands and stepped back.

Almost before the sound could reverberate through the practice hall, the Japanese fighter backpedaled about thirty feet. The crowd was flabbergasted. He was too far away for dueling pistols, let alone a fistfight. Coach Cheng looked over quizzically at Deputy Leader Jiao, who shrugged his shoulders in response.

The Japanese fighter was wired. He ran forward several steps and then backpedaled to where he stood before, ten yards away from his opponent. He repeated this several times. It was like he suffered from physical autism.

"What does this stupid egg think he's doing?" Deqing asked of no one in particular. "Feinting?" It was a surreal sight watching this karateka repeatedly charge forward and then dash back, as if his opponent lacked any depth perception and would therefore be fooled into thinking that the object in front of him was closer than it appeared.

Finally, after thirty seconds of this nonsense, the Japanese fighter finally found his courage and charged like a bull. Coach Cheng waited until his opponent was close, then lunged forward with a left side kick. The Japanese fighter was knocked back a dozen feet. Instead of continuing his attack, he backpedaled thirty feet again, where he restarted the process all over again, charging several feet and then retreating. It was like he needed to rev his courage into the red zone before he was able to attack. After another fifteen seconds or so of back and forth, he charged again. This time Coach Cheng waited an instant longer to strike, jabbing his huge left hand into the Japanese fighter's face to stop his forward motion and pin him in place. He followed the punch almost instantaneously with a lightning-quick right roundhouse kick to the face.

The kick flattened the Japanese fighter's face. He fell to his knees clutching his nose. Blood gushed through his fingers. His translator ran over with a towel.

Coach Cheng stood still for several moments to make certain the fight was actually over. When the translator waved his arms in the air, Coach Cheng shrugged his shoulders and shuffled off with a sheepish grin on his face. As he was walking away, the Japanese fighter shouted something at him in Japanese, which the translator refused to translate.

The translator must have spoken up later. Because at the banquet held at the dining hall in Coach Cheng's honor, everyone was buzzing about what the Japanese fighter had said.

Coach Cheng kept shaking his head. "So this Japanese guy said, 'You have beaten me today, but I will be back in exactly five years to fight you again. I will train every day and defeat you.'"

"He challenged you to a fight five years in the future?" I asked, incredulous.

"That is so typical of the Japanese," Coach Cheng said. "They love to plan ahead. They are always thinking far into the future. They spent thirty years planning their previous invasion of China. I bet you they've spent the last fifty planning their next one."

All the Chinese drank to that.

"If I beat this guy in five years, he will want to fight me again in ten," Coach Cheng said. "He will want to keep fighting me until I am dead. And then he will challenge me in the next life."

One of the monks muttered to himself, "Fuck their mothers."

Upon hearing the curse, the Chinese drank to that, too. All racism is local.

Unlike Americans, the Chinese don't pretend to believe in equality. However, while most of the social hierarchy was fairly clear—older above younger, men above women, rich above poor, city folk above rural folk, Communist Party members and their families above everyone else—it was not absolute. There was a certain circumstantial fluidity. For example, a husband was supposed to have the upper hand in a marriage, but if he refused or was incapable of wearing the pants, his wife would take charge with a vengeance. On more than one occasion I witnessed a scrawny man who had spent all night drinking with his buddies being chased down the street by his wife. She'd run after him wearing one flip-flop and striking him over the head with the other, all the while screaming so the neighbors could hear what a *jiu guizi* (drunken devil) he was and how he'd spent his entire paycheck on booze.

Coach Cheng had a girlfriend like this. She was as emotionally excessive as Coach Cheng was muted. You could hear her high-pitched, hysterical voice from the other end of the compound. Every time I was with Deqing and we heard her screech, he'd just shake his head and say, "What can you do with this type of woman?" I nicknamed her "Shou Ting," because I have a weakness for bad puns, and deep down inside I'm not a very nice person.

Coach Cheng was twenty-eight. I'd estimate that Shou Ting was slightly older, although I was never foolish enough to ask. She lived in Zheng Zhou but visited Coach Cheng regularly.

Curious about the amount of free time she had, I once asked her what she did for a living.

"I have a business."

"What kind of business?"

"The type of business that buys and sells things."

"What type of things?"

"Why is it so important to you?" Shou Ting shouted, her voice cracking, tears forming in her eyes.

"So sorry, I was just trying to be a good friend."

She pointed at Coach Cheng who had his back to her and was pretending like he couldn't hear her. He was teaching one of the younger monks a new move.

"Well, why don't you be a good friend and tell Coach Cheng to be nicer to me," she said.

"He is a coach here. I'm just a student. I can't tell him what to do."

The tears were now streaming down her face.

"Oh, he will listen to you. He respects you. You're educated, not some illiterate peasant kungfu coach who refuses to visit me in Zheng Zhou, so I have to risk my life driving along that awful road."

Since being insulted by your woman in front of subordinates was considered a serious loss of face, I tried to change the subject, "How was your trip? Safe, I hope."

"Safe? Ha! I was nearly killed ten times. But what do I care of life? With a man like him, I might as well be dead! He wouldn't shed a single tear!"

As the resident relationship expert, I found myself falling into the role of couples counselor. The problem was simple: Shou Ting wanted to marry Coach Cheng, and he didn't want to marry her. All he would say on the subject was, "What would I do with a wife like that?" Still he wouldn't break up with her, either.

One day after practice she finally broke down in despair. "Why is he so cold to me?"

"I don't know," I said quietly. Per usual, Coach Cheng had his back to us and was pretending like he wasn't listening.

"After all I've done for him," she paused for dramatic effect. "Did you know he was in jail?"

"No, I didn't."

"He was in jail. And I paid the fine to get him released. I had to sell my car, my business. I lost everything. I did it for him. That is what you get for loving someone, *Bao Mosi*. Promise me you'll never fall in love. Promise me."

She was crying so I promised.

"But you didn't tell me why he was in jail," I said.

Without missing a sniffle, Shou Ting said, "Oh, I had some trouble with a client. He owed me money and refused to pay it back. We argued and the man slapped me. I told Mr. Kickboxing and what does the stupid egg do? He hits the man over the head with nunchakus. Puts the guy in the hospital. The police arrest him and I have to sell everything to pay the fine."

Not able to take it anymore, Coach Cheng finally stopped pretending he wasn't listening and turned around.

"He called you a *chioniu*," he said. "Whore."

"So what? You hit him over the head with nunchakus? Why didn't you just punch him?"

"Because I'd have hurt him worse if I'd punched him," he said.

"Oh, you see, *Bao Mosi*, that is male logic for you. The fine is less for punching someone than striking with a weapon."

"It sounds like he was defending your reputation."

"I don't need my reputation. I need my car back. It took me three years to purchase a new one and it isn't as good."

One morning as I was walking through the halls of the Shaolin Wushu Center, I could feel the fear in the air before I reached the performance hall. I saw Little Wang, one of the junior kungfu coaches, scurry out a back door carrying a suitcase.

"What's going on?" I asked him.

"My older brother got into a fight. The cops are looking for him."

"Why are you leaving?"

Little Wang smiled awkwardly as he ducked out a back door. "I don't want them to use me to get to him."

Big Wang was an important player in the Wushu Center leadership, but it wasn't clear what his actual job was. As far as I could tell, he was responsible for overseeing Coach Yan, who in turn oversaw the monks. Big Wang owed his position at the Wushu Center to his father, who had been one of the most famous and popular instructors at Shaolin. Because Coach Wang's father was master to so many current instructors, Coach Wang, as first son, was everyone's "big brother."

Like many sons of famous men who can't live up to their fathers, Big Wang covered up his insecurity with a belligerent jocularity. Or to put it another way, he was an annoying prick who thought he was hilarious. He liked to make his power known by publicly berating other instructors. But because the offenses were usually innocuous, these chew-out sessions had a certain ritual feel to them. Often Big Wang was unable to call up the energy to make his anger seem real.

Instead he'd say in a mock-outraged voice laced with amusement, "What the hell is the matter with you? Your students are terrible. I went by your class yesterday, and you weren't even there.

What were you doing? Visiting your girlfriend? How are students supposed to improve without a coach, eh? I ought to strangle you."

The instructors' role in this dance was to keep their heads down and keep quiet until he had finished. Coach Cheng was a frequent target. Big Wang envied his greater kungfu skill.

Big Wang didn't know what to do with me. He knew I didn't like him because of the way he treated Coach Cheng. But as long as I paid up each month, I was outside his sphere of influence. So he'd often call out to me, "*Bao Mosi*, look at you. You're too skinny. I know what would fatten you up. You need a woman. I know this prostitute who could use some American dollars. Why don't I get her for you? You'd like her."

He never ceased to find this joke hysterical.

Curious about the situation, I went to Deqing and Cheng Hao's room to ask them why Big Wang was in trouble with the law.

"You know Big Wang's wife works as a waitress in one of the nearby restaurants, right?" Deqing said.

"No, I didn't."

"Well, a customer complained about the food. She said something rude to him. I think she called him a dog-eater."

"He was from the south?"

"Right, so he refused to pay. She said something ruder. He slapped her across the face."

I could picture the scene in my mind. In the Chinese hierarchy, there were few positions lower than waitress. They were always women, usually young and single, and their job was to serve you food. It was almost a requirement to harass them. I often thought that for many Chinese men this opportunity was the major attraction of eating out. The waitresses usually took the verbal abuse, but Shaolin women were made out of rougher cloth than city girls. All of them had either a boyfriend or husband who was a kungfu master. Only a stupid egg would make the mistake of striking one of them.

"How did Big Wang find out?" I asked.

"Little Tiger was at the restaurant," Deqing said. "He ran back to Big Wang's office. Coach Cheng and I were there with him. Little Tiger told Big Wang a man was beating his wife. Big Wang was out the room so fast that Coach Cheng and I had to run full speed just to keep him in sight.

"*Bao Mosi*, I've never seen anything like it. Big Wang blasted the man into a wall with a flying side kick. Then he elbowed him in the face five times. When the man went down, Big Wang started jumping up and down on his chest. When the man's wife tried to intervene, Big Wang punched her in the face. The man tried to get up to protect his wife, but Coach Cheng laid him out with a blow to the back of his neck."

"Did you do anything?"

"No, there wasn't time," Deqing laughed with embarrassment. "It was over in seconds."

I looked at him with disbelief. There wasn't anyone in Shaolin faster than Deqing.

"So you just stood there?" I asked.

"Well, I pulled Big Wang off the woman. He was strangling her," Deqing said. "I thought he was going to hit me. He was crazed."

"But why did Big Wang have to run from the cops?" I asked.

"The man is in the hospital," Deqing said. "He has two broken ribs, a broken nose, a broken jaw, a broken arm, and a punctured lung. His wife's nose is shattered."

"Right, but why did Big Wang have to run? He's Big Wang."

Cheng Hao understood my question. Big Wang had good *guanxi* with the cops. Many had been disciples of his father. And while the cops didn't like it when tourists got hurt—it was bad for business, and the cops took a cut of the gate—their basic attitude was Darwinian: Any tourist dumb enough to provoke a fight in Shaolin was too stupid to live. I'd been in a restaurant where two drunken tourists were giving everyone the evil eye. I had turned my chair so I couldn't see them stare at me. The next thing I knew they were being bounced off the walls like pinballs. After ten minutes of being used like kicking dummies, they had to crawl on their hands and knees to the police station. There weren't any repercussions.

"Because the man is the nephew of Canton Province's minister of tourism," Cheng Hao said.

"So? This isn't Canton. This is Shaolin."

With a tone of bitterness I'd never heard out of him before, Cheng Hao said, "*Bao Mosi*, this is China. The leaders' children are like the descendants of Heaven. This is their world, not ours."

After a moment of silence, Deqing said, "The Canton minister of tourism called the Henan minister of tourism and threatened to ban all Cantonese from traveling to Shaolin. You know what that means?"

I did. Because China's economic reform had started in Canton, the Cantonese were richer than the rest of the country and consequently the biggest group of tourists. The problem was that they took great pleasure in rubbing their wealth in the face of resentful and envious Northerners, forever talking about how much their designer clothes cost in the annoyingly sing-song way they spoke Mandarin, ending each sentence with "la." One local wag had even nicknamed them "the la la people" to widespread approval. (Okay, that wag was me.) Although rare, most fights at Shaolin were with Cantonese tourists.

"So the Henan minister called the Shaolin cops," Deqing continued. "The chief of police called Big Wang to give him a head start."

"What's he going to do?"

Deqing said, "Well, he could pay them 60,000RMB to make the matter go away."

"Big Wang has 60,000RMB?"

"This is Shaolin, not Shanghai," Deqing said. "If he had 60,000RMB, he'd be running the place. So he has to negotiate."

"How?"

"He sends a representative to talk to the cops. The minister wants 60,000. His representative counters with 1,000. What can the cops do? They don't have him in custody. The longer he stays free, the lower the price. As long as the cops don't catch him, he's fine."

"What happens if they catch him?"

"They send him to prison," Cheng Hao said. "And you don't want to go to a Chinese prison."

"What do they do to you in a Chinese prison?"

"The guards beat you."

"That's it?"

"They are very good at it around here. Most of them are Shaolin trained."

It suddenly occurred to me who else was implicated in this fiasco.

"Is Coach Cheng around?" I asked.

"Yes."

"Do you know where?"

Deqing cocked his head and cupped his hand behind his ear, and sure enough I could hear Shou Ting's voice in the distance. I followed the sound of Shou Ting's cries and curses to the training hall. "You stupid egg! You want to go back to prison? I won't bail you out this time!"

Coach Cheng was trying to look abashed, but his smile ruined the effect.

"Why are you still here?" I asked him.

"No one recognized me. They only told the cops about Big Wang."

At the sound of his name, Shou Ting was off on another line of attack. "Why do you always follow him around? You are a fool to do his bidding."

"He's my martial arts older brother."

"So you'll follow him to jail? I won't bail you out this time. I'm warning you—"

"His father was my master."

And with that, Coach Cheng went to the police station to negotiate for Big Wang.

It took five weeks before Big Wang returned. He tried to laugh it off, but he was clearly ashamed.

The final price of his fine was settled at 6,000RMB ($750). It was more than the average Henan farmer made in two years. It was also less than half of what I spent per month at Shaolin.

6

THE SACRED AND
THE PROFANE

For a Buddhist monastery, there wasn't much Buddhism happening at the Shaolin Temple. Under Mao and especially during the Cultural Revolution, the government had been openly hostile to religion, banning the opiate of the masses, throwing monks in jail. With the shift to the profit principle of capitalism, the attitude changed to one of indifference. Tourists paid to see performances; they weren't interested in buying tickets to watch monks sit quietly and meditate. It is not exactly riveting entertainment. The younger monks, adapting quickly to changing values, recognized that their worth depended on their martial skills, not their spiritual depth, and they arranged their focus accordingly.

As a student of Eastern religions, this was a profound disappointment. As long as I had gone to all this trouble to journey to Shaolin, I wanted the complete package-tour experience. I didn't just want to be a badass; I wanted to be an enlightened badass.

"What happened to all the Buddhism?" I asked Deqing one day.

"There is some," he smiled embarrassedly. "But we should do more. We should do more. Sometimes I try to meditate before breakfast."

I tried to do the same, once my body had adjusted to the rigors of daily practice and I no longer had to sleep ten to twelve hours a night to recover. Deqing taught me the basics. The practitioner sits in lotus or half-lotus—or if he is particularly inflexible like me, Indian style. Men are supposed to place the left palm on top of the right in their laps, while women do it the other way around (the reason for this had been lost, but the tradition remained and was insisted upon). Eyelids are half-closed and the eyes are to focus on the tip of the nose without crossing. The breathing is in through the mouth and out through the nose. And the mind is to remain completely blank. Repetition of the phrase *Amituofo* is used to help extinguish all extraneous thoughts.

That's the theory at least. For the beginner, the reality is more like ten seconds of blankness, before various random trains of thought start pulling into the station: *my back itches . . . my friends are probably still in bed . . . no, it's a fourteen-hour time difference, they are probably out partying . . . this is the single dumbest decision of your entire dumb life . . . I miss ice cream . . . I hope the Chiefs make the playoffs this year . . . no, I miss peanut butter more.* Each one of these trains of thought is quickly interrupted by self-recrimination: *stop thinking . . . focus on your breathing . . . you lack discipline.* And then the random thoughts start again.

After what seems like hours of this back and forth, the desire to look at your watch becomes overwhelming. The goal is thirty minutes, and surely you have passed that mark. A quick glance down reveals it has been slightly less than three minutes since you first sat down. Then begins the internal debate (interrupted with more calls to focus) about whether it is okay to reset the goal for fifteen minutes, because you are after all just a beginner and no one finishes the marathon their first time out on the track, or if this would simply be the latest in the long mental list of abandoned resolutions.

It was at this stage that I found my earlier religious training in Catholic guilt particularly useful. I found I could eat up ten more minutes in self-laceration before it became too mentally painful to sit there trying and failing to clear my mind. I also found that it worked better if I repeated, Our Fathers and Hail Marys instead of *Amituofo*s. The Catholic monk Thomas Merton called this practice deep prayer. But it was more like daily penance to me. I never made it past twenty-five minutes in my two years at Shaolin, and my best guess for the longest amount of time my mind was blank is thirty seconds.

The technique that helped my deep prayer the most was physical exhaustion. It was a discovery that shed a different light on the balance between Buddhism and kungfu. At Shaolin, it was a life-cycle relationship. When the monks were young and full of piss and vinegar, their focus was primarily on hard kungfu: it burned off the excess energy and taught them physical and mental discipline. The monks in their late twenties shifted their attention from the hard stuff to softer styles like Chen-style tai chi. And at the age when American men begin to feel that an eventful day is rearranging themselves on the Barcalounger while sipping a beer and watching younger men exert themselves on TV, the monks shift their focus to more sedentary forms of Buddhist practice like meditation and chanting.

I realized Deqing had been chewing over my criticism of Shaolin's lack of religious practice, because one Sunday night he came to my room and invited me to see a Buddhist ceremony at the temple. Ever the staunch defender of Shaolin's reputation, he wanted to prove to me there was still some devotion to the old ways, however attenuated.

When we arrived at the temple, we were held up by the guard at Shaolin's back gate. He didn't recognize Deqing and refused to let us pass without paying him. The argument quickly grew heated. Deqing was as surprised as I was by the guard's rude tone. People tended to take one look at Deqing with the sword scars on his face and hands like pincushions and make way for him. Finally, Deqing—who by the cataclysmic expression on his face was clearly calculating the numerous ways he could hospitalize the guard—grabbed him by the shoulders, lifted him in the air like a toddler, and set him to the side. We walked past the stunned guard and into the temple.

By the time we made it to the central prayer hall—a large room with a gigantic statue of Buddha in the center—the ceremony was already underway. After straightening his robes, Deqing joined the other monks who were walking round and round the Buddha statue while chanting ancient Buddhist prayers and banging wooden bells at rhythmic intervals. The room was filled with a dense, silvery, sweet-smelling smoke from burning incense sticks.

What struck me the most was not the devotion of the monks, which was evident, but rather an overwhelming feeling of alienation. Standing in that room, I felt as alone as I'd ever felt, a stranger in a strange land. Suddenly, I realized how desperately far away from home I was. It took my breath away, and I had to fight an instinct to flee the room. I'd never felt so Catholic in all my life as I did at that moment, and I barely managed to avoid crossing myself when the ceremony thankfully ended a half-hour later.

Eager to think about something other than my fears, I asked Deqing as we walked back to the Wushu Center, "Do the old monks practice sitting meditation?"

"They do, but they do it on their own, not in groups like in the past. With all the tourists, it is impossible to meditate together during the day. But you should keep meditating in the morning. It will help your focus in studying kungfu."

Deqing didn't understand why that made me laugh. Kungfu had started as physical exercises meant to help the monks focus on their sitting meditation. Now sitting meditation was used to help the monks focus on their kungfu. The evolution was complete. I had come to Shaolin interested in both Buddhism and kungfu, but it was obvious to me now that at Shaolin they were one and the same. Kungfu practice was the way they practiced Buddhism—the traditional forms were a kind of moving meditation. Like the young monks, I decided to make that my focus.

In college, I'd become obsessed with mystical experiences as a result of a problem that had been itching at my brain and soul since I was thirteen. One day I had been riding my bike home from middle school when it struck me that according to the scientific method—observation, hypothesis, experimentation, theory—religious doctrine could be neither proved nor disproved, relying as it did on events too far in the past for any of us to observe. This insight caused a crisis of faith and it left me torn between rationality and strongly held religious beliefs.

But in the mystics, I felt I'd discovered a bridge between the dichotomy of science and faith. Their spiritual experiences were like data points that could be indirectly observed, assuming that they were being honest and were not suffering from some sort of delusion. These indirect observations could be compared and contrasted against each other, and on this basis certain working theories could be developed about the nature of God.

What I discovered from studying the Zen monks, the Sufi mystics, and the Catholic saints was a similarity in the descriptions of their experiences. They used different images, metaphors, and theological concepts, but they seemed to me to be pointing in the same direction. It brought to mind a saying from the Upanishads I'd always liked: "God is one, but the scholars call him by many different names." Whatever their faith, mystics experienced an overwhelming power that for a brief moment extinguished their sense of self, an explosion of divinity that created a feeling in them of tremendous peace or ecstasy, a moment so transcendent that words could never fully capture it. As Lao-tzu put it, "The sayers do not know and the knowers do not say."

From these similarities, I followed along Aldous Huxley's path and started to develop what I jokingly called my Unified Field Theory of Religion. My working hypothesis was that the cosmos was made up of spirit and matter, heaven and earth, and that humans consisted of both elements, a body and a soul, dust and divinity. The mystical experience was what happened when the divine or God or Allah or whatever name you prefer breaks through the mundane in a particular soul and exposes it to the universal spirit.

As I studied the subject more and more in college, I'd find myself in these odd conversations. When I'd mention on a plane or over a lunch counter or at a party that my major was religion and my focus was mysticism, a surprising number of times ordinary people would start talking excitedly about some extraordinary spiritual experience they had experienced. Feelings, visions, miracles (usually involving cancer) are apparently fairly commonplace. After several years of these conversations, I felt both reassured and envious. Why hadn't it happened to me? Which is to say, I was more than open to the possibility of a mystical experience, I was actively seeking it, praying for it. It is one thing to hear others tell of these moments, quite another to experience it for oneself—the difference between indirect and indisputable proof.

It was during the afternoon practice on November 10, eight weeks into my study at Shaolin, that it finally happened to me. I had just completed a series of one of Shaolin's eighteen basic movements, which had a 360-degree spinning kick. It was a movement I had done hundreds of times (in Zen Buddhism the repetition of physical movements—washing pans, archery, the tea ceremony—is considered a crucial means for achieving enlightenment). As I turned at the end of the mat to repeat the same movement back across, I was overwhelmed by a feeling of absolute peace. It wasn't visual, aural, or tactile. It was emotional. And it was like nothing I'd ever experienced before. It was like all the background noise in my soul—the stress, the anxiety, the worry—suddenly went silent, like all the static in the universe stopped, and for a moment there was only God.

I froze and turned to Deqing, my mind unable to find the right words to describe what was happening. All I could say was, "I feel peaceful." I must have been smiling in a beatific way, because Deqing grinned and nodded back at me like he knew what I meant, and waited patiently for me to return. I wandered the room in no particular direction. It struck me that this was what Heaven must feel like. I immediately understood why mystics and monks would give up all the pleasures of the world for their spiritual journey: This experience seemed worth any sacrifice.

I can't say how long the feeling of absolute peace lasted, less than a minute probably. But it seemed longer, long enough for me to think that if this was not definitive proof I couldn't imagine what would be; long enough to believe this was absolute proof; long enough to know I'd never doubt again.

Time stopped. I lost all awareness of self.

But then a niggling thought, a worm in the apple, nudged itself through the heavenly clouds of my consciousness. Deqing hadn't said anything to me when I told him what I was feeling. He knew but hadn't said. But I'd said something. Had I jinxed it? Would I ever feel like this again?

And just like that, the sensation of absolute peace was gone, replaced by all the old anxiety and stress and worry. The static was deafening. My soul was pressed by this crushing certainty, as sad as cancer, that I'd never touch the divine again. Not in this life, at least. My soul wasn't wise enough to pass over to the other side while in this world.

After that training session, a debilitating depression fell over me, like true love lost. It lasted for days. I wandered through practices listless.

But at some point the darkness lifted. I'd had my proof, my miracle. I might not make it, but I'd seen the Promised Land. And that alone made the decision to come to Shaolin the best of my life.

The to-do list flashed in my head:

THINGS THAT ARE WRONG WITH MATT

1. Cowardly
2. Still a boy/not a man
3. Unattractive to the opposite sex
4. ~~Spiritually confused~~

In November, a different kind of prayer was answered: God sent an English-speaking *laowai* to Shaolin. Carlos was from Spain. He was in his thirties, a husband and father. His face was gaunt, which made his prominent Roman nose and moist brown eyes seem outsized. His passion was teaching kungfu, but his school back home was small and he had to supplement his income by teaching driving lessons. He'd saved for years to come to Shaolin for a month or two, thinking of it as a kind of graduate school where he could acquire the necessary accreditation to attract more kungfu students.

He was a charming man, but by his own repeated admissions a nightmare as a husband. Watching and listening to him I was fascinated by how he represented the seamless reconciliation of Catholic guilt and Mediterranean libido.

"Oh, Mateo, you do not know how wonderful my wife is—a saint—and how I make her suffer so," he'd say, eyes wet, each night at dinner. "I have been with so many women, too many. I must change. These women who want to learn stick shift, oh you have to see them. There was this *mujer bonita*—my, oh my!—she kept missing the shift and grabbing my leg. My poor wife! But what was I to do?"

And so it would go for hours as he alternated between his poor wife and tales of his conquests, only pausing when this particular waitress, a young country girl with whom he was obsessed, came over to our table, whereupon he'd focus his entire attention upon her, flirting in his pidgin Chinese, trying to get her to "visit" him in his room.

"She likes me," he'd say, after she left us. "Don't you think she likes me?"

I'd play my part, reassuring him that of course she liked him (she didn't) but that he had to understand that we were in rural China, and the sexual mores were very conservative. If she ever went alone to his room, first, everyone would hear about it immediately, second, she'd be considered worse than a whore, and third, she would have to leave the village in shame. I explained that despite his obvious charms, he was offering her the equivalent of a scarlet letter, and maybe he ought to tone down the seduction offensive.

After I finished with the gentle reprimand, Carlos would sigh and return to his sainted, suffering wife and more stories of romantic liaisons past, until the waitress walked past our table again.

One of Carlos's equally quixotic desires was to perform a two-finger handstand. It is what had drawn him to Shaolin. A Shaolin photo-book had attracted quite a deal of attention in Europe when the monks had visited in 1990. In it was a picture of a monk performing a two-finger handstand. He was holding the entire weight of his body upright, perpendicular to the earth, with only his right index and middle fingers. Carlos had been training to accomplish this feat for the last two years, and he'd come to Shaolin to meet the monk in the photo.

I didn't have the heart to tell him the handstand was impossible for him. He'd never be able to complete it. The monk in the photo was Lipeng, Doc's son. I'd asked Lipeng about the photo previously. It was taken when Lipeng was sixteen, and even he couldn't do the two-finger handstand any longer. It was a stunt only teenagers could perform, before their muscles and bones acquired a greater density. At twenty years of age, Lipeng was only a few pounds heavier but that was too much for his fingers to support.

I introduced Carlos to Lipeng, who told him he didn't do the two-finger handstand any longer, but Carlos was undaunted. He even tried to convert me to his two-finger practice routine. The beginner starts in the upright push-up position on all ten fingers, instead of the fists or palms, and simply holds it for as long as possible. Once you are able to hold for five minutes, you start over again but without the pinkie fingers of both hands. Again, after five minutes, you remove the ring finger. Then the thumbs. Then the left hand. After that, you start elevating your body: first feet on a chair, then higher and higher until you reach ninety degrees.

After two years of practice, Carlos could do three minutes with the index and middle fingers of both hands in the push-up position. During my first session with all five fingers, I passed my pain threshold at around two minutes.

"Hurts, doesn't it?" Carlos said, smiling.

"It's positively arthritic," I replied.

My hands were frozen claws. They refused to return to full use for ten minutes. Despite his encouragement, that was my last session. I decided to stick to banging my forearms against trees.

When Carlos arrived, Deqing volunteered to teach the foreigners, so he took over from Monk Chen, one of the older monks who had taken over from Cheng Hao. Two foreigners were better than one, and at least Carlos would leave relatively soon and give him a tip for his troubles.

Deqing's success at Shaolin had been built on a relentless love of hard training, and as he'd watched me he felt that the Shaolin method for training foreigners—all smiles and encouragement—was too soft. He was going to train us like they train their own Chinese students: "To curse is to care, to hit is to love."

Now, there was a good reason for the variation in methodology besides cultural differences. We were older and obviously self-motivated or we wouldn't be here. A rough guess was that of the 10,000 or so teenage kungfu students in the Shaolin village, about half had been sent by their parents rather than volunteered. They were the type of hyperactive boys who refused to study and got into fights. Shaolin was China's version of a reform school; kungfu was their Ritalin.

But I agreed with Deqing that at the very least it was an appearance problem, so I didn't mind when he brought out the stick and whacked us. What did bother me was how he conducted stretching time. Deqing's approach was hands-on and feet-on. When we were in the split position, he'd climb on top of our legs and bounce to the point of breaking us. Then he'd have us lie on our backs, pin one leg and push the other toward our faces until we screamed for mercy.

But it wasn't the pain as much as the fact that we were objects of amusement for the other monks that infuriated Carlos and me. After the first day of screaming, we began to gather a crowd. The younger monks would suddenly appear in the training room at stretch time, take a seat, and wait for the entertainment to begin, holding their breaths until we started begging for mercy and then laugh and laugh. Actually, only one of us begged for mercy. ("Please, master, you're going to break my leg. Please, God, I beg you!") Carlos was tougher than me and therefore able to refrain from screaming anything coherent.

"They sure enjoy watching the foreigners suffer," I said to Deqing once, after a session.

"They don't have TV," he replied, not catching my hint.

After a week of this, it occurred to me that none of them spoke English, so I switched from begging to cursing in my native language, running through the gamut of four letter words, spicing it up with Oedipal accusations and questions about Deqing's parentage, and promises to commit an astounding variety of X-rated acts to various parts of his anatomy. I had to stop, however, when Little Tiger, following one of my tirades, yelled, "Fack youah, madafacka, fack, shat, madafacka, I kah you."

As the banner in the performance hall said, "Cultural Exchange Mutual Benefit."

After a couple weeks of this, when it became obvious the younger monks weren't going to grow tired of watching our torture sessions, Carlos and I decided to speak to Deqing about it. I explained that we didn't mind the tough training, but having the younger monks laugh at us "made us lose face." Deqing visibly blanched. He explained that the monks weren't laughing at us so much as laughing at the memory of when they had been beginners and their coaches had made them scream and beg for mercy. I explained that whatever their reason it still bothered us. He nodded, and the younger monks never showed up in our class again for stretch time.

After class, however, I did gain a constant companion. Once he had heard me curse in English, Little Tiger followed me around every day, begging me to teach him more.

He'd run up to me and say in English, "Fack, madafacka, fack."

"Little Tiger, don't use those words," I said.

"Am I saying them correctly?"

"You shouldn't use bad words."

"But what do they mean?"

"I'm not going to tell you."

"But why?"

"Because you're too young and a Buddhist monk," I said.

Who needs that kind of karmic debt?

After weeks of unsuccessfully attempting to cajole me into teaching him, Little Tiger finally hit upon a winning strategy: slighting my patriotic pride.

"Chinese culture is so much deeper than American culture," he said one day. "I bet our curse words are worse than yours."

"Oh, really, you think so?"

"Absolutely. Let's compare."

I sighed, torn between the choice of spending the next life as a dung beetle or letting one Chinese boy think his culture was better than mine.

"All right, all right, all right," I relented.

Little Tiger gave me a crash course on Chinese curses. The lower-level Chinese curses revolve around dogs and eggs: running dog, stupid egg. Turtle's egg was the worst and likely to cause a fight, although no one could explain to me why. The more extreme curses involve a sexual act performed on various members of your enemy's family: mom, of course, dad, older brother, dad's older brother, dad's father, mom's father, mom's older sister.

Confucianism placed the patriarchal family at the center of society to serve as the model for all relationships. Much like the Eskimos and the word "snow," the Chinese had multiple words for each familial relation. They distinguished between older and younger siblings and relations on the mother's or father's side of the family. For example, there are five different words for "uncle": father's older brother (*bofu*), father's younger brother (*shufu*), father's sister's husband (*gufu*), mother's brother (*jiufu*), mother's sister's husband (*yifu*). Even strangers are often addressed, usually when a favor is being asked, by a kinship term. At Shaolin, I learned to address old men as "grandfather," middle-aged men as "uncle," and males of a similar age as either "older brother" (*gege*) or "younger brother" (*didi*).

"The standard form is *wo cao ni made ge bi*," Little Tiger said with *South Park* glee. "I fucked your mother's pussy."

"That's pretty bad," I said.

"And then you just replace 'mother' with some other relative," he continued. "Can you do better than that?"

"It's not easy," I said, preparing to pull out my trump card. "But those curses are not as bad as 'motherfucker.'"

"Madafacka," Little Tiger attempted.

"Motherfucker."

"Madafucker."

"Better."

"What's it mean?"

The best I could do for a translation was: "You are the kind of man who makes love to his own mother."

Little Tiger scrunched up his face, "I don't understand."

Have you heard the story about a Greek king named Oedipus? A doctor named Freud? Do you understand how a husband and wife make babies? Now imagine the husband is the wife's son and the wife is his mother—I tried several times before Little Tiger grasped the concept, a sure sign I was going to hell for this.

"That's bad, really bad," Little Tiger said. "But I don't think it is as bad as this: 'I fucked your eighteen generations.'"

Given Chinese respect for their ancestors, it was their harshest curse.

I had to give it up. "You're right. That is worse."

Little Tiger was triumphant. "I told you so. I told you so. I told you so. Chinese curses are the worst."

It was a bitter defeat.

On Carlos's last day of his six-week stay, his eyes welled up and tears trickled down his face at breakfast. I thought he was weeping because he was leaving Shaolin.

"It's okay, Carlos, we'll stay in touch."

"No, Mateo, you don't understand. It was just so incredible."

"What?"

"Jesus spoke to me last night."

I instantly knew I believed him, because my first reaction wasn't skepticism but envy. My first thought wasn't: *Isn't Shaolin a little outside of His jurisdiction?* It was: *Carlos gets a lecture from the Son of God and all I got was some crappy little moment of absolute peace. That's not fair, I have seniority here!*

"What happened?" I asked.

"I was in bed, praying for my family, when I heard this voice, and I knew it was Jesus. It was so incredible."

"What did he say?"

"I can't remember most of it. It was so fast, the words rushed over me. I remember him saying, 'I am energy. This is the answer. I am energy. You are energy. Everything is energy.'"

We were silent for the rest of the meal.

BOOK THREE

INITIATE

February–April 1993

酒令大如军令。

"Drinking games are to be observed
even more seriously than military orders."

—DREAM OF THE RED CHAMBER

1

KICKBOXING

Shaolin's students take a winter break instead of summer vacation, because the winters are so brutal in the mountains. The monks spent my first Shaolin winter being treated like kings during their tour of Thailand, the only country on earth where kickboxing is the national pastime and Buddhism the state religion. I tried to stay and keep training, but because neither the hotel nor the training halls had any heating system, I had to keep adding layers of clothing. I trained until it was impossible either to sleep or warm up enough to be able to stretch my legs and practice. I finally broke down and went home for Christmas.

Back in Topeka, my friends took me out to local watering holes. Wanting to test the extent of my Shaolin training, they purposely picked the rowdiest bars in town, the kinds of places where brawls were not only frequent but also had a come-one-come-all quality that tended to metastasize, filling the bar with swinging fists and boots before spreading out into the parking lot. Watching from the sidelines, I became reacquainted with just how big they grow them on the farms in Kansas. Despite my three months of studying traditional kungfu forms, I was still not any more confident that I could protect myself than I was before I left.

After that first bar brawl, I decided to switch from traditional forms to kickboxing, because the best fighters at Shaolin were the kickboxers. And since the best kickboxer was Coach Cheng, I was determined to become his student.

When I returned to Shaolin in early February, after the Chinese New Year, I informed Deputy Leader Jiao that I wanted to study *sanda* with Coach Cheng. I knew this was a rather outrageous demand, because the Wushu Center did not have a kickboxing team and Coach Cheng was not an employee.

"Our focus is on foreign tours and performances for tourists," Deputy Leader Jiao told me. "*Sanda* is difficult to stage for performances."

Having anticipated this line of argument, I said, "There is no doubt that the Wushu Center has the best performance team in Shaolin, but Taguo has the best kickboxers. Administrators at Taguo have told me they think the Wushu Center performers aren't the toughest martial artists in town."

Deputy Leader Jiao graced me with a rare smile, a professional manipulator's nod to a precocious amateur's entrance into the big leagues.

"Interesting," he said. "Very interesting."

Privately owned Taguo was the main rival to the government-run Wushu Center. With its superior infrastructure and indoor training facilities, not to mention its access to Shaolin monks, the Wushu Center had a clear, structural advantage in performance kungfu. In response, Taguo had lowered its tuition and developed a reputation as the toughest place in town where the toughest *sanda* fighters were forged, attracting nearly 3,000 Chinese students as compared to the Wushu Center's 300. With its sheer mass of young students banging on each other year after year until only the strongest were still standing, Taguo's meat grinder had produced a disproportionate percentage of China's national kickboxing champions.

Wanting to leverage its growing national reputation and tuition revenue, Taguo had plans to build a restaurant, hotel, and performance hall to compete with the Wushu Center's core business. It was also working back channels to obtain the right to train *laowai*. Prior to the winter break, Taguo administrators had invited me over for a tour and a sales pitch. News of my visit made it back to the Wushu Center leaders the same day.

"Yes," I said to Deputy Leader Jiao. "It is interesting."

Within a week of my discussion with Deputy Leader Jiao, I was told that the Wushu Center had decided to form its own kickboxing team. Coach Cheng had been hired to train his own handpicked members, all of whom would receive a monthly stipend. The leaders had decided to take the New York Yankees' approach and buy themselves a championship team . . . with my money. While my teammates were all going to be expert kickboxers, I was to be the rank beginner who had to buy his way on to the team. I knew they were going to start off hating me, because everyone hates a rich dilettante, especially if they are indebted to him. The only way to win them over and become a true member of the team was to prove I could eat as much bitter as they could.

The first day of kickboxing practice, the thirteen members of our team lined up by weight class, which in *sanda* are 48 kg. (105.8 lb.), 52 kg. (114.6 lb.), 56 kg. (123.5 lb.), 60 kg. (132 lb.), 65 kg. (143 lb.), 70 kg. (154 lb.), 75 kg. (165 lb.), 80 kg. (176 lb.) and up. There were two fighters per category up to 70 kg. Fighters above 75 kg were rare in China, given the genetics, diet, and lack of weight training, equipment, and steroids. Also, because it was an amateur sport, there was no financial incentive to move up to a more popular weight class. So *sanda* fighters were like American collegiate wrestlers, always trying to drop kilograms so they could get down to a weight class where they were stronger than their opponents.

Sanda class started like forms class. We ran around the room, we did drills up and down the mat, and then we stretched. After the stretching, we paired up with the other guy in our weight class, who would be both a partner and a rival for the top spot. Having already dropped down to 150 lb., I was in the 70 kg. class along with Baotong, the team's strongest fighter. He was a pugnacious-looking dude about my age. While we were nearly the same weight, I was four inches taller, so he was a good deal broader and thicker than I. His physique looked like it had been chiseled by Michelangelo, with special attention paid to the calves, which were bigger than my thighs. In fact, his calves were bigger than his own thighs, too.

The first drill was to practice *sanda*'s basic techniques against a kungfu shield, a thick pad that covered the forearm, held by our partner. Unlike traditional Shaolin forms, *sanda* had the simplicity of a Chuck Norris movie: four basic punches (straight, hook, uppercut, and overhand), five basic kicks (forward thrust, roundhouse, side kick, spinning hook, and spinning sweep), and three throws (leg catch and sweep, head lock and hip throw, and the waist grab and trip). Hundreds of techniques had been boiled down to a dozen, driven by the rules of Chinese-style kickboxing, the limitations of the human body, and the merciless logic of skilled opponents fighting each other over and over again. Only the most effective techniques survived.

After we finished with the punches, we moved on to the kicks. The front side kick is the standard opening attack in *sanda* and the cornerstone of the style, because *sanda*, unlike most other kickboxing styles, rewards contestants for throwing each other to the ground, and the side kick is a powerful, long-ranged attack that is difficult to grab. (Styles make the fights, but rules make the styles.) To execute the front side kick, you take a big step forward with your lead foot, then slide your back foot up to meet your front, and in one motion lift your front leg into the air, chamber it against the side of his body, and turn at a ninety-degree angle to your opponent. When done properly, the body looks like a compressed accordion for an instant before you fire the front leg directly at your opponent with as much speed as possible, snapping it like a whip at the last moment.

The second most popular kick is the roundhouse. For this kick, you lift your knee and twist your upper body, while at the same time swinging your leg around in a circular motion like a baseball bat. It is the fastest of the three major *sanda* kicks and the best for head shots, but it is also the easiest to grab.

The least popular is the thrust kick. For a right thrust, you plant your left foot, raise your right knee up into your chest so that the sole of your right foot is pointing at your opponent, and then drive the foot forward like you're a fireman kicking open a locked door. It is a powerful kick used to jackhammer an opponent backward and is difficult to grab because it comes in at a straight angle, but it is slow and easy to dodge.

Despite my three years of martial arts training in college and three months of Shaolin forms, I was terrible at every technique, particularly the side kick. Baotong, who had been kickboxing in Shaolin for the last seven years, was in a different league. But still, he seemed bored as he practiced his front thrust and side kicks. It wasn't until he got to his roundhouse that he brightened considerably. He picked up his right leg with its massive calf on the end and swung it like a mace, hitting the shield so hard I thought he had dislocated my shoulder. He smirked at the look of pain on my face. If anything, on his next kick he tried even harder to hurt me. After two kicks, I had to use two arms to hold the pad.

The next drill was throws. *Sanda* differs from most other styles of kickboxing because a fighter can score two points by throwing, sweeping, or knocking his opponent to the canvas. This must be done quickly. The referee will step in to break the fighters apart two seconds after they have started to grapple. And once one fighter goes down, the referee steps in until he can get back up—there is no ground fighting. These rules are meant to keep a kickboxing fight from turning into a wrestling match. So throws have to be quick and efficient. While it is legal to just charge your opponent, grab him around the waist or head and throw him to the mat, such throws are easy to defend against and therefore hard to complete within the two-second limit. The most effective throws involve anticipating your opponent's kicks, catching or trapping his kicking leg and then sweeping the standing leg.

The other pairs were drilling at half speed. One partner would gently toss out his leg, the other would catch it, gently sweep the standing leg, and cradle his partner to the ground. They were going slowly to perfect the motion. Not Baotong. When I gently tossed out my leg, he grabbed it hard, chopped at my standing leg with his massive roundhouse sweep, and smashed me to the ground. When I got back up, he had a bigger smirk on his face that said, *Bitter, ain't it, rich boy?* I kicked slowly again with the same results. The wind knocked out of me from the fall, I stood up more slowly, a rage building inside.

The rest of the team was now half-practicing and half-watching us to see what would happen next. It was Baotong's turn to kick. Instead of putting out his leg for me to easily grab, he kicked me full force, jamming my thumb. On the next kick, I grabbed his leg and moved slowly to sweep his leg, but he grabbed me roughly around my neck, refusing to go down. The rest of the team had stopped to watch. I was back on the playground. My face felt hot with anger and shame. On his next kick, I grabbed his leg hard, turned, pulled his leg in a circle, and swept his back leg with as forceful a kick as I was capable of. He went sprawling to the mat. He blinked a couple of times, looking up at me.

Snarling, I stood over him, "Get up. Let's go again."

He kicked me hard again. I caught his kick. He tried to grab my neck. I ducked him and threw him to ground as hard as I could.

"Don't waste time," I shouted. "Get up. Let's go again."

Baotong looked over at Coach Cheng and started laughing. Coach Cheng smiled. Clearly, I had just passed some unspoken test. The *laowai* wasn't such a wimp after all. For the rest of practice, Baotong and I went at each other full force. He banged me up pretty good, but he wasn't smirking anymore.

After the morning practice, I was so wrecked I didn't think I could make it back to the hotel, so I went up to Deqing and Cheng Hao's room above the performance hall instead. As I sat on Deqing's bed looking at the kungfu movie posters on the wall, I tried to keep from quivering with exhaustion.

"How was *sanda* class?" Deqing asked.

"Baotong was trying to kill me," I said.

"He wanted to see if you were afraid," Cheng Hao laughed.

"He's powerful but slow." Deqing said. "You have to stay out of his range." I tried to smile, but my body was shaking too violently from exhaustion and adrenaline letdown. "Are you okay?"

"No problem," I said, sitting on my hands to try to make them stop quivering.

"He's tired to death," Cheng Hao said. He cracked their door open and shouted, "Little Tiger, come here!"

Little Tiger ran over to their room. "What is it?"

"*Bao Mosi* is tired to death. Go get some sugar and hot water."

"Where do I get the sugar?"

"From the restaurant."

"They'll want money."

"Tell them it's for the *laowai*."

"What if they still want money?"

"Don't argue, get going!"

Little Tiger ran off. As the youngest monk, he was used to the *wushu* team's seniority system: crappy errands rolled down the hierarchy of age. He came back ten minutes later with a packet of sugar and a thermos bottle. Deqing poured the boiling water and sugar into a bowl.

"Here, drink this," he said. "It will help stop the shaking."

I tried to bring the bowl to my lips, but my hands were quivering too badly. I spilled the boiling water into my lap.

"Here I'll hold it for you," Deqing said, grabbing the bowl and putting it to my lips. "Just like a little baby. You okay?"

"No problem."

I drank down as much as I could. Everything was fine for a moment, but suddenly I was bent over their wastebasket, vomiting.

"I'm sorry, I'm sorry, I'm sorry," I said.

"No problem," Deqing said.

"He's an American," Cheng Hao said to Deqing. "They don't like hot drinks. We should have gotten him a Coke."

"Maybe."

One of the younger monks, Genming, was walking past the room.

"Genming, come here!" Cheng Hao shouted.

"What is it?"

"Get *Bao Mosi* a Coke. Here's 4RMB. Also take this trash out and clean it."

"Get Little Tiger to do it."

"Don't argue. Do what you're told."

Genming walked into the hallway. I heard him shout, "Little Tiger, come here. Cheng Hao wants you to clean out this basket."

Little Tiger must have dreamed of the day when someone younger than him joined the monastery.

I managed a couple of swigs of Coke before Deqing forced me to lie down in his bed and take a nap. I woke up just before three P.M. It took everything I had to drag my bruised body out of bed and back down to the practice room. Deqing saw me just before I entered.

"*Bao Mosi*, you should go back to bed," he said.

"I don't want Baotong to think he's beaten me."

He nodded. "That is the right attitude."

I limped into class. Coach Cheng looked at me. He raised his eyebrows and smiled slightly. He must have heard about my being sick.

"You are here," he said with a mixture of surprise and amusement.

"Correct. I am here."

"Good. Let's start class."

I dragged through the early drills, barely keeping up. Baotong, seeing how bad off I was, took pity on me. He ran through the throwing drills with me at half-speed, letting me sweep him to the ground without much of a struggle.

Watching us sleepwalking through the drills, Coach Cheng decided to raise the stakes.

"Enough!" he shouted. "All right, it looks like it's time for some sparring."

He sent one of my teammates to get the pads.

Sanda matches take place on a *leitai*, a raised canvas platform, a boxing ring without the ropes. In ancient times, traveling performance troups would erect a wooden platform in the middle of town and the kungfu expert of the group would offer an open challenge to the town, just as John L. Sullivan did in 1890s America. The winner was the last man standing on the platform, a kungfu version of king of the hill.

The Wushu Center didn't have a *leitai*, so Coach Cheng marked off the dimensions of a regulation *leitai* with the kicking shields. He threw the two sets of protective gear into the center of the ring and then went to sit down outside the marked-off area.

"Baotong."

"Yes, Coach."

"You first," Coach Cheng pointed at the center of the ring.

He looked around the team. Every other member of the team dropped their eyes: none of them wanted to spar with Baotong. This realization hit me a second too late. I was still looking at Coach Cheng when we made eye contact.

"You."

"Me?"

"Yes, you."

The rest of the team was smiling, happy they had avoided facing the toughest fighter on the team. I turned my back on Baotong as I started to put on the protective gear.

The Chinese government designed the modern rules of *sanda*

with an eye toward international amateur competitions like the Olympics. Because these are tournaments where each contestant will have to fight multiple opponents within a period of a few days, the two big concerns are exhaustion and injury disqualifications, so the matches are kept short (two-minute rounds, best two out of three rounds wins the match), and there is a great deal of protective padding: headgear, mouthpiece, chest pad, boxing gloves, cup, shin guards, and mini-footpads to protect the fragile bones on the top of the foot.

When I was done putting on my armor, I felt like the Michelin Man. Baotong was waiting for me, wearing only a cup protector and his boxing gloves, clearly unconcerned about the possibility that I might hurt him. My pride, still tender from the morning practice, flared again. I threw my headgear off and started pulling off the chest protector. Coach Cheng intervened, "No, no, no, Matt. It is your first time."

I compromised. Baotong did after all have massive calves. I left the headgear off, but wore everything else, including, thankfully, the cup.

Scoring in *sanda* is relatively simple:

Punch = 1 point
Basic kick below the head = 2 points
Basic kick to the head = 3 points
Advanced spinning kick = 3 points
Knocking opponent down while remaining standing = 2 points
Knocking opponent off the platform = 4 points

Coach Cheng slapped his hands together and stepped back. I bounced nervously on my toes, wanting very much to be somewhere else. Baotong jumped forward and raised his left leg as if he intended to kick me with a front side kick. Still a jangle of nerves, I jumped back two steps. He put his foot on the ground. Then, like in a nightmare, he made the exact same motion, jump-stepping and feinting a kick. And I had the exact same response, jumping back two steps. But this time, I had reached the end of the marked-off space, my foot tangled in the handle of one of the kicking shields. I found myself tipping backward in slow motion, my arms windmilling cartoonishly as

I tried to remain standing. I failed, flopping back onto the ground. Without touching me, Baotong had knocked me out of the ring.

4-0.

My teammates were laughing.

Coach Cheng shouted at them, "You dare laugh? Do you want to fight Baotong?"

Shamed, they shut up. I stood up and walked back into the center of the ring.

Still testing me, Baotong faked another left side kick, but this time I didn't move. He smiled slightly. The fog of fighting had lifted. I faked a jab, jumped, and kicked him in the chest. Baotong's smile broadened: I'd scored, and now the games could begin.

4-2.

Next he charged forward and let loose a right roundhouse kick with that massive right calf hurtling toward me. Turning, I caught the blow on my left tricep. 6-2. It knocked me two feet to the side. Baotong stepped in closer and kicked me in the other arm with a left roundhouse. 8-2. He was pinballing me left and right around the ring. 10-2, 12-2, 14-2. He clearly intended to keep chopping away at my torso until I toppled. I had to strike back.

With a minute left in the first round, I lifted my right leg to roundhouse him in the chest. At the same moment, he was lifting his left leg. The timing was unfortunate for me. My right leg swung around on a slightly higher plane; his left chambered exactly below it, sliding along the underside of my leg. Time froze for just an instant and I knew not only what was going to happen but that I was helpless to stop it. My foot was inches from his chest when his slammed into my protective cup.

It cracked.

Coach Cheng must have dismissed the class while I was writhing on the ground, because when I was finally able to open my eyes, he and I were alone. He pulled me to my feet. I found it hard to meet his gaze.

"Look at me," Coach Cheng said.

I looked up. He raised his right fist, as if to strike. Like some abused Pavlovian dog, I flinched and ducked behind my hands. I looked up to see that his fist hadn't moved.

"What are you afraid of?"

"Being hit."

"Why?"

"The pain."

He looked at me for a long time.

"When you were little, did they beat you?"

His question caught me off guard. My eyes got hot.

"Classmates?"

I nodded.

"Okay."

He picked up a boxing glove and put it on his right hand. He punched at me in slow motion. I held firm. The glove lightly tapped my head. He pulled his fist back and punched at about half speed. I braced but didn't flinch. The modest blow knocked my head back a couple of inches. Coach Cheng reared back again. This time the punch was pretty close to full speed. I blinked right before my head snapped back. I stumbled to a knee before catching my balance.

I stood up slowly, my head ringing.

Coach Cheng looked at me with a slight smile on his face. "You still alive?"

"Unless this is hell," I said.

"Was it too painful?"

"I don't know. I can't feel my face. I think I'm okay."

"You're okay, and you didn't die. So what do you have to fear?"

"Brain damage," I offered.

Coach Cheng laughed. "Don't worry, even with a damaged brain you would still be too smart to be a kickboxer."

He took off his glove and turned his back on me. Suddenly, he twirled swinging his naked fist at my face. I froze. He pulled his fist up short just millimeters from my nose.

"I didn't move," I said.

He grabbed my nose between his fingers and tweaked it.

"In this case, you should move," he said.

2

MEDIA MATTERS

C hina had four state-run TV channels, but Shaolin received only two of them. The programming mostly served propaganda purposes. The dramas were overwhelmingly World War II serials, in which noble Communist peasant-soldiers battled against vicious Japanese imperialists and corrupt Chinese nationalists, pushing both out of the country: the Japanese to Nippon, the nationalists to Taiwan.

The news programming was tedious, government boosterism:

> This year Henan Province produced 512,000 metric tons of wheat, 304,000 metric tons of rice, and 211,000 metric tons of [something]. Henan's governor said this represented a strong improvement on last year's numbers of 454,000 metric tons of wheat, 281,000 metric tons of rice, and 145,000 metric tons of [something], but the people of Henan must pull together to further increase our contribution to China's growing economy. The Henan government has invested 50 million yuan in agriculture projects. It has also invested 100 million yuan in transportation and other developments. In other news, this year Henan has produced 600,000 metric tons of coal . . .

The only other staple was show trials: no jury, a court dominated by judges in police uniforms, and a stricken-looking defendant who said next to nothing, because the outcome was preordained. Depending on the point the government was trying to make, they'd reshow the same trial for weeks at a time.

When I first arrived, the big trial was of a man who had made and sold knockoff Maotai, the most expensive brand of *baijiu* in China. He bought empty bottles of Maotai, filled them with a cheaper version of *baijiu*, dipped the cork in real Maotai so customers would be fooled by the distinctive Maotai scent, and sold hundreds of thousands of RMB worth to stores and restaurants around the country. He had also apparently exported some of it, which was the core problem. The head judge went on at great length about the potential impact on the Chinese economy if foreigners lost confidence in Chinese quality. China was applying for membership in the World Trade Organization at the time, and black market and pirated goods were a sticking point in negotiations.

At the end of the thirty-minute program, the defendant was convicted and sentenced to "death." The first time I watched the trial, I grabbed my Chinese-English dictionary, not quite believing I'd translated what they'd said correctly. The death penalty for selling knockoff booze? They won't even execute you for that in Texas! But Deng was a big believer in capital punishment. Besides murder, a Chinese citizen could get a bullet in the back of the skull for rape, arson, embezzlement, armed robbery, pimping, and organizing a secret society, like the Falun Gong.

There was only one decent program on TV while I was at Shaolin. In China the TV event of the year was a twenty-plus-part miniseries called *Beijingers in New York*. It was so popular that the government showed it twice. While it was on, almost every monk on the performance team crowded into my room on a nightly basis.

The story line featured a Beijing couple who move to New York City in search of a better life but end up miserable. The woman can only find a job in an illegal sweatshop in Queens. Her husband has to work as a delivery boy in a Chinese restaurant. The stress of trying to survive strains their marriage. Then the woman's boss—a devious, Chinese-speaking *laowai*, who unfortunately bore a striking resemblance to me—seduces her. The couple divorces. The husband takes up with a Chinese woman who owns a restaurant/bar.

It was pure propaganda, of course, and more than a little bit xenophobic. But the writing and acting were so good that even I enjoyed it. The husband delivered the best line of the series. One night, he's drinking beers and ranting about how hateful *laowai* are. He concludes, "Do you know why *laowai* are so hairy? Because when we were human, they were still monkeys."

The monks doubled over with laughter. For weeks afterward, they'd reenact the scene.

After the series was over, I asked Cheng Hao, "Do you still want to go to America?"

"Yes. It was just a show," he said. "Besides, even the worst life in America is better than what we have to endure here."

With most TV programming so dull, the boys at Shaolin were kungfu movie freaks, constantly visiting Shaolin's multiplex to watch the latest blood-spattered Hong Kong releases on VHS. Once a year, the Wushu Center leaders threw a white tarp over a two-story stone wall and played an old print of Jet Li's *Shaolin Temple*. The night had the feeling of a religious service.

In Hong Kong chop-socky flicks, the bad guys, or at least the bad guys' henchmen, are more frequently than not *laowai*. A white guy is never the hero, and only rarely does a foreigner get to be the hero's buddy. Within the industry there is a subset of *laowai* actors, usually Australian, who appear near the end of these films, shout something like, "Ha! You Chinese dog, your kungfu is no match for mine," and then display their good but distinctly inferior martial arts skills against the Chinese hero for a minute or two of screen time before being dispatched in a humiliating manner.

When you are the only *laowai* in a village of 10,000 Chinese martial artists and you've sat through several dozen films where a white man shouts, "You Chinese dog," before getting his ass kicked, it starts to irritate you. We all need role models.

Wanting to undermine the assumption that *laowai* suck at martial arts, I brought VHS copies of Steven Seagal's *Above the Law*, David Carradine's *Kung Fu*, and Jean-Claude Van Damme's *Lionheart* back from winter vacation.

We watched Seagal's movie first. It is very roughly based on his life (according to his somewhat suspect publicity bio) as an aikido instructor in Japan who became involved with the CIA. A Japanese aikido school had performed at the Shaolin Temple prior to my arrival, so all the monks retold stories of the visit during the first half of the movie.

"But what do you think of the actor?" I asked, finally. "His kungfu is pretty good, isn't it?"

Little Tiger said, with the honesty of youth, "He's not bad . . . for a *laowai*."

"Oh," I said, wounded.

"But he is very fierce," Deqing politely interjected. He cuffed Little Tiger across the back of the head when he thought I wasn't looking.

"What did I do wrong?" Little Tiger asked.

Deqing said, "Pay attention to his eyes. He looks like he enjoys hurting people."

The monks were used to highly fictionalized portrayals of the Shaolin Temple, so they weren't bothered by the fantasy version of Shaolin in David Carradine's *Kung Fu*. They were, however, shocked by the casting of David Carradine.

"How can he be a Shaolin monk?" Little Tiger asked. "He's a *laowai*."

"Actually in the story he's half-Chinese, half-*laowai*," I said.

"He doesn't look like a *hun xui*," Little Tiger said. "Mixed blood."

Deqing cuffed Little Tiger across the back of the head again. "Don't use bad words."

"The actor is a *laowai*," I said. "He's pretending to be half-Chinese."

"That explains why his kungfu is so terrible," Little Tiger said, as he ducked to the back row to avoid another cuff.

For the rest of the movie I ignored the slights about Carradine's kungfu skills, which were admittedly poor. (To be fair, however, he did capture that California New Age, faux-Zen blankness perfectly.) I was waiting for the climactic moment that nearly every American male who was alive in the early 1970s remembers: the scene where Carradine lifts a burning chalice to pass the final Shaolin test, permanently branding a dragon on one forearm and a tiger on the other. I hadn't seen or heard anything like this legend since my arrival, but I had to know.

"Is this story true?" I asked. "Did that used to be the final test for Shaolin monks?"

"No," Deqing said. "Why would we want to burn our arms like that? You might end up a cripple, never be able to make a fist again in your life. What kind of kungfu test would that be?"

"Americans have excellent imaginations, however," Little Tiger offered as consolation. "Don't you agree, Deqing?"

"They make good movies," Deqing conceded.

Jean-Claude Van Damme impressed the monks the most, especially his bodybuilder physique.

"Look, he has muscles on his muscles," Little Tiger shouted. "I wouldn't want to wrestle him."

"But muscles that are too big reduce the quickness of your technique," Deqing said. "Power is generated by speed, not size. You saw what a tiny bullet can do."

Little Tiger shouted, "I know! I shot a gun at the range! Bam! Bam! Bam!"

The monks were also intrigued by Van Damme's signature move: a jumping, spinning hook kick. Van Damme does a full split while in the air. The monks did theirs with one leg tucked under their body.

"His flexibility is very good," Cheng Hao said.

"But why would he split his legs?" Deqing asked. "You generate more speed with your right kick if you keep your left foot tucked."

"He studied, um, what is the Chinese word for the French traditional form of dance?" I said.

Lipeng, who was one of only four monks assigned to Shaolin's first trip to Paris two years before, said, "Ballet."

"Right, right, ballet." I said.

"It looks pretty," Little Tiger said.

"But it is not as fast," Deqing repeated.

We watched in silence for another thirty minutes before Little Tiger tugged on my sleeve.

"When does he die?" he asked.

Confused, I asked, "Who dies?"

"The *laowai*."

"Which *laowai*?"

"The one with all the muscles."

I was even more confused, "But he's the hero."

"Right, so when does he die?"

"He doesn't. Heroes don't die in American movies."

"They do in Chinese movies."

"I know, but not in American movies."

"Then they aren't heroes."

"Why do you say that?"

Little Tiger paused to think. "I don't know. They're just not."

Feeling like I was on to something important, I pressed. "But why do you think that?"

Little Tiger dropped his head and shrugged his shoulders.

Deqing, who had been following the exchange, said, "Because it doesn't take much courage to fight when you still believe you can win. What takes real courage is to keep fighting when all hope is gone."

3

IRON FOREARM BOY

Along the sidewalk of Shaolin's road, there were half a dozen ancient women who sold tiny clay cats that meowed when the attached string was pulled. But since the sound was more like a bleating "mao" and the price point was, coincidentally, 5 Mao, which is half a RMB (about six cents), they were nicknamed the "Mao Mao Grandmothers." Every day as the tourists passed their wooden stands with the clay cats displayed, they'd plaintively pull on the string of one of the cats in a desperate effort to entice someone to make a purchase. *Mao! Mao! Mao!* It was highly irritating, like alley cats in heat.

But it was hard not to feel sorry for them. They were too poor to retire as they should have at their venerable age, and they spent all day trying to sell something that nobody wanted. What tourist visiting a famous kungfu monastery wants to buy an annoying-sounding clay cat? I often wondered if it wasn't a subtle form of begging. *Money! Money! Money!*

One day I was walking down the street with my new supply of Cokes when I saw one of the tourists, a thirtysomething Chinese male, slap a cat out of the hand of a Mao Mao Grandmother and stomp on it. I was about fifty yards away and didn't know how to react. I can't say I hadn't thought of doing the same on more than one occasion. But then Grandmother said something I couldn't hear, and the tourist slapped her. I pushed through the crowd that had stopped to watch.

Grandmother pointed at him and blurted something else, which

I assumed was a curse, because the tourist's face turned red, and he took a swing at her with a closed fist. The punch was amateurish, and Grandmother was able to dodge it as she darted around the table, putting it between them for protection. Embarrassed and angry, the tourist knocked over her table and stomped each one of her cats flat. When finished, he twirled around and started to walk away from her, but she cursed him again.

The tourist whirled, caught her by the arm as she tried to flee, and kicked her twice in the butt. His kicking wasn't much better than his punching—the equivalent of a couple of gentle spanks—but I couldn't stand by and watch a man in his prime kick an elderly lady in her backside, whatever the cause of the dispute.

As I moved purposefully toward the Mao Mao Grandmother, the tourist's friend grabbed him around the waist, pulled him away, and turned him around, pleading, "Enough. Enough. Enough."

I stepped into the vacated space between the two antagonists. Grandmother was behind me and I was facing the tourist's back. Grandmother cursed him again, claiming to have fucked one of his relatives, but her accent was so thick, I couldn't translate which one. The tourist whirled and was about to charge until he saw me standing in the way. He stopped in his tracks. His face was still red with rage, his eyes still wild, but this look of bafflement danced across his visage. One moment he was knocking around a peasant who had offended him, the next he was face-to-face with a very tall *laowai*. He couldn't get his mind around it.

Sensing the shift in the balance of power, Grandmother rained curses down upon him. She must have been from a nearby mountain village with its own slang, because I didn't understand anything she said—and thanks to Little Tiger, I had become a dedicated student of local curses.

The friend grabbed the tourist around the waist again, which freed the tourist to give the appearance of trying to charge Grandmother without actually moving forward. It was a Mexican standoff.

I wasn't particularly worried. I'd seen he couldn't fight and knew there were only two of them. Besides, what chance did they have against Iron Forearm Boy? I played out the scenario in my mind. If he broke free, I'd snap a left kick to stop his forward momentum and then clobber him over the side of the head with the bag of eight Cokes I had gripped in my right hand. That would take him down and make his friend less likely to enter the fray. My biggest worry at that moment was whether I had enough money on me to buy eight new cans of Coke.

"Grandmother, would you please, please, please shut up!" I shouted over my shoulder.

Finally, after a minute more of this, the friend was able to convince the tourist to walk away. "It's not worth it. It's not worth it. It's not worth it." He dragged his friend all the way down the road.

When he was far enough away, I turned to Grandmother who was still cursing in her local dialect.

"Are you okay?" I asked.

She walked over to her smashed cats and picked them up, one by one. When she'd finished, the old crone handed me one. As magical trinkets go, it was not particularly inspiring.

Looking at the crowd that was dispersing unsatisfied, I noticed Little Tiger for the first time. I waved him over, but he turned and scurried back to the Wushu Center.

When I got back, I went straight to Deqing's room. I was feeling pretty pleased with my minor heroics and good deed for the day.

I sat on his bed and said as casually as I was capable, "I had an interesting afternoon today . . ."

"I heard what you did," Deqing said.

"Little Tiger didn't waste any time."

I was expecting praise. Instead, he said, "*Bao Mosi*, you shouldn't have involved yourself."

"But Deqing, the man was beating on an old lady who couldn't defend herself," I protested.

"But you don't know why he was doing it."

"What possible reason would justify kicking a grandmother in the butt?"

"I don't know. Maybe she cheated him."

I paused to consider this. "Well, even if she did, he kicked her before I had a chance to stop him, so he got his revenge."

"You shouldn't have done it."

"But what good is learning kungfu if you don't use the skill to help people?"

"You believe you were correct to help, but you are a foreigner here. It isn't proper for you to involve yourself in the people's business."

We soon changed the subject and talked about other things, but I was sore at him for rebuking me and left his room as soon as propriety allowed.

It took me half a year to discover that I was not the only foreigner studying in Shaolin. I was walking past the Shaolin Wushu University watching the Chinese adolescents practice their basic movement one day when I stopped in my tracks. Something was wrong with this picture. Even though he dressed in the same jogging suit and shoes as the rest of the boys, one of the young men stuck out. His cheekbones were too high, his skin was too reddish brown, and his torso was too long in proportion to his body. He clearly wasn't Han Chinese.

He had seen me staring and must have guessed the reason because he waved. I waved back. When his class was over, he came over to greet me.

He said in broken English, "Hello, my name, um, Ahmed. Happy you meet. I hear, um, American, um, Wushu Center."

"It is an honor to meet you," I said in English. But then, I continued in Chinese, "Do you speak Chinese?

"Better my English . . . a little bit," he replied in Chinese. "Thank you."

"I didn't know there were any other *laowai* in Shaolin. What country are you from?"

"Afghanistan."

"Your kungfu is very good. How long have you been here?"

"Three years."

"That's a long time," I said, somewhat miffed to discover I wasn't the toughest *laowai* in town.

"Yes."

"And you like it here?" I asked.

"Yes."

"And you live with the other Chinese students?" I asked, incredulously.

I had long since realized that if I had to live like the Chinese students—eight to a room, straw-mat bed, no toilet, no shower—I never would have had the strength to survive three weeks let alone three years, especially if my Chinese were as rough as his.

"My dorm over there."

"So how long are you planning on staying?"

"As long as I can. My brother works embassy Beijing. He help me get here. It's much better than home."

I was dumbfounded. In my spectrum of experience, Shaolin was as bad as it got. I knew very little about Afghanistan. Like most of my fellow countrymen, I preferred not to learn too much about dysfunctional countries until after my government invaded them. It's emotionally easier that way.

"But isn't the war with Russia over?"

"It worse now."

Even though his poor Chinese made conversation difficult, I tried to visit Ahmed as frequently as possible after that. He was a great guy—the kind you want to have a drink with and to have your back in a fight. Deqing often joined me in these trips, because he had a number of friends at the Wushu University.

Deqing, Ahmed, and I were sitting with our backs against the Wushu University outer wall one day when we saw a posse of adolescents leading a teenager like a prisoner. They had a rope around his neck and *wushu* spears pointed at his back. The boy holding the rope had a samurai dagger pressed against the prisoner's throat. As they marched him toward Wushu University, the boys took turns punching him in the gut and across the side of the head.

As they got closer, the prisoner noticed Deqing and shouted something to him in a dialect I couldn't understand.

Deqing exploded off the ground and jetted himself toward the posse.

"What the fuck do you think you're doing? What has he done that you treat him this way?"

"What business is it of yours?" the boy with the dagger and the lasso asked.

"What business? Listen to your tone! I am Wang Deqing," he said, using his full family name. "You all know me."

"So? Who is this turtle's egg to you?"

"He is from Zhejiang. I am from Zhejiang. That puts him under my protection."

Identity politics in China were primarily geographical. Shaolin had boys from all over the country, so provincial loyalty was particularly strong. The only connection more powerful was devotion to one's schoolmates. As the highest-ranking person in Shaolin from Zhejiang, Deqing was in effect every Zhejianger's big brother. He took the role seriously. Young Zhejiang boys who arrived with little money, as Deqing had, sought him out for loans, favors, and advice. Twice a week he taught a class for Zhejiangers who were too poor to afford tuition at one of the schools.

The posse didn't want to relinquish their prey. "He borrowed money from one of our classmates. When he asked for the money back, this prick beat him."

There were six well-armed boys, but Deqing was older and on the edge of exploding. He knocked the dagger out of the leader's hands. He pushed the spears down. He yanked the prisoner away and pulled the rope off his neck.

"I don't care what he did," Deqing said. "This is excessive. You dare to rope and beat him like he's a dog? I ought to do the same to you."

The boys refused to back down. It looked like a fight was imminent. Ahmed and I flanked Deqing. I was scared shitless. The spears were light and blunt; at best, they'd take out an eye. But a samurai dagger in skilled hands would leave a man lying in a puddle of his own blood.

Our presence tipped the balance. Ahmed was a classmate of theirs. And seeing me pulled Deqing back from the brink.

"We will settle this tonight when the cops are asleep," Deqing said, pushing the prisoner into my arms. "*Bao Mosi*, you take him back to my room."

The leader pointed at the boy and said to Deqing, "He's your responsibility now. If you don't bring him back tonight, we are coming after you."

"Why, you disrespectful prick. I was your coach's coach. You dare talk to me like that?"

They continued to argue as I walked the shaken boy back to the Wushu Center. Deqing arrived twenty minutes later. He grabbed the boy roughly and slapped him hard across the face, "What are you, a thief? You take money and then beat the boy you borrowed it from? You've made all Zhejiangers lose face! I should strangle you to death to restore our honor. Do you have the money?"

"No."

"You stupid egg!" Deqing slapped the boy again. "Okay, I'll take care of it. Now get out of here. And tell the others to meet me outside the Wushu Center at midnight. And you better be there, too, or you will wish I had let those boys beat you."

After the boy left the room, Deqing's quicksilver mood shifted 180 degrees. He laughed and shook his head. "This is really difficult," he said. "What the boy did was wrong, and they have every right to punish him for it. But I couldn't allow them to be so excessive to a Zhejianger in front of me."

At 11:30 P.M. I knocked on Deqing's door. He opened it. He and Cheng Hao were laying out weapons.

"What are you doing here?"

"I came to fight with you."

Deqing's started laughing in disbelief. "Oh no, you can't fight with us."

"Why? You don't think my kungfu is good enough?"

This made Deqing really laugh. "No, no, no, but you're a *laowai*."

Deqing's mood shifted and he looked at me with fondness. He pinched my cheek.

"You're the best. You really are the best," he said. Then he rocked back and laughed in disbelief again. "No, no, no, I can't let you fight."

"Why not?"

"You're a *laowai*."

"So?"

"One of us gets hurt, no one cares. But if you get hurt . . ." Deqing trailed off. "Do you think Beijing wants to read in *The New
York Times* that an American got killed at the Shaolin Temple? It
would turn a simple little fight into an international incident. It
would make the government lose face, and then all of us would be
arrested."

Deqing finally spied the two samurai daggers he and Cheng Hao
had given me tucked into my waistband. This really made him
howl.

"You brought weapons! Oh, you really are the best. I can't believe it. You really are the best. Isn't he the best, Cheng Hao?"

Cheng Hao, who had remained quiet during this entire exchange, leveled a look at me.

"I think he's crazy to want to fight when he doesn't have to."

"He might be crazy, but he's still the best."

Deqing sent me back to my room. Still smarting, I jumped the
wall instead and waited in a dark corner. How was I supposed to
prove my courage if no one would let me fight?

Deqing led a group of about fifty monks and Zhejiangers toward
the university. He had a firm grip on the neck of the prisoner. I
waited for them to get a hundred yards ahead and then followed
quietly. I was fairly certain I wouldn't be seen. There were street
lamps in Shaolin, but they were few and far between.

Waiting for them in front of Wushu University must have been
300 boys, about half the school. They were armed with spears,
swords, staffs, nine-section whips, the whole array of weapons taught
at Shaolin. It struck me as a fairly equal matchup.

Deqing's side stopped and formed a line fifty yards from the
other group. Deqing separated from the group with the prisoner in
tow. From the other side came the posse leader and another boy,
whom I assumed was the aggrieved party.

When they met in the middle, words were exchanged, but I was
too far away to hear them. Then Deqing forced the prisoner to his
knees. He handed the disputed amount of money to the aggrieved
party, who slapped the prisoner in the face.

Deqing raised his hands in the air to indicate the matter was
settled. The Wushu University students were the first to leave.
Then the monks and the Zhejiangers turned back. Deqing said

something to the prisoner. It must have been to stay where he was, because the boy remained after everyone else had left.

I thought seriously about sneaking back, but I was bursting with too much pride. Deqing began laughing when he saw me come out of the shadows.

"You naughty boy. I should slap you."

"I was only going to fight if our side started losing," I said.

Deqing pinched my cheek. "You're the best. You really are the best."

The author as ninety-eight-pound weakling.

Monk Chen, the author, and Coach Yan.

Monk Deqing demonstrating a counterattack on the author in his hotel room.

High-kicking Monk Deqing and the author inside the Shaolin Temple.

Monk Cheng Hao, the author's first instructor and an expert in Eagle Claw kungfu.

Monk Lipeng performing a two-finger handstand.

Senior monks standing in front of the Shaolin Temple's legendary entrance.

Coach Cheng lets loose a flying sidekick
on a Western student inside the Shaolin Temple.

An expert in Chinese-style kickboxing,
Coach Cheng was Shaolin's champion fighter.

Iron crotch expert Monk Dong pulling a five-hundred-pound stone roller. Yes, the rope is attached to his "dong."

For some reason, Monk Dong was quite popular with the ladies.

Monk Lipeng demonstrating his iron stomach kungfu at a Wushu Center performance for tourists. They are trying and failing to dislodge the bowl, which Lipeng has suctioned to his belly.

Coach Yan, the head instructor of the Shaolin Wushu Center monks.

Deputy Leader Jiao: former Shaolin monk, member of the Chinese Communist Party, and second-in-command at the Shaolin Wushu Center.

Monks practicing in the Wushu Center performance hall.

Baotong, the author's sparring partner. Needless to say, his kicks really, really hurt.

Monks at play in the Wushu Center courtyard.

The author marching in the Zheng Zhou International Wushu Tournament's opening parade.

Back at home in Kansas, the author shows off his silver medal.

A special Wushu Tournament edition of the city newspaper showing the seventy-kilogram champion and the author.

4

TAIWAN TUNES

I had just finished practice in the training hall when one of the older monks came up to me and asked me embarrassedly, "Is it true?"

"Is what true?"

"Is it true that in America there are homosexuals?"

"Yes, it's true."

He shivered. "It is not human."

"No, no, no, it's very human."

He shook his head, "You Americans are too strange."

"China also has homosexuals."

"No, we do not," he said with conviction. "It is a foreign problem."

"You're wrong. It is not a problem," I said. "And China has homosexuals."

He refused to believe me. And when I made polite inquiries into the matter I found no one else at Shaolin believed there were any gay Chinese. I realized there was no homophobia at Shaolin, because it is difficult to be phobic of something you don't believe exists. Men could walk around holding hands because no one would think anything of it.

Of course, the monks were wrong. Mainland China certainly wasn't like Hong Kong, which under a century and a half of British rule had developed a fairly open gay culture. But it was an open secret that there were certain parks in the big cities like Beijing and Shanghai where gay men met at night. What surprised me the most about the denial of the monks, though, was that they seemed not to notice that Monk Xingming, a senior monk at the temple, was obviously gay.

I first met Monk Xingming in the performance hall. He was sitting with Deqing and the others. Deqing introduced him as the younger monks' Buddhism instructor. He was a university graduate and clearly held in high regard by the monks, most of whom hadn't graduated from anything more than grade school. Monk Xingming was a sprightly senior citizen with a cherubic face, sad eyes, and a warm smile.

I bowed. *"Amituofo."*

He looked at me and said in almost a falsetto, "You are so cute."

It was the most effeminate voice I'd ever heard out of a Chinese man, like a Mandarin Truman Capote. He offered his hand to shake, which I did. He held on to it while motioning me to sit next to him. He asked me where I was from, how long I had been here, what I was studying. As we talked he gently stroked the top of my hand with the tips of his fingers. Even for China, this was a little too friendly.

Little Tiger jumped into the conversation. "Master Xingming loves American songs. He sings them very beautifully."

"That is very nice to hear," I said, gently pulling my hand away. "Master Xingming, what American songs do you like?"

"Broadway songs," he replied. "And Barbra Streisand."

"Wo mingbai le," I said. "Oh, I see."

Little Tiger urged Monk Xingming to sing something. After much encouragement, which he halfheartedly tried to deflect, he launched into one of Babs's songs. Or at least I assume it was. It was hard to make out the mangle of Chinglish he was humming. I stared at the other monks, trying to see why it was they couldn't see what was so obvious.

They were looking at me expectantly—the arbiter of Monk Xingming's English singing talent. It had been a truly gong-worthy performance.

It was all I could do to smile and praise his singing.

"That's one of my favorite songs," I said.

I bumped into Monk Xingming around the Wushu Center frequently. He was usually accompanied by a young man who was the not-so-platonic ideal of a boy toy: sweet of nature, broad of shoulder, dumb as a post. None of the monks seemed to think it was odd, so I didn't say anything. I once asked Deqing what their relationship was, but he didn't catch my meaning.

"Master Xingming is his Buddhism instructor," he said.

Every time I met him, Monk Xingming was always the kindest, gentlest of men, so it was a surprise to walk into the performance hall one day and discover him railing about politics. The monks were gathered around him. He was holding up a Chinese newspaper and holding court. Everyone went silent when I walked up. My heart dropped when I saw the photos above the fold: three F-16 fighter jets. I braced for the worst.

"What has happened?" I asked.

"Your president sold military planes to Taiwan," Deqing said.

I was relieved. I had been afraid there had been some military skirmish between our countries. It is always the danger for ex-pats from the world's hegemon. You never know when your host country's embassy in Belgrade is going to "accidentally" get hit by a missile, or some spy plane is going to crash land, or your president is going to sell military equipment to a rival country. It was the first time I ever wished I were Canadian. It wouldn't be the last.

The mood of the room was hostile. I retreated into a platitude that usually worked to deflect such situations.

"This is a difficulty between our governments, not our people," I said.

It was a useful formulation for dealing with situations where a Chinese person had a bee in his bonnet over one or another of America's foreign-policy positions related to China. The Chinese were usually very good about distinguishing between the American government and the American people.

"Taiwan is a part of China," Monk Xingming shouted at me. "I will go to war with America over Taiwan."

I was thunderstruck. It's not every day that a Broadway tune–singing, sixty-five-year-old Buddhist monk, who has dedicated himself to a life of peace, says he's ready to march into battle against the marines.

Monk Xingming's fervor caught up the younger men. Several of the other monks said that they too would fight the Americans for Taiwan if it came down to that. This wasn't quite so weird, since teenage boys are socially engineered to serve as cannon fodder. But still, it was a level of nationalistic fervor I had not seen before at Shaolin.

For a brief moment I wondered if it had anything to do with the rumor I had heard a couple of months earlier that a secret Communist cell had recently been sent to spy on activities in town. When a friendly restaurant owner in town told me this as a warning, I had tried to make a joke of it. "What do they want to do? Find out the black-market price for American dollars?"

The government had recently discontinued FEC and allowed Chinese to trade RMB directly for U.S. currency. But they had pegged the exchange rate at a ridiculous level of 8 to 1, which had set off a speculative frenzy because the Chinese are at heart hard-core gamblers. "Shanja mahnie?" The black-market rate would rise to 12 to 1 before the bubble finally burst.

"No, they are worried about the spiritual pollution of Western ideas," he said, nodding at me, the only Westerner in Shaolin, and, one would have to suspect, the Typhoid Mary of Shaolin's nascent democracy movement.

I studied the monks, but it was obvious they were sincere in their patriotic fever. Each one proclaimed his devotion to China, his denunciation of Taiwan as a rebel state, and his willingness to fight America if necessary.

"What do you think of that?" one of them asked me.

What I thought about that was what the U.S. government thinks about that: While Taiwan is a part of China, the dispute should be resolved peacefully, which the F-16s were meant to ensure. What I thought was: Taiwan isn't Hong Kong, and America isn't England. What I thought was: China has a long way to go before it can absorb Taiwan without destabilizing itself, and the wiser Beijing leaders probably know this but can't admit it because the threat of Taiwanese independence is such a useful patriotic rallying cry. What I said instead was, "It is complicated."

Deqing, bless his heart, came to my rescue. When Monk Xingming repeated his vow to fight the Americans, Deqing asked him, "And how will you fight them, master? Sing them to death?"

This broke the fever. The younger monks laughed. And after a moment, so did Monk Xingming.

"Naughty boy," he said to Deqing. "You love my singing."

"No, I just pretend I do," Deqing said, smiling to take the sting out of it.

5

PLAYING HANDS

Other than kungfu, Shaolin's only other serious pastime was *hua quan*, which roughly translates as the "Hand Game," or more directly as "Playing Hands." It was the most popular drinking game in rural China, played almost exclusively by men in restaurants across the countryside on a nightly basis.

The Hand Game is similar to Rock, Paper, Scissors. But instead of three options, there are six. Each opponent throws out a number of fingers (zero to five) on one hand, while shouting out a number he believes will be the sum (zero to ten) of both players' hands. If one player guesses correctly while the other does not, the loser drinks. If both are mistaken or both are correct, they try again. For example, if you put out three fingers and shouted "six" while your opponent put out two fingers and shouted "five," you'd drink. On the next round, if you put out a fist (zero) and shouted "four" while he put out four fingers and shouted "eight," he'd drink. As the drinks flowed, the shouting invariably grew louder, which was why city sophisticates frowned upon the game.

Playing Hands is an inspired game because of the limitations of the human brain. If two random-number-generating computers played each other, they'd each win exactly 50 percent of the time. But human minds and motor skills operate in patterns that tend to repeat, especially when alcohol is involved. This is what makes it a skill game. If you are able to discover your opponent's pattern (say, after putting out five fingers, he always puts out a fist or his thumb) while disguising your own, you dramatically increase your odds of winning. And as your wins pile up and your opponent sinks into a stupor, his ability to see your patterns decreases while his repetitions increase. Once this tipping point happens you go in for the victory by blackout.

The perfect Hand Game champion would possess the mental acuity of Stephen Hawking, the manual dexterity of Rachmaninoff, and the alcohol tolerance of F. Scott Fitzgerald. The closest to this ideal at Shaolin was Coach Yan, the calculating coach of the Wushu Center monks. He looked like a movie villain and possessed a dangerous temper to match. And he was to the Hand Game what Coach Cheng was to challenge matches. Whenever an outsider came into town and proved himself good at the game, Coach Yan was called in to drown him in thimble-sized shots of *baijiu*. When he sat down at a table—and the rule was you had to play everyone round-robin style, with the number of shots usually ten per person, although that was negotiable—the nonalcoholics found excuses to leave early.

I decided to seek him out as my Hand Game coach, because, despite possessing the recuperative powers of a twenty-one-year-old, the Chinese were killing me. At every banquet the Wushu Center threw, the leaders brought me over so the visiting VIPs could enjoy the novelty of beating a *laowai* at the Hand Game (not to mention the sadistic pleasure every Chinese party hack feels when he watches a *laowai* trying to choke down a shot of *baijiu*). I had to get better at the game—if not for my pride, then for my liver. The problem was that Coach Yan was the coach of the other coaches at the Wushu Center. Basically, he was the dean of the faculty, and like most deans he was a bit aloof from the students, even one with special status like me.

My strategy was to appeal to Coach Yan's competitive instincts. I invited him, Deqing, Cheng Hao, and several other monks to a mini-banquet, because that was where all decisions in China were made. As the drinks were being poured, I cleared a space and pulled out a quarter.

"The Hand Game is very interesting. But it can't compare to America's favorite drinking game."

"I don't believe you," Coach Yan said. "What kind of game is it?"

"It's called twenty-five cents," I said, translating as best I could.

"The goal is to bounce this coin off the table and into the glass. If I succeed and you fail, you drink."

I demonstrated the basic thumb–index finger bounce, and then asked Coach Yan if he wanted to play me first. It was a beautiful sight watching him miss and miss and have to drink and drink. When he finally got one in, I switched to rolling it off my elbow. Then to rub it in I said I would drink the shot for him unless I made the next one off my nose. I made it.

As we walked home—them stumbling, me laughing—Coach Yan clapped me on the shoulder. "Let me borrow your American coin," he slurred.

Shaolin monks spend a lifetime mastering an art that requires a complete devotion to mental and physical conditioning. I have met a lot of athletes who are stronger or more powerful but few as coordinated or balanced. And none as competitive. So I probably should not have been surprised when two days later, Coach Yan joined me at my dinner table and pulled out the quarter. Nor should I have been shocked when he proceeded to whip me in ten straight games. In two days he had supplanted the skills I had misspent countless weekends of my youth perfecting.

"Did you sleep?" I asked. "Or have you been practicing straight for forty-eight hours?"

"I didn't have the angle right last time we played," he said. "And I still cannot do the nose."

"Yours is not big enough."

Coach Yan laughed, "So your big nose *is* useful!"

After establishing his dominance in this new game, he soon agreed to become my Hand Game coach. I knew the basic rules of Playing Hands. Coach Yan taught me the subtleties. The first set of lessons involved social customs. In every nation there is at least one finger combination that will get you into trouble: in England it is the "two fingers," in America "the bird." China, suiting its long history, had acquired many combinations that were considered somewhere between rude and downright offensive. Pointing your index and middle finger at someone meant you wanted to poke out his eyes. Pointing the index finger and the thumb meant you wanted to shoot him. But pointing and shaking your pinkie finger at someone—"you're a small man"—would start a fight. And if it didn't you could increase the insult by pointing your thumb at yourself at the same time—"you're a small man, and I'm a big man." So trying to put out the number "two" was a complicated affair. I was left with either the bird or the heavy-metal devil horns.

Next, Coach Yan taught me the tricks.

- **PERIPHERAL VISION:** Instead of throwing your fingers in front of your opponent, you move your hand in random directions around his peripheral vision, so it takes his tipsy mind longer to register the number of fingers, and thus any patterns.

- **PACING:** There is no rule about how fast you have to play the game. The expert and sober tend to play faster than the beginner and the blasted. It usually takes a couple of rounds before an unspoken understanding about the pace is established. But if you wanted, you could suddenly start shouting numbers and throwing fingers rapidly, causing your opponent to catch up, disturbing his ability to rethink his strategy between rounds.

- **DECOYS:** Straight out of the Sun Tzu playbook, you pretend to have fallen into a fairly obvious repetitive cycle, and then switch out of it just as your opponent tries to capitalize. The key with this one is timing.

- **ACT DRUNK:** A tactic known to most high school girls, this one is obvious.

As Coach Yan and I played for hours, night after night, my lubricated brain started to see Playing Hands as a grand metaphor for China. Between rounds, I pulled together pieces of the argument in my head.

Earlier European and American writers called the Chinese fatalistic and passive. This was a mistake. They aren't passive; they are introverts. They study the patterns and wait for their opportunity. But if opportunities were continually deferred, they exploded.

This was the reason why *luan* (chaos) was the most feared word in the language.

Consider the first thing that China's first emperor, Qin Shi Huang, did after he'd conquered and unified the various competing kingdoms in 221 B.C.: He built the Great Wall, the only introverted Wonder of the Ancient World. The ancient Egyptians were obsessed with death (the Pyramids), the Greeks with exploration and trade (the Lighthouse of Alexandria), the Mesopotamians with fertility and beauty (the Hanging Gardens of Babylon), but the Chinese just wanted to tend their own garden without any interference from the barbarians on the northern steppe. This was the society, after all, that invented gunpowder but preferred to use it for fireworks. This was the society that arguably discovered the New World seventy-one years before Columbus (according to Gavin Menzies's book, *1421: The Year China Discovered America*) but didn't think it was worth the trouble to colonize. The introversion is even enshrined in the country's name: *Zhong guo* literally means "center country," or, if you are more poetically inclined, "Middle Kingdom." That is why *laowai* like me were literally "outsiders."

While China had some extroverts, like Deqing, introversion was the masculine ideal. You could guess who was the most powerful man at any banquet in China by seeing who talked the least. Unlike in America, where having power means everyone else has to politely listen to your blather, in China power means those lower on the totem pole play the clown while you observe the patterns.

One day when Doc was working on my leg, he gave me some advice. "Every man has two faces. The outer face he presents to the world, and the inner face he saves only for himself and his family. Your feelings are too obvious. You must hide them."

As we played the Hand Game, I came to the conclusion that the Chinese were not, as early Western observers had pejoratively termed them, "inscrutable." In truth, they were poker-faced. The first European visitors had simply not been interested enough or spent enough time to learn the tells. The forced smile, the wandering gaze, the subtle shifts in vocal tone, these were all calculated gestures to bluff or sucker or misdirect an opponent in order to achieve a particular goal. The contemporary American obsession with "keeping it real," "being true to yourself," "conveying a sense of who you are" was not only alien to them—it was anathema. (The Chinese don't tend to write confessional memoirs.) The reason why Chinese interaction so often seemed stilted to me was because both parties were trying to get one over on the other. The instant group topic of conversation after one person departed was not whether he had lied, but why. What was his angle?

In this sense, the Hand Game was more than a metaphor; it was a training regime for the skills a Chinese man needed to succeed.

After a month of nightly training in the Hand Game, Coach Yan waved me over to a table where Deputy Leader Jiao was entertaining five VIPs—one politician (brown suit, bad shoes), two army officers (green uniforms), and two police officers (oversize sunglasses). The reason for my invitation was that they were discussing America. A tour promoter had booked the Wushu Center monks to perform in America, and these were the men the Wushu Center was going to pad the tour list with to curry political favor.

Coach Yan had been crushing them in the Hand Game, so the VIPs had reached that point in all-male inebriation rituals where the conversation turns to sex, or in the case of corrupt, ugly old men, prostitutes.

"What do American women charge to *wan yi wan*?" one of the police officers asked me. "Party."

When I said I didn't know, Deputy Leader Jiao ribbed me, "Oh come on, I know you love to party, young guy like you. I see the way you look at these waitresses."

The rest of the table joined in.

"Okay, okay, okay, I don't know myself," I said finally. "But I've heard it is around $300."

This set off a round of exclamations of surprise and concern.

"So much!"

"How can it cost so much money?"

"Are they all that expensive?"

And then Deputy Leader Jiao said something I'll never forget, because it perfectly encapsulated the difference between our two countries: "Of course, it's that much. America is so wealthy the poor people are fatter than the rich."

"Deputy Leader Jiao," Coach Yan interjected with an expression of complete innocence, "you should play hands with *Bao Mosi.*"

He said no, until the pleas of the VIPs changed his mind. This was entertainment of the first order.

"Bring out the snake alcohol," the VIPs shouted.

A waitress was sent to fetch a large glass jar filled with four poisonous snakes fermenting in *baijiu.* The Chinese considered snake alcohol medicinal. Doc had several jars in his home under the staircase. But the VIPs wanted it just to fuck with me, because it tasted much worse than regular *baijiu,* if such a thing was possible, and looking at the jar sent a chill up your spine.

As the waitress poured ten shots of *baijiu* into thimble-size shot glasses, I tapped the table with my index and middle finger three times. It was the modern Chinese custom for saying thanks. The reason, according to my favorite version of the story, was that in ancient times you had to stand when a waitress served you. But when a long-ago emperor's legs had been severely wounded in battle, his underlings started tapping the table with two fingers as a symbol for standing because they didn't want to remind him of his injury.

After I tapped the table, the politician nudged the PLA officer. "*Ta dong shi,*" he said. "He understands things."

It was also the custom that the first four shots in the Hand Game are toasts. Deputy Leader Jiao and I clinked our thimbles. I made certain that the lip of my thimble touched the bottom of his. It was a polite custom that signified, "You're higher, and I'm lower."

The VIPs shouted their approval. "Hey, the *laowai* is a China expert!"

I choked down the shot and chased it with a swig of Coke, which I had discovered was the only way I could drink *baijiu* without gagging.

As we raised the second shot, the PLA officer tested me, "Why do we toast twice?"

"Because a man cannot walk on one leg." I said, repeating the traditional Chinese saying.

More cheers, as the four shot glasses were refilled.

As the game began, Deputy Leader Jiao took the early lead, but I figured out his pattern toward the end—he tended to follow five fingers with one. I evened the score at 5-5.

Deputy Leader Jiao was upset and wanted to play another ten shots. I tried to beg off, saying it was a little early in the day for me. The only thing worse than waking up in the morning with a *baijiu* hangover is waking up in the evening with a *baijiu* hangover and knowing you're going to be up all night alone battling suicidal thoughts.

Deputy Leader Jiao was having none of it.

"See, I told you," he said to the rest of the table. "Americans can't outdrink the Chinese."

The Chinese had a firm belief that they possessed the highest tolerance of any people on earth, a rather bold claim considering the competition (my money is on the Russians). While normally I find this very male tendency to try to turn a vice into a virtue charming, it annoyed me that Deputy Leader Jiao was trying to egg me into playing him again. And even more that he was going to succeed.

"I'm *Irish*-American," I said as I poured the ten shots.

I crushed him, 8-2. To rub it in, I drank his last two shots, a courtesy usually performed for an opponent who has had too much to drink. In this case, I was patronizing him.

Deputy Leader Jiao was furious. Watching Coach Yan try to stifle a smile, it hit me that he had been planning this little revenge since he had started training me in the Hand Game. He was Deputy Leader Jiao's little martial arts brother and owed his position at the Wushu Center to him, so there had no doubt been multiple slights over the years. To him, I was simply an arrow in his quiver.

6

CRAZY NEGOTIATIONS

s my skills at the Hand Game grew, I also found myself improving in the most important survival skill in China: negotiating. Almost everything in China was subject to a
negotiation because the Chinese believe all situations are contex-
tual. The price depended on who you were. There was the Chinese
friend price (deep *guanxi*), the Chinese friend-of-friend price
(shallow *guanxi*), the Chinese stranger price (no *guanxi*), the
smart *laowai* price (he knew what the Chinese price was), and
the sucker *laowai* price (usually 100 to 200 percent higher than
the smart *laowai* price). Taking their cues from the government,
which had instituted different prices for Chinese and foreigners at
tourist attractions, hotels, and friendship stores, the local merchants felt no unease in gouging a *laowai* like me.

It was part Marxian "from each according to his ability, to each
according to his need" and part postcolonial revenge. The Chinese
expected the white man to pay more for his burden because the
British, the Pablo Escobar of imperialists, had forced them to buy
opium from India in 1850 and had stolen Hong Kong. Even the
most uneducated merchant had the most obscure details of the
Opium War at his fingertips if I asked to pay the Chinese price.
Merchants would actually get offended at the suggestion: "But, but,
but . . . you're a *laowai*!"

Having come from a fixed-price culture (a late nineteenth-
century American invention), I spent months being gouged so frequently I felt like a pincushion until, finally, I had my first successful

negotiation. Being a serious Cokehead, my biggest daily expense was to get my sugar, caffeine, and carbonation fix. Every couple days I'd go to Grandfather, who had sold me my first can at Shaolin, and drag a half-case back to my room. My addiction was such that I had singlehandedly created a Coke market in the village. As the other merchants, who sat in stalls right next to each other with almost identical merchandise, watched me walk by day after day they started stocking up on Coke.

By the time I left Shaolin, the merchants had converted almost all of Shaolin's other students from Jianlibao to Coke—making me a bona fide cultural imperialist, an army of one. But in those early months, I was the only buyer, and there were dozens of desperate sellers. I liked Grandfather, but he was charging me 4RMB a can, and with other suppliers to choose from I had the leverage. For days I'd stroll slowly in front of these other merchants, swinging the two bags of cans I'd just bought tantalizingly, waiting for one of them to break the Coke cartel. It was a social taboo to undercut the prices of your neighboring merchants.

Finally one day it was too much for one of the women. She called out, "You see, I have your American drink now. You can buy from me."

This elicited a hiss from the other sellers. It was the moment for a reverse auction.

"Grandfather is charging 4RMB," I told her. "Will you sell to me for 3.5RMB?"

"Yes."

I turned to the merchant to her right. "She says 3.5RMB. What will you sell it to me for?"

"3.2RMB?"

Stepping back and addressing them all I said, "Who will sell at 3RMB?"

Four stalls down I had a willing seller. From that point it was tougher, but I eventually found a seller at 2.7RMB, the floor for a smart *laowai*.

From that day on, Grandfather would shake his head and call me "China expert" whenever I walked by. And he never forgave me.

My other major expense was the $1,300 a month I was paying the Wushu Center for room, board, and tuition. It took four months before I learned I was the sucker *laowai*. A German karate instructor had visited the Wushu Center for two weeks of training. As he was leaving I asked as nonchalantly as possible what he had paid the Wushu Center. I'd grown suspicious. For two weeks he paid $225, which meant that $550 per month was the smart *laowai* rate. Leader Liu and Deputy Leader Jiao had been away when the German had arrived, so he'd had the luck to negotiate the price with Vice Deputy Leader Me, the number three man and the one honest broker of the bunch.

It is one thing to overpay a poor peasant merchant for a can of Coke—it is almost like charity. But when I discovered I was being ripped off by members of the Chinese Communist Party, something in me snapped. It might not have been so bad if I hadn't been feeling so intensely guilty about being just another overprivileged Gen-X twit spending daddy's hard-earned money trying to find himself in some exotic locale. There is nothing as sharp as the shards of hate that have first been ground on the whetstone of one's own soul. These turtle eggs had been stealing from my family and had made me their unwitting accomplice, or so I told myself over the next two weeks as I stirred the poison in my heart and waited for my monthly visit from Comrade Fish to collect my fee.

When he finally came to my room that day, instead of paying him right away as I usually did, I sat him down and poured him a glass of tea, which is what the Chinese do right before they reopen negotiations.

"Do you have the money?" he asked nervously.

"I have $550 for you." I said, sitting down.

"Then you can go to the bank in Zheng Zhou to get the rest of the money tomorrow, right?"

The only way to get American cash was to go to the Bank of China in Zheng Zhou. On the second floor, they had a machine connected to the American Express office in Beijing. After an average of four hours of fiddling with the machine, taking tea breaks, and filling out multiple forms, they would dole out thirteen U.S. one-hundred-dollar bills. It was like spending an afternoon at the DMV every month.

"I have the money," I said. "But I'm only going to pay the Wushu Center $550 per month from now on. That is what the correct price is, right?"

Comrade Fish put down his teacup. "But you agreed to pay $1,300."

"Yes. But the German only had to pay the equivalent of $550 per month. And he only stayed for two weeks. I am staying for a year. Besides, my *guanxi* is much deeper than his. It's not fair."

"But you agreed to $1,300 a month."

This set the pattern for the negotiation. I was using the Chinese value system: price depended on *guanxi*, and agreements are frequently renegotiated even after a deal has been struck. And he was using what he perceived to be the Western value of keeping your word, honoring a verbal contract.

This went on for an hour. He tried all the possible emotional combinations: friendly cajoling, abject pleading, angry threats. He referenced obscure "regulations"—a favorite tactic of Chinese bureaucrats. I remained monotone. It wasn't fair, because my *guanxi* was deeper. I wasn't going to pay more than $550, I insisted, leaving unstated: *And what are you going to do about it?*

He couldn't do anything about it. He and I both knew he didn't have the power to renegotiate the fee. He grew increasingly agitated as it became obvious he was fated to be the messenger of bad news to Leader Liu.

"Then you will have to leave," he said angrily as he walked out of the room.

This was the calculated risk. I had nowhere else to go. (Taguo still couldn't accept foreign students.) But I assumed his threat was a bluff. The Chinese pride themselves on being good hosts, which they are, and they find it shameful to kick a guest out. I was also counting on the leaders' greed. Even at $550 a month, I was bringing in steady revenue to cover operational costs of the hotel and restaurant and support the expense of the new *sanda* team. Many nights and many meals I was the Wushu Center's only paying customer. And the monks didn't get a bonus for teaching me. So my tuition fee was pure profit for the party leaders.

Word that the foreigner had refused to pay spread quickly at the center, probably because Leader Liu screamed at Comrade Fish so loudly that everyone in the hallway outside his office could hear. Leader Liu also called in Vice Deputy Leader Me to chew him out as well. In Communist China, honesty was not the best policy. Leader Me's punishment was to join Comrade Fish in a tag-team negotiation to persuade me to pay the $1,300.

Deputy Leader Me and Comrade Fish arrived at the same time the next day. Their approach was to play the victim card. Didn't I understand that the Wushu Center in particular and China in general was very poor in comparison to a wealthy country like America? Didn't I think it was my duty to help out my new friends and teachers?

I replied that Leader Liu did not seem so poor to me with his Toyota Santana and chauffeur. But I'd be happy to pay my teachers the original amount of tuition money if I were allowed to pay them directly instead of the Wushu Center.

It was hard to tell, but I think Leader Me smiled slightly when I finished.

Comrade Fish did not. He knew he was in a more vulnerable position in the hierarchy and would receive the bulk of Leader Liu's wrath.

"That is unacceptable," Comrade Fish said. "You must pay the money now!"

"Okay, I'll give you $550."

"Unacceptable. You will pay $1,300."

"No."

And then we repeated the scene, Comrade Fish playing the bad cop, Vice Deputy Leader Me the good, and me the belligerent criminal. After an hour, they finally left. That was the last I saw of Leader Me on the subject, but not Comrade Fish. He showed up every afternoon for the next six days with someone new. One day it was Deqing looking uncomfortable and unhappy to be there. Another day it was Coach Cheng. On the fourth day it was Coach Yan. Comrade Fish was trying to find the right combination of *guanxi* to unlock my wallet. If I didn't care about helping the school, surely I didn't want to disappoint my instructors, he'd say.

But I knew that the monks agreed with me. I had made certain to invite all of my teachers out to dinner after the first confrontation in order to pick their brains. They had all advised me to hold firm. Chinese negotiating strategy is based on patience and persistence.

They will try to outlast the opponent, banging away at a single point until the other side gets frustrated and agrees to the unfavorable terms. This is particularly the case with *laowai*, who are more anxious to make deals than the Chinese. Every foreign investor in China has experienced the first-night banquet where they are cajoled into drinking as much as possible, but few understand its underlying purpose: Nothing increases the desire to cut a quick deal so you can return home like a vicious *baijiu* hangover. But I wasn't going anywhere, so I had the longer time horizon. They'd need my money before I'd need to leave.

Still, Comrade Fish was growing more desperate, and his threats that I wouldn't be allowed to practice anymore unless I paid were starting to concern me. Even missing a few days of training could make me rusty, and this was dragging on.

The morning of the seventh day of negotiations, Coach Yan came to visit me. Despite my concerns, I was feeling rather elated. I was finally standing up to injustice. I wasn't rolling over and allowing myself to be walked over. Coach Yan, however, was pessimistic about the situation.

"You can't simply refuse to pay any longer," he said.

"But it is unfair," I insisted, repeating my arguments.

"Yes, but you are making Leader Liu lose face in front of the entire school," he explained. "If you can defy him, then what stops someone else from doing it?"

"But Leader Liu hasn't even come to see me."

"Of course not. He can't allow you to defy him in person. Then he would have to do something about it. He sends Comrade Fish, so it is Comrade Fish's fault, not his. But still you are making Leader Liu lose face."

"But it isn't fair."

"This is China," Coach Yan said. "What does fairness have to do with anything?"

"You have a point," I said. "What should I do, master?"

The most important relationships at Shaolin were between master and disciple: Both sides had an obligation to help the other in times of need. It was one of the reasons I had tried to have as many coaches as possible, especially the coaches with deep *guanxi* like Coach Yan.

"Where do you get this money?" Coach Yan asked. "From your father, right?"

"More or less."

"The Chinese people have great respect for the family."

"Yes, I know."

"We also know that sometimes families can have money problems. You understand?" he said, staring at me until I understood what he meant.

A piece of face-saving fiction was called for, and it was up to me to craft it if I wanted to stay and pay only $550 a month.

I started to spin: "I was too ashamed to admit this before, but my father is not happy with me being here." All good lies start with the truth . . . "He has stopped sending me money." Shift to a plausible untruth . . . "So I had to ask my grandfather for the money." Followed by the big lie . . . "But he is just a farmer." Embroidered with honest details . . . "So he can't send me more than $550 per month." And sympathetic bullshit.

Coach Yan stood up, bowed slightly, and left.

Amituofo.

Comrade Fish's mood and approach were transformed when he arrived the next day. He came as a supplicant with all the bowing and scraping and pleading that entails in China.

"Oh, this is so embarrassing. I hate to trouble you, *Bao Mosi.* You were probably resting. But we have a problem, and we need your help. The Wushu Center needs to borrow $600," he said, hands fluttering upward to the ceiling as if begging for divine intervention.

"Why?"

"To pay the dancing teachers."

Every night for the past two weeks, the leaders of the school and their wives, plus some of the waitresses and other village officials, had turned the Wushu Center's performance hall into a dance studio. Besides karaoke and drinking, the favorite recreational activity of the older generation of Chinese was Lawrence Welk–era dancing. They loved nothing more than to waltz around nightclubs or outdoors in parks during the summer months. The younger generation preferred dancing to Western and Hong Kong pop. At the Zheng Zhou International Hotel's nightclub, the DJ would play four or five waltzes in a row for the older crowd, then switch to Western style music for the kiddies.

But I had the feeling I was being conned.

"Why are you bothering me with this? Surely Leader Liu has that much money," I said, my voice hardening into the imperious, guttural tone the Chinese use when they really want to see the supplicant get down on his knees and kowtow.

"What can I say? It is a difficult problem. The teachers insist on being paid in American dollars. Leader Liu only has Chinese money at the moment. You have always been such a good friend of the Shaolin Temple and this school, won't you help?"

"But I told you. I was only going to pay $550 a month. Is this a trick to raise the price to $600?"

"I will give you the $50 in Chinese money, okay?"

I paid him the money, he left, and that was that. Comrade Fish did not come back again until a month later. And he did not argue when I paid him $550.

After it was all over, I took Coach Yan out to dinner. After many rounds of Playing Hands, he admitted that he had taken my story back to Leader Liu.

"He was going to kick you out. But Chinese people love family relationships," he explained

"Chinese people also love saving face."

"Yes. Empty your glass." Coach Yan slapped me on the back. We continued my Playing Hands training well into the evening.

One day during training, Doc asked me to visit him after class. When I arrived, he poured me tea. I readied myself to be hit up for a favor.

"I want to start a business selling Chinese medicine," he said. "But I need a grinder, so I can turn the leaves, roots, and skin into powder. It's easier to package that way."

"Where can you buy a grinder?"

"Zheng Zhou."

I sighed internally. He sat quietly, waiting for me to finish calculating the *guanxi* debt I owed him for teaching me iron forearm kungfu and fixing my knees and realizing it was far more than a day trip to Zheng Zhou and the cost of a grinder.

"Okay, I'll go with you to Zheng Zhou and buy you one."

The trip was uneventful. We found a store, bought a $95 electric grinder, and brought it back. The grinder lasted two days before the motor broke.

Doc invited me over that night to show me the offending object and its sputtering engine. I shrugged. What did he expect? Everything with more than two moving parts broke in China. But Doc had decided he wanted to return it and get a refund. I was less enthusiastic. Chinese stores' return policies are so notoriously caveat emptor that the country even has a traditional proverb on the subject: "Once the goods are carried out of the store, the owner will refuse to acknowledge them." But Doc was insistent, and I wasn't inclined to argue with a man whose hobby was breaking river stones with his palm.

Still, I tried to weasel out of my obligations. If he had only fixed my knees, I could have just said no, but I hadn't paid off my debt to him yet for teaching me iron forearm kungfu.

"What good will me coming along do you? Stores don't return money for broken goods."

He chewed on the end of his cigarette for several moments before saying, "Maybe he won't want to lose face in front of a foreigner."

"Doc, the grinder cost 750RMB. That's very expensive face."

Doc considered this. "You can always scare him."

"How am I going to do that?"

Doc smiled, a rare event for him. "*Bao Mosi*, you have lived in China for many months. Tell me, what is the general Chinese prejudice about *laowai*?"

I immediately quoted *Beijingers in New York*: "Do you know why foreigners are so hairy? Because when we were human, they were still monkeys."

Doc laughed out loud. "Exactly. *Laowai* make us nervous. You are so emotional, so unpredictable, like very tall children. We never know what you are going to say or do next."

When we returned to the store, I stood behind Doc, while he initiated a discussion with the owner. He had the receipt and anyone could see the grinder was broken. The storeowner agreed that it certainly was broken, but it hadn't been broken when he sold it. It had broken while Doc was its owner. Doc explained that he had followed the instructions, and it was clear that the machine was faulty. The proprietor was certain that Doc was an honest man, although most were not these days. But how was he to know if Doc might not be mistaken? Maybe he had, without realizing it, of course, done something wrong, and therefore the mistake was his, not the machine's. How was he to know the real cause? And if he couldn't know for certain, why should he return the money? Doc said he didn't want the grinder any longer. He wanted the money back instead. The proprietor wondered why *he* should want a broken grinder. He preferred the money, thank you very much.

This continued for several minutes before the histrionic level was ratcheted up to more personalized attacks. This was to be expected. Negotiations in China frequently took a turn toward the melodramatic—it's one of the few times the Chinese feel free to display emotion, even if it is feigned. This was one legacy of China's favor-based (*guanxi*) economy. The problem with favors is that they are very hard to quantify, to secure an agreement at the market exchange rate. If a friend helped you secure a meeting with a town official so you could obtain a zoning permit for your new store last year, how many days are you obligated to loan him your truck so he can haul lumber? One, three, or seven? How many days before you have repaid your obligation, and he starts owing you another favor? As anyone with a difficult mother-in-law knows, one way to up the perceived value of a favor is to complain bitterly about how much sacrifice it will entail before granting it.

Doc's difficulty was that he was asking the merchant to do something he wasn't obliged to do without offering anything in return. It was my job to change the merchant's calculation from benefits to potential costs. When he called Doc a peasant and poked him in the chest, Doc stepped back and gave me a nod.

Having received my cue, I went ballistic. I bugged out my eyes, stomped the floor, threw my hands wide into the air, and yelled in Chinese, "You dare touch my master? You stupid egg! Do you know who he is? This is one of Shaolin's greatest kungfu masters! And you just touched him. So disrespectful! Do you not want life? You sell him this piece of shit and now you don't want to take responsibility. Look at it"—at which point I kicked the grinder, knocking it dangerously close to a display case—"it is worthless and so are you."

"What are you doing?" the stunned merchant cried out, "You dare kick it?"

"I dare! I dare kick everything in this backwards store!"

I went over to the display case and smacked it with my palm hard enough to make it shake but not break the glass.

I could almost see the merchant's mind whirling like a cash register as he calculated the price of replacing the glass against reimbursing us for the grinder. I learned the glass was cheaper when he said, "What is the matter with you? Are you sick in your mind?"

"You are sick in your mind if you think you can cheat and insult my master without consequences!" I said, towering over him. "I'll destroy this entire store."

I picked up the grinder and charged the storefront window as if I meant to throw it through the glass.

"Is he crazy?" the merchant asked Doc. "You must stop him."

Doc shrugged his shoulders. "What can I do? Foreigners are strange."

The storefront window must have been expensive, because the storeowner relented.

"I'll give you 50 percent," he said.

I snapped out of it and put the grinder down—it was heavy and I didn't think the merchant would offer a better deal.

"Okay," I said. "That's 375RMB."

On the way back to Shaolin, Doc and I howled as we replayed the incident.

"You should teach that as a special kungfu," I said.

"Yes," he said. "I'll call it Crazy Foreigner Kungfu."

7

TAKING A BEATING

C oach Cheng believed that before a fighter could learn how to win, he first had to master losing. He had to experience defeat after defeat until there was nothing new to it and thus nothing left to fear. The ideal Chinese kickboxer stepped onto the *leitai* with indifference, nonchalance—just another day on the job. It was an approach Coach Cheng felt crucial for me to develop, because the fear of physical confrontation left me paralyzed.

For my lessons on Zen and the Art of an Ass Whipping, Baotong was Coach Cheng's jolly teaching assistant. While Baotong was not by inclination a particularly creative fighter—he preferred to fix his opponents with a quick side kick or a jab so he could chop at their torsos with massive roundhouse kicks, a limited approach that had kept him out of the top ranking in China—my helplessness inspired him to employ the full range of kickboxing techniques. After a few sessions banging me around with roundhouses, he grew restive and actually tried some throws, which worked so beautifully that he spiced it up with some spinning sweeps to great applause. Buoyed, he actually went back to the basics and started to throw kick and punch combinations, something he normally would have sneered at as being for those weak fighters who lacked his thunderous roundhouse kick.

And as he explored the wide variety of ways to pummel me, I became his best critic, a human punching bag with an analytic mind. He'd catch my leg and toss me across the room. And I'd get up and say, "Nice execution." He'd level me with a thrusting kick to my chest and I'd shout out from the ground, "Real power. But maybe you want to try a straighter angle."

As I learned to watch my devastations with an aesthetic detachment, my fear of losing started to fade. I'd wake in the morning wondering how I was going to lose that day. And I'd spend the evening massaging the various bruises that I wore like blue badges of courage, while replaying the bouts in my head, looking for opportunities missed. In the ring, I no longer bounced nervously on my toes, and I ran only when that roundhouse was aimed above my shoulders. When it came to being bullied I was already something of an expert, and under the tutelage of Baotong's fists and feet I quickly became a master.

Switching from traditional forms to kickboxing was like finding love again after a bad relationship. All my vices were now virtues, all my flaws strengths. Instead of being too tall and awkward, I suddenly had a reach advantage. The simplicity of *sanda*'s techniques allowed me to focus all my attention on just a few moves.

And unlike those who view combat sports as brutal, I found *sanda* beautiful. The opposite of barbarism, I saw it as the height of civilization. A defined space with rules, judges, a referee, and two men, who have of their own free will volunteered to ask and answer one of the most basic questions men ask: Who is the better fighter with the better techniques? In this, I saw the *leitai* as no different from a courtroom (who has the better lawyer and legal arguments?) or a parliament (which side has the more persuasive politicians and policies?). Single combat has always been, according to the military historian John Keegan, the primitive but certainly less bloody way to resolve tribal conflicts short of total war (see also David v. Goliath, Tom Wolfe's *The Right Stuff*, or, if you prefer beefcake, *Troy*). As far as I was concerned, barbarism was what happened outside the ring where inevitably it was the strong, relatively certain of victory, who attacked the weak. Stepping alone onto the platform, no matter how good you are, is always an act of courage because you can never be certain of the outcome. One foolish mistake, one lucky punch, and even the mightiest can fall.

Before anyone expected, I was ready for the next stage. Six weeks into my *sanda* training I shocked everyone.

We always had "sparring-only" days on Saturday mornings,

because Sunday was our day off and we could use the time to nurse any injuries, usually strained shoulders, cuts along the forearms, and bruising on the shins and tops of the feet. On the sixth Saturday of my *sanda* training, I was in the middle of the ring with Baotong when he kicked me with one of his thunderous roundhouses to the chest. Instead of retreating, I stood my ground and kicked him with my roundhouse to the chest. He kicked me again. I kicked him back. We stood there and exchanged six or seven kicks before Baotong stepped back, a look of surprise in his eyes and a grin on his face, and bowed.

Amituofo.

I bowed back. We continued fighting, and he outscored me on points, but it was close, close enough that our teammates razzed him afterward about losing to the *laowai*.

After class, Coach Cheng asked me to come up to his room. He was silent for a long time, which I was used to, but this time he kept shaking his head like he was trying to work out a problem.

Finally, he said, "I don't understand it. I just don't understand it."

"What don't you understand, Coach?"

"I don't understand how you could improve so quickly. Usually it takes years. I don't know, maybe it's because you're a college student that you learn so fast." He fell silent for several minutes before continuing, "China has a proverb, 'The martial arts and cultural learning are two halves of the whole.' So that must be it. You are a college student, so you grasp basic principles quickly."

He shook his head again and fell silent. It was so quiet he could almost hear me purring.

Coach Cheng went to his desk, pulled out a rolled-up poster, and unfurled it. It was a poster for the Zheng Zhou International Wushu Festival, which would be held in September.

"Henan Province is the birthplace of kungfu and tai chi," Coach Cheng said. "So the government throws a festival every two years to encourage tourism. Martial artists from dozens of countries come to compete. I want you to fight for me."

"But Coach," I said, "that is in less than eight months."

The best *sanda* fighters in Shaolin had been training for at least eight years. Baotong was very good, but he wasn't the best in China. I'd be lucky to survive one round with a nationally ranked Chinese fighter.

"It's impossible," I said.

"If you keep working as hard as you are and improving as rapidly, you will be ready."

It was completely crazy, so as a crazy *laowai* I agreed to do it. It was a great opportunity for Coach Cheng. Not only was I a beginner, I was a foreigner. If he could make me competitive at the national level in eight months, he'd establish himself as a miracle worker.

BOOK FOUR

APPRENTICE

April–June 1993

棍子伤肉，恶语伤骨。

"A club hurts the flesh, but evil words hurt the bone."

—*TRADITIONAL CHINESE PROVERB*

1

HAPPY ENDINGS

It only took five months of self-imposed celibacy before my libido went nuclear. One night it conspired with my subconscious to produce an erotic dream that was rather more, shall we say, "Grecian" than I had ever experienced previously. I'd like to say that I was such a mature, secure, liberal-minded guy that I wasn't concerned when I awoke. But I was raised in a part of the country where it is strongly believed that if a man has to put something inside another man it had better be a bullet. As soon as I opened my eyes, a new list flashed in my head:

THINGS THAT ARE WRONG WITH MATT

1. Gay?
2. Gay?!
3. (Not that there's anything wrong with that, but . . .) GAY?!?!

That was it for my vow of celibacy. But there was just one tiny problem. There weren't any women who wanted to have sex with me. Not any nearby, at any rate. Shaolin had at most a hundred women, and all of them were either underage, married, or otherwise spoken for. A couple of the waitresses at the Wushu Center restaurant might not have had beaus, but they would never sleep with me. As I had explained to Carlos, it would have been social death.

But it wasn't just the social stigma. It was also part of the legal code. Any Chinese woman found alone in a room with a *laowai* after midnight was automatically considered a prostitute and the foreigner her john. The *laowai* and the woman were fined $1,000 apiece, which in practice meant $2,000 to the foreigner because no Chinese woman had $1,000 on her. A Shaolin policeman had once told me with great relish the story of an Italian businessman who had made the mistake of bringing his Beijing girlfriend with him on a trip to Zheng Zhou. (The police in Beijing were lax about the law, because there were so many important diplomats and businessmen in the city.) The key girl on his hotel floor called the cops, and the businessman was $2,000 poorer.

If late-night sex with a local was automatically considered prostitution, then the only answer was to skip the amateurs and go straight to a professional—during the day. Here I was in some luck to be a member of the *sanda* team. My teammates were not monks. They were jocks, and like jocks everywhere, they talked constantly about women and sex. When we ran up the mountain, we talked about women and sex. When we did drills, we talked about women and sex. The only times we weren't talking about women and sex was when we were talking about *sanda*.

Most of them were still virgins (they likewise suffered from the local shortage of women, if not the social and legal dilemmas I faced). But if anything, that made the subject of sex all the more fascinating to them. Especially because they had in their midst an honest-to-God American, a citizen of the country that gave the world *Baywatch*. They wanted to know everything I knew about women and sex, which admittedly wasn't much, but was a great deal more than they did. In exchange, they would tell me what little they did know. One thing they knew was that the barbershop next to the Zheng Zhou International Hotel doubled as a massage parlor. Whether the female hairdressers' services were limited to *happy endings* or if they included *lie down dancing*, they could not say, because none had ever gone. But they wanted more than anything else in the world for me to go and give them the vicarious details.

After days of internal debate, I settled on the excuse that I would simply go to see what it was like. As a student and visitor, it was my job to learn about the culture. At the very least, it would make for a good story.

Deeply conflicted, I opened the door to the barbershop next to the Zheng Zhou International Hotel. There was nothing to indicate it was anything other than a hair salon. Four barber chairs faced a wall-length mirror, a special basin for washing hair was at the far end of the salon, a cash register over a glass cabinet with hair products for sale was next to the door. A matronly Chinese woman stood behind the cash register. A young hairstylist, maybe twenty years old, stood next to her chair.

After I sat down, the hairstylist asked, "Do you want your hair washed first?"

"Okay."

She led me over to the basin in the corner of the room. With a certain amount of relief mixed with a dash of disappointment, I decided the massage-parlor rumors were either unfounded or I had stepped into the wrong salon.

But then she started washing my hair. There was nothing overt about her technique. But my fevered brain, having spent way too long in an isolated monastery, inferred erotic intent in her proximity (too close), her touch (too sensuous), and her thoroughness (too long). By the time the wash was over, I already was light-headed. She led me by the hand back to her chair, as I shuffled with a jake leg waddle trying to hide the effect her hair washing technique had had on me. The list flashed in my head.

THINGS THAT ARE WRONG WITH MATT

1. ~~Gay?~~
2. Cowardly
3. Still a boy/not a man
4. Unattractive to the opposite sex

As I settled back into the chair with some subtle readjusting, my stylist stood behind me and gently kneaded my shoulders. This was quite nice and necessary, but not really sufficient. If this was Henan's idea of a massage parlor, I would need to arrange a trip to a coastal city.

She leaned in and whispered in my ear, "Would you like a massage?"

Thinking she was asking me if I wanted her to continue rubbing my shoulders, I nodded.

Just then a thirtyish harpie wearing too much makeup and too tight a sequined dress burst through the front door and upon seeing me started squawking like a molted macaw, *"Laowai! Laowai! Laowai!"* as she dashed across the room. She opened a door to a room in back and exited stage right. Now I knew that my teammates had been right.

The facade shattered, my stylist led me by the hand to that back room. Here was the massage parlor half of the business. A windowless room with only one door. Nine flat beds, barely wide enough for an anorexic, sat next to nine chairs. Each pairing was divided by five-foot cubicle walls to the left and right. And the fluorescent lights were bright. The whole effect was about as erotic as a dentist's waiting room—and less private. I clearly wasn't the only one who thought so, because it was completely empty. My stylists led me to the massage cube farthest from the door.

Still the macaw did try to get a gander at what was happening as I lay down. She dashed down the row of cubicles, leaned her head around the final partition, and then fell back in mock disbelief. *"Laowai! Laowai! Laowai!"*

My stylist leaned in close and said sotto voce, "You are lucky she was out to lunch, and you got me. Her character is very low. She would have cheated you."

This put me at ease. You haven't really established a relationship with a Chinese person until they feel comfortable enough with you to bad-mouth one of their colleagues.

I said, "I trust you will be very fair."

And with that bond established, she started massaging my shoulders. She wasn't nearly as good at this as she was with the hair washing, but it would have been all right if she had just kept quiet. But now that we were fellow travelers she felt the need to unburden herself.

"I'm new to the city," she said. "I grew up on the countryside."

"Ah."

"You can't trust city people. They are too *jiaohua,*" she said. "Slick."

"Right."

"It's not like the countryside. The people there are *laoshi,*" she said. "Honest."

"If you don't like the city, why don't you go back?" I asked.

This was a mistake. I had come here for a happy ending. Instead I received a depressing backstory.

"I can't go back. My father doesn't understand me. He never listens to me. Does he ever consider what I want? His ideas are backward, but China is changing. He can't accept it. He always says, 'China was very poor, but we were equally poor.'"

I sighed internally. There is no bigger turnoff than a woman talking about why she dislikes her father. If she can't stand the man who helped create her, how long before she decides she hates me?

After ten minutes more of why her father didn't understand his massage-parlor daughter (apparently the sex industry is not the best place to find women with positive father/daughter relationships), she asked in a sad, hesitant voice, "Do you want to turn over?"

I couldn't go through with it. It was obvious she didn't want me to say yes. But then again I didn't want her to feel I was rejecting her, so I blurted out, "I can give you a backrub."

She looked at me like I was insane. I briefly considered trying to explain that in college, exchanging backrubs was the equivalent of a first date, but I didn't think it would help things.

". . . or not."

"Perhaps I should cut your hair now," she said.

"Good idea."

When I returned to Shaolin, my teammates didn't believe me when I told them I had gotten only a haircut.

"The *laowai* is too *jiaohua*," they said, laughing.

2

IRON CROTCH KUNGFU

Being specialists, the Beijing *wushu* team had more gymnastic talent than the Shaolin Temple, and Wuhan's kickboxing team was better in the ring than our *sanda* fighers, but considering the sheer range of martial arts displayed—from modern *wushu* to traditional forms, from kickboxing to iron kungfus—the Shaolin martial monks gave the best kungfu performances in the world. They were also the only live entertainment in town. So for months I had attended every single demonstration. But a steady diet of the same dish, no matter how rich, dulls the palate, and over time I was skipping more and more of their smaller performances, only attending the big shows they reserved for VIPs and foreign tour groups, where they pulled out all the stops. After several elaborate performances, I thought I had seen everything. The monks were as awesome as always, but it wasn't fresh anymore.

One night in March there was a huge buzz at dinner about an upcoming performance later that night. Prominent party officials from Beijing were bringing down a delegation of high-ranking German politicians to see the monks perform. Word was this would be the best performance yet. The Wushu Center had brought back some former monks to add their talents to the mix.

As part of the festivities, the Henan provincial army regiment had sent its marching band to open the show. So by the time the monks started to perform, the hall was filled with members of the marching band, the politicos, and various locals who had heard rumors of a big show. The performance was amazing as always, but I didn't lean forward until a monk I'd never seen before entered from a side door. He was not a pretty man. His face was acned, his cheeks too wide for his recessed jaw, his torso too short for his legs.

The new monk walked into the center of the hall. He began with some *qigong* breathing exercises, the prelude to an iron kungfu demonstration. He was breathing in and out of his nose, and his hands roamed around his body. You can usually guess which extremity is about to take the abuse among iron kungfu masters because the hands will focus on that part of the body, directing the *qi* energy out of the palms and onto the limb in question as a kind of protective covering. This monk started with his neck, so I assumed he was an iron neck practitioner, of which there were a number in Shaolin. They usually stuck the points of spears into the notch in their throat that had so obsessed Ralph Fiennes in *The English Patient* and bent the spears in half. But after rubbing his neck, this monk moved his hands down and around his groin area. It was like a bad Chippendale impression. He kept at it long enough that there were soon some embarrassed coughs from the German contingent.

Finally, to everyone's great relief, he stopped massaging himself. Deqing came out onto the floor to invite audience members to participate in the demonstration. After all the crotch rubbing, the audience was understandably a little reluctant. Deqing pantomimed to the audience that they were invited to punch the monk in the throat. No one volunteered, and in fact most recoiled when Deqing entreated their section. To demonstrate that this was all perfectly safe and they had no reason to worry, Deqing walked back over to the monk, who had clenched his jaw to tighten the muscles around his neck, pulled back his fist and faster than the eye could follow popped the monk in the throat. I jumped out of my seat in awe. The throat is arguably the most vulnerable part of the human body. It takes very little force to break the trachea, a lethal blow. This is one reason fighters are always told to keep their chins down. (The other is because a blow to the chin—specifically the points about a centimeter to the left and right of the tip of the chin, known as the "button"—is one of the surest ways to be knocked unconscious.) Here was a man doing exactly the opposite, tipping his head back, holding his chin high, leaving his throat completely exposed, and inviting a free shot. His trachea's only protection was the flexed neck muscles on either side of it. If something went wrong, he'd be dead, his last minutes on earth spent writhing on the floor like a fish on dry land, his brain desperate for oxygenated blood as his lungs, no longer able to access fresh air, filled with carbon dioxide.

Deqing finally convinced one of the women from the marching band, a trumpet player, to come out on stage with a friend. They both, after much coaxing, made halfhearted attempts to punch him in the throat. They giggled and tried to return to their seats. Deqing stopped them. They were not done. Deqing wanted them to help demonstrate one more of the monk's iron kungfu specialties.

While the throat is the most vulnerable part of the human body, it is not, in the case of the male half of the species, the most tender. Deqing was asking these two women to stand in front of 400 people—including their direct army superiors, a collection of foreign diplomats, and a half-dozen national party officials—and kick a Shaolin monk in the nuts. Even Deqing was not fast enough to catch them as they fled to their seats, shaking their heads in horror.

Deqing pleaded with others in the audience, but there were no takers. The Beijing officials were trying to push their German counterparts out of their seats, which they were gripping for dear life. None of them was foolish enough to risk the possibility of the international papers acquiring a photo of a German politician kicking a Chinese Buddhist monk in the balls. Deqing walked away from the Germans and returned to the monk, who calmly spread his legs and thrust his hips forward. Deqing slipped the shoe off his right foot, reared back and snapped a kick into the monk's groin that was so vicious it literally lifted him off the ground.

Without realizing it, I was up on my feet shouting in English, "You've got to be fucking kidding me!"

Deqing saw me standing there like a fool. He motioned me over. I shook my head. I was intimately familiar with what being "racked," as we called it on the playgrounds of Topeka, felt like. I wasn't going to do that to another man, even if he were volunteering for it. Deqing took a couple steps toward me and motioned again with a sharper movement, his eyes narrowing, letting me know this wasn't a request. I'd pay for a refusal during the next stretching session.

Better him than me, I decided.

Amituofo.

The monk waited for me, legs spread, hips thrust out. I hauled back and let him have it, lifting him off the ground with the blow. He seemed completely unaffected by the kick. I could feel the top of my foot throbbing. His groin was harder than my foot.

"Again," Deqing said.

Annoyed that I'd hurt myself, I kicked him again and again and again, trying to get some reaction. I lifted him off the ground—two inches, four inches, six—but the expression on his face never changed. Finally, I stopped. My foot was numb. The crowd erupted in applause. I bowed to him and turned to my seat, but Deqing stopped me and pointed to the monk's throat.

My first punch was self-conscious, fluttering with the fear that I might kill him. But it bounced harmlessly off his neck muscles, which felt like hardened rubber. My concern switched to annoyance: Was he smirking at me? The crowd began shouting. I'd give them a show. I threw a flurry of punches, right, left, right, left, right, knocking him back step by step with each blow. My last right flew a little high, however, landing smack on the button of his chin. The monk's eyes flew wide with surprise. My eyes went wide with fear.

"I'm sorry, master, extremely sorry, so very sorry, sorry, sorry, sorry," I groveled, pressing my hands together and bowing.

After a long pause, he said, "No problem," and bowed back.

His demonstration was over.

The performance hall was rocking after the show, the atmosphere like there'd just been a last-minute championship victory by the home team. No one wanted to leave. Everyone wanted to talk about the star player's mastery of one of mankind's most primal fears. The monks and I gathered outside the hall to discuss the evening's hero, who I decided to nickname, in tribute to John Hughes, "Long Duk Dong," or "Monk Dong" for short.

Little Tiger imitated Monk Dong's routine: legs wide, hips forward, and popping up and down on his feet as if he were being kicked.

"He was amazing," Little Tiger said. "His penis must be made of stone."

As we laughed, Deqing tried to hush him, "Don't use that word."

He seemed slightly miffed that Monk Dong's performance had eclipsed his own.

"*Bao Mosi*, what did you think?" Little Tiger continued.

"My foot is bruised," I said.

"He's invulnerable. He could go into a fight like this," Little Tiger said, spreading his legs farther and tipping his head back as he walked forward.

"Do you practice iron crotch kungfu?" I asked Deqing.

"Oh no, I'm not crazy," Deqing laughed.

"How does he do it?" I asked.

Deqing turned to Monk Chen, who was an older instructor at the school, somewhere in his midthirties. He had been my teacher for several weeks and was the kindest monk at the temple, always smiling, always helpful. The only thing that seemed to bother him was his expanding waistline, which he was always trying to reduce with little success.

"Teacher Chen, you lived with him for several weeks, right?" Deqing asked.

Chen burped a short embarrassed laugh.

"Yes, we were roommates when we toured in Europe. Every morning he gets up and puts his thing and its two friends on the desk and then—WHAP! WHAP!—he smacks it with his hand. Too weird, too weird. Thirty minutes every day. Think about waking up every morning to that. Too weird, too weird."

At the other end of the hallway, there was a small group of women from the army marching band. I had been watching them out of the corner of my eye as we were talking about Monk Dong. They were having an animated discussion about the same subject. After several minutes, the group collectively pushed one of the women, the trumpet player Deqing had convinced to punch Monk Dong in the throat, in our direction. She walked toward us slowly with her head down.

Stopping just outside our group, she whispered a question. Deqing asked her to repeat herself. She asked again in a quavering voice, "Is it real?"

"Is what real?" Deqing asked her politely.

"Him, what he did . . . his thing . . . is it real?"

Deqing looked confused.

I couldn't help myself, "She wants to know if his penis is real."

All the boys cracked up. The girl covered her face with her hands and ran off in embarrassment. It was the high school locker room all over again.

Chen shook his head at me with a fatherly smile, "*Bao Mosi*, you shouldn't talk like that."

"She just wants to know if his penis is real," I said. "Think of what kind of lovemaking master he must be. He could do it standing up without using his arms. How much weight do you figure he can lift with that thing?"

As I demonstrated the concept, Chen kept shaking his head at me, trying not to laugh out loud. The rest of the monks, particularly Little Tiger, were in hysterics.

"You are all naughty boys," Chen said.

The trumpet player had stopped halfway down the hall, trapped between the two groups, unable to go back without an answer but too embarrassed to ask us again. Finally, the need to know won out.

She returned to ask again, "Is it real? Is it real? Is it real?"

"How are we supposed to know if his penis is real?" I said. "Why don't you take a look and tell us?"

This was too much for her. She ran back to her friends, as the naughty boys continued to snicker and giggle.

My Catholic guilt kicking in, I looked over at the group of women to see if the trumpet woman was okay. The women were leaning toward her as she recounted what had happened. Several minutes later Monk Dong walked out of one of the back offices and straight into this group of clucking hens. He smiled at them as he continued to walk forward. But as if operating with a single communal brain, all of them surrounded him and the most incredible thing in a night of amazing things happened: The women started— at first tentatively and then with more urgency—to touch him, his arms, his chest, his back, with reverence and fear, like they were trying to confirm that he was real, a man of this world and not some resurrected deity. It was both erotic and spooky, particularly the fact that Monk Dong was smiling pleasantly as if this happened to him all the time.

After lolling for a stint in a crowd of awed women, Monk Dong finally pulled away from his worshippers and made his way to us. I made sure to apologize to him again for hitting him in the face when I saw that his chin was still red from where I'd punched him.

"No problem," he said, rubbing his jaw. "You've got a strong punch, but no problem."

I apologized again. Not only were his crotch and neck impervious, I had hit him with my best right punch right on the knockout button and he had barely moved. There was no way to hurt this guy, short of shooting him.

Then he startled me by asking, "Would you like to learn iron crotch kungfu?"

"Hmm, that's a very interesting proposal," I hedged, trying not to imagine mornings spent punching the family jewels. "I will have to think about it."

"You are staying here tonight. So am I. Let us talk more."

As we walked away, I looked back at Deqing. I felt a little sluttish running after the latest kungfu expert, but Monk Dong was too intriguing to ignore.

Later that night we went to his room. It was unusual for visiting monks to be put up in the hotel; they usually had to stay with friends. Clearly, the Wushu Center was giving him the star treatment. Monk Dong asked me what the focus of my training was. I told him I was studying *sanda*.

"With your height, that is good. *Sanda* was one of my specialties. Have you ever been to Anhui Province?"

"No, I haven't."

"I'm from there. I'm leaving tomorrow for home. Do you want to make the trip with me? Even if you don't want to learn iron crotch, I can show you some *sanda* techniques."

I readily agreed. Anhui Province was where Pearl S. Buck had set her Pulitzer Prize–winning novel, *The Good Earth*, and I hadn't visited it yet.

The next morning, as I was brushing my teeth, I heard a door open down the hallway, followed by some whispered conversation. I cracked my door open and peeked my head out.

Walking down the hall was the trumpeter from the marching band who had asked us the big question. She was leaving Monk

Dong's room. She froze when she saw me. She thought about turning around, but the staircase was at the other end of the hallway.

As she walked past, the devil made me say, "So, miss, was it real?"

She ran the rest of the way to the staircase.

When I went to meet Monk Dong, I was surprised to find that Tiger Man was with him and obviously prepared to travel with us. I didn't think Tiger Man had any friends.

I had met him a month earlier. I had been in the practice hall with some of the monks when Tiger Man showed up unannounced. Everything about him was outsize—his head, his body, his bulbous nose. So was his personality. Upon seeing a *laowai*, he dropped down in front of me and launched into an Ali-like rap about his greatness.

"I am the best martial artist in Shaolin," he proclaimed. "You're American? I was just touring in America. They loved me. They'd never seen anyone like me before. I once fought fifty men and beat them all." Each time he said the word "I" he would jab his huge nose with his huge thumb.

I looked over to Deqing to see if this guy was for real. Deqing rolled his eyes. Tiger Man continued on with his "I am this, I am that" monologue for thirty minutes before growing annoyed with my failure to fawn over him. He jumped up and launched into his unique version of Tiger form to demonstrate his great skill. After he finally left, Deqing told me he got the nickname Tiger Man because the Tiger form was the only one he knew. His only other skill was breaking bricks over his huge forehead. That afternoon he had broken five for my benefit.

Tiger Man was Shaolin's buffoon and con man, proof that the nuts Shaolin attracted weren't just foreigners. He had hoodwinked the organizer of the American tour into giving him a spot. He had also conned some of the Shaolin's younger students into teaching fees. When they discovered he didn't know any kungfu beyond Tiger form and brick breaking, they chased him out of the village. Deqing described with great delight the scene of a dozen teenage boys running after the giant as he fled town.

As a con artist, Tiger Man wasn't unique. The transition from communism to capitalism had given rise to a large number of grifters. Salaries at state-run industries had remained relatively fixed for years, but inflation was running at 10 to 15 percent and the country was being flooded with all those tempting Western goods: microwaves, stereos, refrigerators, computers, home karaoke machines, mopeds, cars, and, most desirable of all, cellular phones—called in Chinese *dage da* (big brother big) because Motorola cell phones circa 1992 were the size of bricks. Class differences had returned with a vengeance, and the working class was being squeezed at the same time it was being tempted with a lifestyle it couldn't afford. To bridge the gap many were leaving their state-industry jobs to start their own businesses, a terror-filled act captured by the Chinese phrase that they used to describe it—*xia hai*, diving into the ocean.

The more criminally inclined chose to become *pianzi* (con men, tricksters). It was their only reasonable option in a country without guns and with a government that practiced a true "zero tolerance" policy toward violent offenders. The root of *pianzi*—*pian* (to con, to trick)—was one of the most frequently used and pungent words in conversation. If someone didn't believe what you'd just said, they'd ask, "Are you *pian* me?" The proper response was: "Why would I want to *pian* you?" You could always pick out the grifter, because his pitch was inevitably punctuated with the phrase, "I wouldn't *pian* you"—the Chinese equivalent of "trust me." Tiger Man used the phrase ad nauseum.

But the most fascinating thing about that first conversation with Tiger Man was that he had flagrantly violated China's taboo about tooting your own horn. According to a traditional Chinese proverb, "An able person does not boast. A boaster is not able."

Whereas in America most conversation between strangers getting to know each other begins with a recitation of their résumés—occupation, education background, accomplishments—in China, conversations began with you complimenting the person you've just met as extravagantly as possible and your new acquaintance deflecting those compliments as self-effacingly as possible. There were several options for false modesty: straight denial like "No, no, no, my Chinese is terrible," a general rejection of flattery such as "No need to be polite," or the classic, "Where? Where? Where?"—as if the flattery must have been aimed in a direction other than yours.

(When Mao Zedong's attractive wife first visited America, the American translator said to her in Chinese, "You are very beautiful." She replied, "Where? Where? Where?" Not understanding this was a generic response, he answered, "Your face is beautiful, your eyes, your body, um, your hands.")

In China, bragging was a tag-team affair. Your friends would introduce you to strangers you wanted to impress with extravagant praise, which allowed you to humbly deny everything—"Where? Where? Where?" Then when your friends needed to impress someone, you took your turn bragging about them, so they could act humble. I had assumed that Tiger Man did his own bragging because he didn't have any friends who would take up the assigned role. But Monk Dong had traveled with him during the American tour, and they had apparently struck up an odd sort of camaraderie: the star and the fool, both outcasts in a way.

Whatever the reason, I was stuck on a very long bus, then train, then bus again ride with Tiger Man, who was in full form the entire trip. In the old days, Shaolin warriors often traveled with a blanket wrapped around a kungfu staff strapped to their back. Tiger Man, who wore the orange robes and kept his head shaved despite the fact that he wasn't a Shaolin monk, carried a rolled, laminated, three-by-five-foot enlarged photo of himself with one of China's top-ranking politicians. I didn't recognize who it was, but he must have been important, because whenever we changed transport Tiger Man unfurled his poster and proudly displayed it to the peasants who were traveling with us. They all seemed impressed. Tiger Man would tell them how he had performed in Beijing and so thrilled this important comrade that he had personally requested they take a photo together. (Somehow I doubt this politician was carrying a laminated photo of Tiger Man.) This would lead naturally to a riff on his deep *guanxi* with national party officials, and not content to merely imply that he was a man who could get things done, he would spell it out.

"All of you agree that most people you meet *mei you yong*," Tiger Man said. "Have no usefulness."

In a country where even the simplest task was complicated by yards of red tape, this was one of the harshest things you could say about someone.

"True, true, true," one farmer said.

"Not me, my friends. I have *benshi*," he continued. "The talent to get things done."

After this set piece, he would edge toward whomever he thought was the richest and focus his attention on him, promising the man he could help him with whatever he might need—for a reasonable fee to be discussed later, of course. During lulls between performances, he would sit next to me and tell me detailed stories about the many times he'd conned businessmen out of money. After each story, he'd ask me if I needed anything done for a reasonable fee, his eyes big and innocent, completely convinced of his own sincerity. I'd stare at him in amazement until he became self-conscious again, a shiftiness creeping back into his eyes. Then he'd turn away from me and launch into another one of his public routines. It was the damndest thing I've ever seen. He reminded me of a common Chinese saying: "To trick others, trick yourself first."

It was a fifteen-hour trip. By the end, we were both having difficulty pretending we could stand each other.

At Tongling, the capital of Anhui Province, we left the train to catch a bus to Anqing. Monk Dong's home was located somewhere between the two cities. I thought we had finally arrived when he asked the bus driver to stop and we all got off. After walking for fifteen minutes, we reached a small house. An attractive woman—his wife?—bounded out, insisting we stay. Monk Dong demurred. We had to be going. Her son clung shyly to his mother's leg. Monk Dong pinched the boy's high cheekbones and pockmarked face. It took another hour's worth of promises to return soon before Monk Dong pulled away from his baby's mama.

We went back to the main highway and flagged down another bus and rode for another half hour or so, before the whole scene repeated itself like some Chinese version of *Big Love*. This time it was a daughter with high cheekbones and bad skin. One of the rumors about iron crotch kungfu was that the practice of it made a man impotent. Clearly not. Before the afternoon was over we visited two more of his families. Monk Dong was the Sir James Goldsmith of Anhui Province. Although China had a draconian one-child-per-family policy, Monk Dong had apparently decided to circumvent the rule by having one child with multiple women, restoring the feudal Chinese custom of polygamy. As I stood back with Tiger Man, watching Monk Dong pull away from another woman, I realized what the connection between the two men was: they were both *pianzi*.

It was not until we reached the fifth home and a fifth woman walked out to greet him that I knew our long trip was blessedly over. The woman was his mother. Mama's boys tend to have problems with serious romantic commitments.

Located in the countryside about thirty minutes from Anqing, Dong's home was palatial by Chinese standards: a five-bedroom brick ranch house. I tried to imagine how a man whose primary skill set was an iron crotch made enough money to support five families.

I had my answer that afternoon. He was a kungfu star. Monk Dong had built his own martial arts academy on land near his home. It was common for former Shaolin monks to open schools in their hometowns, proof of Shaolin's continued influence on Chinese society. But this was a major operation. There were about 500 students practicing outside a large barn.

After Monk Dong conferred with the instructors he had left in charge, we had a *sanda* class. He worked diligently on my front side kick for a couple of hours. As we were walking back to the house, he popped the question.

"I could teach you iron crotch kungfu."

"You are too kind," I said.

"For $2,000."

Amituofo.

"I'll have to think about it," I hedged.

That night I weighed the pros and cons. On the positive side, iron crotch kungfu seemed to be the Chinese equivalent of Spanish fly, an aphrodisiac so strong women found even ugly men attractive. It would also make me impervious in a fight. On the other hand, if anyone back home found out about it, I'd be forced into therapy. I kept imagining the look on the psychiatrist's face when he heard I pounded my privates every day before breakfast. *Ka-ching!*

And yet, what a party trick.

The next morning I woke up to the sound of a man grunting. I walked into the hallway. The sound was coming from Monk Dong's room. Was he having sex with yet another woman? The door was slightly ajar. Overcome with curiosity, I peeked through the crack.

Monk Dong, naked from the waist down, had placed his testicles on a wooden desk. At regular intervals, he brought down the palm of his right hand hard on his sack. He smacked and grunted. I winced.

After a particularly brutal blow, I involuntarily shouted out in English, "Jesus, Mary, and Joseph!"

He turned to look right at me, and I slunk away in shame. A couple of minutes later, Monk Dong knocked on my door. I expected the worst, but he wasn't bothered at all.

"I was just finishing my morning practice," he said. "Come, I will show you the rest."

As we walked back to an empty courtyard, Monk Dong carefully explained that hardening the groin with daily blows was just one part of iron crotch kungfu. Another key was strengthening the muscles in the area. He was able to contract his muscles, actually pulling his testicles up inside his body. So when I was kicking him at the performance, I was actually striking the muscles in the area. In effect, he was able to turn himself into a living Ken doll.

This took care of the balls, he told me. But there was still "the penis problem"—a subject with which I was well acquainted from my friendship with several women's studies majors in college. To avoid damage, he always taped the little man to his belly before a performance to prevent any painful rebounding between blow and body. This was necessary but not sufficient—strengthening exercises were also required.

As we walked into the courtyard, I saw a large stone roller and several boulders with ropes wrapped around them. The iron crotch method of strengthening Mr. Happy was not the one with which most teenage boys are so familiar. Monk Dong dropped his drawers, picked up the rope attached to the stone roller, and tied it to his Johnson. The roller looked like one of the wheels on Fred Flintstone's car. It must have weighed 500 pounds.

With the rope running between his legs, Monk Dong leaned

forward and pushed with his feet, trying to walk forward. The roller was stuck. The rope was so taut it vibrated. Monk Dong was grunting again, breathing heavily. And then, ever so slowly, the roller began moving forward, step by painful step. It was like watching a porno version of the World's Strongest Man contest on ESPN2.

Five steps into his penis-pull, I knew with certainty there was absolutely no way I was going to take up iron crotch kungfu. Even my masochism had its limits.

After Monk Dong untied himself, I said, "Master, your skills are tremendous. However, I am afraid to eat so much bitterness. I am not a dedicated enough student. I would not want to waste your time."

"It would not be a waste."

"I'm sorry I would not be able to stand it. Tomorrow I should go back to Shaolin."

"I understand."

That evening Monk Dong's mother fixed dinner for Tiger Man, Monk Dong, and me before retiring to her room. I'm not exactly sure what the food was, but the Chinese version of spam played an important role in the main dish. While I picked at my meal, my stomach still a little queasy from my up-close-and-personal look at iron crotch kungfu, Tiger Man retold all of his favorite grifter stories. My Chinese had improved dramatically over the last six months, but by the end of the day my mental translator would still get tired and slow down. When I realized I'd fallen several sentences behind in a conversation and needed to catch up, I'd often repeat, "Right, right, right" to be polite and cover up. Because Tiger Man was a blowhard, I'd stopped listening to him.

"Right, right, right."

He must have assumed that I couldn't understand Chinese very well, because after about twenty minutes, he turned to me, smiling and patting me on the shoulder as if he were about to pay me a compliment, and said in a pleasant voice, "Son, you really should listen more closely when your father speaks to you. You know I fucked your mother's pussy, right?"

Without missing a beat, I smiled back at him, "Right, right, right, my great-grandson. You know I fucked your eighteen generations, right?"

His face fell, and Monk Dong fell off his chair laughing.

For the rest of dinner, Monk Dong relived the moment, "You cursed him thinking he would not understand, but then he cursed you worse. That is too funny!"

Tiger Man did not speak another word for the rest of the meal. *Amituofo.*

The next day Monk Dong decided to join us on the thirty-minute bus ride to Anqing, where Tiger Man and I were to catch a bus back to Zheng Zhou. Feeling guilty about turning him down, I told Monk Dong he shouldn't waste his day, but he said, "It's something I should do." The Chinese were very serious about sending off guests, often taking an entire day to make sure their visitors caught their transportation without trouble. Given the rickety and unpredictable nature of China's transportation infrastructure at the time, and the number of very serious wrecks, it was a useful, as well as polite, custom. Monk Dong took us to the Anqing bus station and, after helping us buy tickets, said his good-byes.

Anqing was the poorest city I had visited yet. The only visible industry was bicycle repair. For lunch, I bought some peanuts and looked for a Coke, but apparently in the soft-drink wars, Anqing had fallen to the Pepsi Empire. I sat down next to Tiger Man on a stone bench in the center of the outdoor bus station. Tiger Man had been very friendly since we left that morning—as if the embarrassment of the night before was totally forgotten, and it may well have been. Looking back at his behavior, I wonder if breaking all those bricks over his forehead hadn't damaged his short-term memory.

In a town this poor and this far away from the coasts, a *laowai* was still a big deal. From the way the people were drawn toward me, I assumed most had never seen one in the flesh before. They were not rude, just extremely curious. They gathered in a semi-circle around me at a respectful distance. As I continued to eat, the crowd grew. I increasingly felt like a circus animal.

After ignoring the fifty people quietly watching me eat for several minutes, I finally looked up and said in Chinese, "Hello. It is very nice to meet you."

A murmur rippled through the crowd: *The foreigner speaks Chinese.*

An ancient woman pointed at my face and said something in the local dialect that I was unable to understand.

"I'm sorry, I can't understand you," I said in Mandarin.

She repeated herself.

Smiling, Tiger Man said to me, "She wants to know if you are blind."

"Why?"

"She has never seen blue eyes before. She wants to know if they are broken. She says you have the eyes of a ghost."

I stood up, put my arms out, and pretended to be blind. I fumbled toward her like a mummy. The crowd tensed. The ancient lady leaned backward, but had nowhere to go. Just in front of her, I stopped, put my hands on her shoulders, looked at her directly, and said, "I can see you, Grandmother."

That broke the spell. The peasants burst into laughter.

The ancient lady smiled at me and said, "Naughty boy!"

The crowd dispersed, and the peasants slapped each other on the back, retelling the story of the ghost-eyed *laowai* who'd given an old woman a scare by pretending to be blind.

3

GETTING SCHOOLED

I t is difficult for my fellow countrymen who have never lived abroad to understand that until a foreign man is about sixty-five, he still thinks, every so often, that under the right circumstances he'd like to punch an American in the face. Even people like the Chinese, who mostly like us, think of us—at least partly—as loud, fat, poorly dressed, overprivileged, hectoring, naive, arrogant, self-righteous bullies with little knowledge and no interest in any culture other than our own. I once had a conversation with a Japanese journalist who said to me, "You don't seem like an American." When I asked him, slightly hurt, why he said that, he replied, "Because you listen."

Once word got out that the *laowai* was pretty good at *sanda*, 10,000 Chinese martial artists suddenly had an American in their midst who they could smack in the face without going to jail for it—the right circumstances. I didn't realize until later that Coach Cheng was acting as my gatekeeper. He turned away dozens of kickboxers who wanted a chance to spar with me. The first person to volunteer who Coach Cheng didn't feel he could turn down was Coach Ming, one of the Wushu Center instructors who taught the Wushu Center's Chinese students. They were of equal status.

Coach Ming and all his fellow coaching buddies were waiting for me when I showed up for a Saturday morning sparring session during my second month. It is a little paranoia-inducing to suddenly discover that you are the student all the teachers want to beat up.

As the match started, I was bouncing on my toes. Coach Ming

looked like he was set in stone. He didn't move when Coach Cheng clapped his hands to start the fight, and since I was the anxious one I attacked first with a front side kick.

The one problem with a "reach advantage" is that longer limbs take longer to arrive at their target, and this is doubly true for beginning students. Because *sanda* allows for throws, slow attacks can be very dangerous. From the time Coach Ming noticed my foot leaving the ground to the time it was inches from his body, he could have sat down and stood back up again. Instead he waited stock still until my foot was almost touching him before flying into motion. He grabbed my ankle, stepped back to straighten out my leg, and then whipped it around and forward in a motion that looked like a man reaching back for a bucket of water and then throwing it on a fire. When done properly, this throw creates a centripetal force that causes the throwee to go flying and spinning through the air like a helicopter without its tail rudder. Being a coach, he did it properly. I was airborne long enough to make two complete rotations before crashing to the floor.

Coach Ming's friends whooped it up.

"That's right. Show the *laowai* how it's done!"

"Did you see how the *laowai* flew?"

"Beat him up!"

"Show him who is the master and who is the student!"

It was like being back on the playground.

I tried to make my next kick, a roundhouse, so fast he couldn't catch it. Instead it unfurled with the languorous pace of a fat man on a humid day. Before it arrived, I knew what was going to happen. Coach Ming grabbed my leg as he had the last time, spun me around again, and threw. Only this time as I was flying past him he stuck out his foot to trip my standing leg. The technique is used to put an opponent down hard and fast, and it did. This time I got up more slowly.

It was the second throw that is taught to beginning students. This wasn't a sparring match to him; it was a teaching seminar. This is what his friends found so funny. He was schooling me, literally. He wasn't going to try to get inside my reach to attack with punches or kicks. He was simply going to sit back and wait for my kicks so he could run through the repertoire of *sanda* throws. It was a good strategy, but I had noticed a flaw on his previous throw. In his overconfidence he was failing to tuck his head when he grabbed my leg with both hands, a necessary precaution because otherwise the face is completely exposed.

So this time when I kicked my slow roundhouse, instead of extending my hips, I kept them tucked to shorten my leg. Coach Ming grabbed it and stepped in to sweep my standing leg as I had anticipated, the third technique taught. With his hands around my leg, his face was defenseless. I torqued my hips and punched a right hook as hard as I could. I wanted to drive his nose into the back of his skull. Stunned, he failed to let go of my leg to protect his face. So I smacked him twice more before he backed away.

Not wanting to give him any time to recover and change his strategy I kicked a slow, short roundhouse again. He caught the leg exactly as he had before. And exactly as before I punched him hard three times in the face. Blood sprayed from his mouth and nose.

This time when he let go, his shock bordered on panic. His eyes darted around the room trying to reconfirm that this was the world he grew up in and not some parallel universe where *laowai* are miraculously able to defeat Chinese kungfu coaches. He bent his knees, testing gravity. He looked out the window and found the sky still blue. He cranked his neck to make certain his fellow instructors were still with him. They were, but they were laughing at him now, which proved the principle of face and shame still held in this universe. With downcast eyes, he raised his arms toward Coach Cheng to indicate he'd had enough.

I could hear his friends continue to laugh at him as they walked away. But none of them ever challenged me. That was the first and last time a Wushu Center coach asked to spar with me.

4

THE SIXTH RACE

As the birthplace of Zen Buddhism and kungfu, Shaolin had become a major stop on most Far East truth-seeking package tours geared for Westerners: a week bathing in the Ganges with your Hindu guru, fourteen days of silence in a Nepalese monastery, several sessions of Zen and the Art of Archery in Kyoto, a trek to Tibet, kungfu with the Shaolin monks.

Over time I grew used to this type of *laowai* and came to appreciate their relative value in buttressing my self-esteem. Compared to them, I was the model of sanity. There was the Belgian woman who spoke to the dead. She claimed she had to leave Shaolin because so many of the souls in the vicinity had died violent deaths and were still seeking revenge. Then there was the Swiss couple that spent half the year collecting welfare benefits at home to pay for their search for inner peace in East Asia. The Shaolin segment of their journey ended after the third night when the husband tied one on and gave his wife a black eye. But the absolute king of the wacko spiritual tourists was a Finn named Mikael.

Nearly four months after my Spanish friend Carlos's departure, Little Tiger rushed into my room to tell me another foreigner had arrived in the village, a young man about my age.

I asked the only question I needed answered.

"Does he speak English?"

"I don't think so, because he didn't respond when I said to him, 'Fucka ah youah, madafacka.'"

"Little Tiger, I told you not to use those bad words with strangers."

"I couldn't help myself. I have no one to practice them with except you."

As acting president and only member of Shaolin's *laowai* welcoming committee, I decided to find out if this foreigner spoke English, as all good foreigners should.

"What is his room number?"

"He is not staying at the Wushu Center. He is at the Shaolin Kungfu Academy."

"Which one is that?" I asked. "I've never heard of it.

"It is far west of the temple. Come, I will take you."

I was so excited at the possibility of another English-speaker that I didn't even notice all the "Hallo"s and "Look, a *laowai*"s directed at me on the tourist-jammed road.

I'd never visited the Shaolin Kungfu Academy before. It was as small as its name was big—just a single stone dormitory with a couple dozen Chinese students practicing outside it. They pointed to a room on the first floor, knowing whom I had come to see. Outside the room was a flatbed truck with four Chinese movers wrestling an upright piano to the ground. I poked my head into the room. In the middle of it was a less skinny version of me: my age and my height with brown hair and light eyes. When he turned to look at me, I could see his eyes were green, not blue, but otherwise the similarity was striking, particularly after being the only white man in town for so long.

I felt like pointing at him and saying in Chinese: "Look, a *laowai*. So tall. Too tall."

Instead, I said in English, "Hi, I'm Matt."

"Nice to meet you. Mikael," he replied with a very faint northern European accent.

I smiled. "I'm sorry to barge in on you. I was just excited to hear there was another Westerner in town. Your arrival has doubled our numbers."

His expression didn't change, and his piercing green eyes stayed fixed on me without blinking. I grew afraid he might know only a few English phrases. But as I quizzed him about where he was from and what he was doing in Shaolin, it became clear that he was fluent.

Mikael had been living and studying kungfu in Beijing for the past year. He had grown bored with his training there and decided to move to Shaolin. His teacher had not been happy about it, but had arranged for him to study with a former Shaolin monk who lived in a town just west of the Shaolin village. When I asked him why he wasn't staying at the Wushu Center, because it was illegal for *laowai* to live anywhere else, he said the Wushu Center was a rip-off and he didn't think he'd have a problem. He didn't mind the spartan living conditions of the Shaolin Kungfu Academy. All he needed was his piano.

As we were getting acquainted, the movers were valiantly trying to drag the upright piano into one corner of the tiny room. I had been studiously avoiding any mention of it, the pink elephant in the room, because it was such a bizarre thing to bring to Shaolin and did not portend well. But he brought it up, so I asked him.

"Where did you get a piano in Henan?"

"I bought it in Beijing."

"You had a piano transported from Beijing to Shaolin?"

"It wasn't very expensive."

"But there's not even a highway connecting Beijing and Zheng Zhou, just back roads."

"Yes, I'll need to retune it. But I love having music around me."

The movers had finally placed the piano where Mikael wanted it. He sat down in front of it and whipped off a better than average rendition of some classical piece I knew I should recognize but didn't. My own piano career, which I tried not to think about very often, had been a short and bitter affair that ended at age eleven. Watching a Finn play his piano in a Shaolin kungfu school in the middle of East Bumfuck, China, was so disconcerting I felt like I had vertigo. As soon as I had listened long enough not to seem rude, I excused myself and invited him to visit me when he settled in.

Mikael visited my room that night, sat down across from me, and, without any preamble, immediately launched into his pitch.

"Matt, have you heard of the sixth race?"

"No, I'm afraid I haven't. What is it?"

"Up until this point in time there have been five evolutions in human consciousness. Were you aware of that?" he asked, staring at me with his piercing green eyes—guru eyes, I thought—and blank expression.

"Um, no, I must have missed the meeting. So you're saying that we are the fifth race of humanity?"

"Exactly. But the sixth race is coming soon. Human consciousness is about to evolve again, creating the sixth race."

"I see," I said, my heart sinking.

"Not everyone will evolve, of course."

"Of course."

"It is Spiritual Darwinism."

"You mean like Social Darwinism but without the Nazis?" I said, hoping he might laugh and reveal that this was some sort of joke, a Scandinavian version of a put-on.

He didn't.

"The sixth race will possess a higher state of consciousness. People will be able to read each other's thoughts, so there will be no more miscommunication. Without miscommunication, there will be no more violence, no more war."

"Really? I would think that knowing what other people actually thought about you would make violence more likely, not less."

"No, the sixth race will exist in a higher state of consciousness, where all those ugly thoughts will be gone. We will see that we are not separate individuals but connected at the same source."

"Like the Hindus believe."

"It won't be belief. It will be knowledge, perception. All that is necessary is for a certain mass of people to join their energies toward this evolution and then the effects will ripple outward."

"And then we'll all be part of the sixth race?"

"No, some will refuse to join and will remain stuck in the lower level of consciousness."

"And what will happen to them?"

"They will disappear."

"Right. So will this be immediate, like a reverse Rapture? Or slowly, like the Neanderthals?"

"It will be like the laws of evolution," he said. "When I came to China, my connection was in Japan. As we were flying over that country, I felt this very negative energy. Most of the Japanese will disappear."

"Okay, so anyone else not going to make the great leap forward?"

"The Germans, they give off the same black energy."

"I see."

I'd given up hope that he was joking, having resigned myself to the fact that he was the latest, albeit the most nutty, of the truth-seekers. But his piercing stare and pose of tranquility bothered me. With your average crazy person, you get a darting gaze and unconscious twitching of the face and hands, as though they're extremely uncomfortable inside their own bodies. But Mikael was acting like he was explaining a simple mathematical proof to an extremely dull student. It was causing the hair on the back of my neck to rise. My kungfu training kicked in. I took in his size, measured the distance between us, and visualized a series of attacks.

"Well, it's nice of you to come over and tell me about all of this," I said. "So you're going to begin your kungfu training tomorrow?"

"I came to Shaolin to recruit people to join their energies to the cause of the sixth race."

"Well, good luck. The Chinese are pretty focused on their economic evolution."

"I knew this was where I had to be after what happened on the train ride from Beijing to Zheng Zhou," he continued. "I was meditating and went to this deep place. And the train car opened up around me. The clouds parted and Odin and Thor descended into my cabin. Do you know them?"

Somehow I managed to keep a straight face.

"Not personally, no," I said.

"Odin is the one-eyed leader of the Norse pantheon. Thor is the god of thunder."

"Right, I played *Dungeons & Dragons* as a kid."

"I told them about the sixth race that is coming. And they thought it was really important, so they agreed to join their energies to the project."

"You told them about the sixth race and then recruited them? Odin and Thor?"

"Yes."

"I realize that Odin and Thor are sort of has-been, B-list deities who have been out of favor for a long time, but you're telling me they didn't know about this sixth race thing?"

"You don't believe me?" he asked, his face finally betraying some emotion. His eyes narrowed with annoyance. Having finally cracked the all-knowing guru facade, I pressed forward.

"I'm a religion major. I've read about too many mystical occurrences to think they don't happen. But all of them had one element in common: The human was overwhelmed by the experience. I've never heard any encounter with a deity being turned into a recruitment meeting."

"You were a religion major?" he asked, leaning forward, his green eyes even more piercing than before.

"Yes."

"So you read about other people's experiences. It is different when you have your own."

"Yes, I know."

"It is different to *believe* something is true than to *know* it is true. How can you know the truth if all you do is read about other people's beliefs?"

I stared at him. He comes into my house and challenges me? Only after an intense internal struggle was I able to check myself.

The knowers do not say; the sayers do not know.

"Okay, Mikael, you're right. I guess I can't *know* the truth," I said, swallowing the bitter aftertaste of pride's backwash. "I guess all I have is my questions and my theories."

"But don't you want to know the truth?"

"Sure, who doesn't?" I said, losing the battle against my ego. "Maybe now that Odin and Thor are on board, you can send them over to my room so they can tell me about the sixth race."

He didn't reply. We stared at each other in silence until I said, "Well, I should get to bed early. I've got practice tomorrow."

He agreed he should as well. We shook hands and promised to meet up again, and basically said all the things you say when you are trying to make nice after a pissing contest.

I figured that was the last I'd see of Mikael. Over the week, various Shaolin monks asked me about him. Mikael had shaved his head and was wandering around town in monk robes, which would normally be considered presumptuous for someone who was not a monk. But the monks, who were inclined to search for a more forgiving explanation, asked me, "Is he a little bit crazy?"

"More than a little bit," I said.

Mikael came to see me in the second week of his visit while I was training. After class was over, he approached me. He'd not forgotten our discussion or given up on recruiting me to the sixth-race movement.

"Last night, I was meditating and Jesus came to see me," he said.

"He seems to visit Shaolin quite often," I said.

"I told him about the sixth race, and he was very excited about it and promised to join his energies to the cause."

"That's great, Mikael. You must be very pleased. Now that you've signed a bankable star, no doubt your project will be green-lighted. I hope your kungfu training is going well. I should get back to my workout."

I was certain that would be it, but Mikael was relentless. But this time when he came back to the Wushu Center a week later, he was slightly shaken. His relationship with his Shaolin instructor had taken a bad turn. He explained that while in Beijing he had developed the "perfect attack." He'd come to Shaolin to test its perfection. He and his master had been lightly sparring in the Shaolin Temple when Mikael decided to unveil his "indefensible" technique. And according to Mikael, it had worked, only too well. His master's failure to overcome it had enraged him and he had attacked Mikael will full force and fury. Mikael showed me the bruises on his arm and chest as proof of this battle in the halls of Shaolin.

By this point, I'd decided to treat Mikael like a wacky cousin. It was hard to hold a grudge against the only other person in a thousand-mile radius who could speak English.

"Well, you shouldn't worry," I said. "It sounds like you don't need to train with him if you have the perfect technique."

"This is true. Would you like to see it?"

One of the things I had learned in Shaolin was that martial artists love to demonstrate their techniques. Unlike martial artists of the past, they feel the need to prove the value of what they've learned. I'd also learned that if you agreed to participate in a demonstration, you invariably ended up bruised and battered and wishing you hadn't. But I knew every attack has a counter, so I was curious to see the crazy Finn's "perfect" attack.

Mikael stood with his dominant right side forward. His right fist was partially extended. His left palm was in front of his face for protection. With his right arm the spear and his left hand the shield, he looked like an unarmed version of an ancient Greek hoplite.

I shifted into a *sanda* stance, my body loose and resting mostly on my back right leg. "So I'm going half-speed," I said as a warning so he wouldn't overreact. I shifted my weight to my left foot in order to bring my right leg around in a roundhouse kick. Halfway through my attack, he stepped toward me, his right foot pinning my left foot to the ground and his right fist jabbing forward the short distance between where it started to the tip of my nose.

"That's your perfect attack?"

"It's all in the timing. See, I have hit you before your kick could land."

"And you created it?"

"It came to me when I was meditating one night in Beijing."

I just stared at him. My geekiness had been offended. He obviously didn't think I was enough of a nerd to have read Bruce Lee's *Tao of Jeet Kune Do*. The attack Mikael had just done was the first technique described by Lee, and the foundation of his style. The jab is the fastest technique because it is the shortest, a straight line from the forward fist to the opponent's head. Boxers normally put their weak side forward and use the jab to set up their cross, which is a more powerful punch.

Bruce Lee's idea was to put the dominant side forward, because a jab is faster and you could make up for its inferior power by using the stronger side of the body. It was a compromise, a clever one certainly, and by all accounts, Lee was able to generate a tremendous amount of power from his dominant side jab, but it wasn't a perfect, no-defense-possible technique. And Mikael certainly didn't think it up.

"Mikael, by any chance when you were meditating that night in Beijing, did Bruce Lee visit you and, in exchange for your insight into the whole sixth-race thing, show you this technique?"

"I don't understand."

"You should, because you didn't create this technique. Bruce Lee did. It's in his book."

"I never read his book," he said.

"It's also in all of his movies. He's always using it. He stands like this," I said, imitating his sideways style, "Bounces on his toes, and as soon as his opponent moves he jumps in and hits him with his right. Now, your punch is more of a straight jab, and his was more of a backhand. But it's the same technique."

"It's not the same. Bruce Lee didn't step on his opponent's foot to pin it down."

"Oh, so now you're saying you created a modification to Bruce Lee's main technique."

"It's perfect."

"No, it's not."

"There is no way to stop it."

"Okay, well then let me show you something."

I stepped back, took a running start, ducked my head, bent at the waist, and tackled him like a football dummy. As my arms were reaching around him, his punch glanced off the back of my head. He ended on his back with me on his chest.

As I stood up, I said, "There are no perfect techniques. All attacks have counters, and all counterattacks have counter-counterattacks. A jab is a high punch, so I ducked low. As a counter to my move, you should have brought your knee up against my face when I was tackling you, because it was unprotected. And by the way, if you're going to shave your head, don't wear the monk's robes. You're not a monk, and the Chinese find it rude. And because we are the only *laowai* here, what you do reflects on me."

Mikael didn't say anything, and he left the Wushu Center that day.

A week later, Mikael had decided to move back to Beijing. He had survived less than a month. It tickled my dark heart that he had survived less than a month.

"Shaolin's energy is bad," he told me as he departed, leaving his piano behind.

"Well, I guess we're shit out of luck when the sixth race comes around," I said. "Give my best to Thor."

That was not, however, the last I saw of Mikael. Once when I was in Beijing, I bumped into him in the lobby of the Great Wall Sheraton. He was flying back from Paris. He'd found some angel investors willing to set him up in his own kungfu/meditation academy in France.

When he told me this, it suddenly all made sense. As the Chinese say, "Not all pilgrims come to worship God." Mikael *was* crazy. Crazy like a fox. He hadn't come to Shaolin searching for the truth. He'd come to pad his New Age résumé.

5

DIRTY JOKES AND BEER

"*Bao Mosi,* you should come to the performance hall," Little Tiger told me one night as I was writing a letter to my mother. "Long Spear is back."

"Who is Long Spear?"

"He was part of the performance team. He went to Wuhan Sports University. He's a national champion in spear and straight-sword form. He's the best."

"Better than Deqing?"

"Yes."

"That's not possible!"

I assumed this was simply Little Tiger's bias. Spear and straight sword tended to be performed by long-limbed and lithe martial artists, because the forms had a number of elegant twists and turns. Staff and machete forms were for broad, muscular stylists, because they emphasized power and acrobatics. Little Tiger was a spear specialist. Deqing was broad and muscular.

I arrived at the performance hall to find Long Spear—spiky hair, angular features, slight frame—performing his spear form. The only other person watching was Deqing, who looked none too happy to have his rival back. As far as technique was concerned, Little Tiger was right. Long Spear executed his form with technical perfection. It was smooth and silky. The best I'd ever seen. He didn't have Deqing's explosive power or leaping ability. But then, no one did.

"You've improved," Deqing said, grudgingly. "I've added some moves to the staff form. Take a look."

Deqing proceeded to power through the form, his leaps slightly higher than normal, his strikes more forceful. But after watching Long Spear, I could detect the slight flaws in his technique, the minor imperfections.

After the challenge match was over, Long Spear said, "Powerful, but it's not regulation."

"We don't do regulation forms here."

"I know."

Then each of them continued working on moves while surreptitiously watching the other. Finally, Deqing dropped his staff and walked out without saying anything to me. He wasn't used to defeat.

Little Tiger introduced me to Long Spear. I invited him to dinner. I wanted to collect some intel. Wuhan Sports University was renowned for having the best kickboxing team in the country. The reigning 70 kg. national champion was at Wuhan, and I expected him to be one of my opponents at the Zheng Zhou tournament in the fall.

After discovering the reasons for my interest, Long Spear offered to take me back with him to Wuhan, show me around his university, and introduce me to the Champ.

"Do you think he'll mind?" I asked.

"Why should he mind? He's the best in the world. He doesn't have anything to worry about."

"I'm sorry to say that's probably true."

After Long Spear had spent a couple of days meeting all his old friends, I arranged for a car to take us to Zheng Zhou, where we caught a train to Wuhan, the capital of Hubei Province. Zheng Zhou was built on the Yellow River, Wuhan on the Yangtze about 400 miles directly south. Wuhan is an industrial city. I could see the smokestacks from the train. It has a subtropical monsoon climate, and it was now the height of summer. The humidity had a fetid, dank feel. I could almost see the soot from the factories hanging in the air. If you're worried about global warming and inclined to despair, you don't want to visit Wuhan.

Long Spear shared a room with seven of his *wushu* teammates. They were a small, yappy, high-energy lot. Introductions were succinct. They needed to brief Long Spear, who was obviously their leader in the latest political machinations. Apparently, a boxer and a wrestler had a disagreement involving one of the young ladies from the women's *wushu* team. This argument had escalated when the entire boxing team decided to challenge the wrestlers' position as the most influential squad in the university. A fight had been scheduled but was canceled once a coach got wind of it. The boxers were appealing to the *wushu* boys for backup.

"The wrestlers are stronger, we'll need to bring weapons," a teammate with a moon face said.

"But the dull ones, not the sharp. We don't want anyone getting killed," the teammate fiddling with a performance sword said.

"The boxers won't fight if we don't back them up," Moonface replied.

"They could go to the kickboxers."

"They never get involved. They think they are above all this."

Long Spear contemplated the situation for a minute before delivering his verdict.

"We will wait until after the fight to see who wins and then pick sides."

The matter settled, they turned their attention to me. They were extremely polite and friendly. I was their leader's new pal. Moonface offered me his bed during my stay.

"Where will you sleep?" I asked. The floors were concrete and filthy.

"I can sleep next to one of the other guys."

"No, no, no, thank you, thank you, thank you," I said. "You are too polite. But I've already rented a bed at the local hotel."

Long Spear stood up and said, "I want to take you to meet someone."

We walked down a hallway past the eight-bunk rooms filled with the gear of various sports—basketball, boxing, soccer. At the end of the hall, Long Spear knocked on a door. A sparkplug of a man opened it. I quickly pegged him for the lieutenant, because sitting in a desk chair was Wrestler #1, who I'd soon discover was the prince of the school. He had the entire room to himself. He was a big bully of guy with a bashed-in face and a ready sneer. He'd clearly chosen fear as his leadership style.

"Ah, Long Spear, you're back from Shaolin? What do you want?"

"I brought someone to meet you, Big Brother," Long Spear said in a supplicant's tone of voice.

"Eh, what, a *laowai*? So what?"

"He's an American. He is training kungfu at Shaolin. He's very talented. He even speaks Chinese."

It was at this moment that I realized why Long Spear had invited me to Wuhan. I'd been in similar situations before. In a country closed off to travel, having a *laowai* friend was a sign of worldliness. Long Spear was the cold, calculating type. He was displaying me to increase his perceived value to Wrestler #1. In return for the favor of introducing me to the Champ, it was my job to impress Wrestler #1.

"It's nice to meet you," I said.

Wrestler #1 looked me dead in the face and then turned away. He knew what Long Spear was doing, too, and he refused to take the bait. He was the big man on campus, and he wasn't going to show deference to some random *laowai*. Long Spear was annoyed but couldn't think how to rescue the situation.

Feeling obliged to Long Spear's hospitality, I said, "Big Brother, I have heard so much about you, I asked Long Spear to introduce us. Everyone says you're the most important man on campus. I want to throw a banquet in your honor."

Picking up the lead, Long Spear said, "Yes, we can invite your entire team and my *wushu* team."

This elicited a grudging smirk, but Wrestler #1 still wouldn't look at us.

"Wednesday," he said.

And with that we were dismissed.

Long Spear invited me to the school cafeteria for lunch. The students were university age, but the place reminded me of high school. Tables in the school cafeteria were divided by team-based cliques. The boys talked of fighting and rivalries. The girls on the *wushu* team were the Heathers—pretty, popular, and mean. The level of sexual tension and physical rivalry was high. Compared to Wuhan, Shaolin was a sea of tranquillity.

That afternoon, Long Spear took me to the kickboxers' practice room. It had the sweaty feel of an old-time boxing gym. In the center of the room was the *leitai*. Two heavyweights were banging on each other with thunderous claps of punches and kicks. They had muscles on their muscles. They looked as juiced as Barry Bonds.

Long Spear brought the Champ over to meet me, explaining why I was here. We exchanged pleasantries as we checked each other out physically, a habit among *sanda* fighters, looking for weaknesses. The Champ didn't have any. His body was the perfect shape: height about five foot ten, legs slightly bulkier than his torso, not an ounce of extra fat on him. He looked at me, measuring the length of my legs. He saw my weakness: With such long legs on a six-foot-three frame, I had a high center of balance, which made me particularly vulnerable to throws. The Champ knew I knew what he was looking at. In a flash he ducked down, grabbed me around the waist and lifted me like a feather into the air.

"You have to protect against that," he said when he'd set me down.

It was a free lesson and also a psyche job. It worked on both levels.

"Thank you," I said just once. "I will try."

We sat on a bench. The Champ cracked open the Sprite I had brought to give him. He was warm with no affectation. National champions in *sanda* were invariably the nicest martial artists I met in China. They were the best and had nothing to prove, but the sport had little fame and no money to swell their heads. The Champ had studied at Taguo before graduating to Wuhan. We discussed mutual acquaintances. After the appropriate interval, he excused himself to return to practice. I stayed to watch. The Wuhan team was awesome. Their skill level was light-years beyond mine.

At Chinese banquets, the seating is always precise. As the honored guest, Wrestler #1 took his seat at one end of the long table, and as host I took mine at the other. The *wushu* team sat on one side, with Long Spear seated next to Wrestler #1. The wrestlers sat on the opposite side.

I observed all the formalities. I opened with two toasts. The first to the friendly relations between our two great nations. The second to Wrestler #1, who had so graciously welcomed me to Wuhan. Then I grabbed four shot glasses and walked around the table to Wrestler #1 and toasted him twice. But Wrestler #1 refused to be impressed. This was all his due. As plates of food filled the table, Long Spear tried to warm Wrestler #1 up, whispering into his ear, but he was annoyed with Long Spear's scheming.

As the banquet was drawing down, Long Spear looked glum, and Wrestler #1 looked ready to leave. The beer and *baijiu* had flowed and the participants were getting bleary. I felt a duty to save the evening for Long Spear. I had a pretty good idea of the temper of the attendees. They were jocks, so I decided to tell the one dirty joke I knew in Chinese. It was a Hail Mary pass.

"Listen up, listen up," I said. "I have a joke I learned in Beijing. You want to hear it?"

"Yes," Long Spear shouted.

"Okay, there was this Beijing girl named Little Fang. And let me tell you, this was one horny girl. I mean she really needed it. All the time. She exhausted her poor boyfriend. Well, one day she and her boyfriend take a *miandi* bus [a van where everyone sits in a circle facing each other] to go shopping. There's only one seat available. So her boyfriend takes it, and she sits on his lap. Well, you know how the roads are. She is bouncing up and down," I said, bouncing up and down on my seat as if I were Little Fang and my chair the boyfriend.

There was dead silence around the table. They had no idea how to react to a *laowai* telling a dirty joke in Chinese. Having passed the point of no return, I continued.

"Pretty soon, she begins to feel her boyfriend's excitement. And this drives her crazy with desire. But what can she do with everyone watching? Per usual she's a wearing a skirt but no panties. So slowly, ever so slowly, she inches up her skirt, reaches around, pulls out her boyfriend's member, and puts it inside her without anyone noticing. But wouldn't you know it? The bus hits a long patch of smooth road. His thing is in her, but she can't move without someone realizing what is happening. She is going insane. What do you think she does next?" I asked the table.

Dead silence.

"She leans over to the man across from her and says"—I lifted myself off the chair about five inches, looked at one of the wrestlers, and said in my best imitation of a high-pitched Chinese girl—" 'Sir, where are you traveling to?' "

I sat back down, then lifted myself up five inches, looked at one of the *wushu* team members, and said in the same falsetto, " 'Grandmother, where are you going?' " Back down. Back up. "Where are you going?" Back down. I was riding the chair, reverse cowboy position, faster and faster. Up. "Where are you going?" Down. Up. "Where are you going?" Down.

Imitating Little Fang as she finally reaches her climax, I clapped my hands and squealed, "We are all going there! We're all going there! We're all going there! So good! So good! So good!"

For a moment as I finished the joke the only sound was of breaths being sucked in, and then Wrestler #1 exploded out of his chair, raised his beer glass, and shouted, "Good! Good! The *laowai* is good!"

As he started howling, the laughter rolled over the table, knocking some of the boys off their chairs. Wrestler #1 had to wipe tears from his eyes.

For the rest of the night, I was the most popular guy at the table. Even Wrestler #1 brought four shots around to my seat to toast me personally.

At some point I wandered outside to take a leak. Not able to find an outhouse, I settled for a tree. Moonface wandered out to do the same. As we stood in the dark, he said, "That was so funny, so funny. 'We're all going there.' So funny."

"Where? Where? Where?" I said.

He didn't speak for a few seconds, as if considering a new thought, and then whispered under his breath, "I wish I were you."

6

PRIDE AND PENANCE

By May, our Saturday-morning sparring class had acquired such a regular audience that it had been moved to the performance hall. When I walked in one Saturday morning, I found a *sanda* coach from Taguo sitting in the front row. Coach Cheng had a slightly embarrassed smile on his face when he told me that the Taguo coach wanted to fight me. Given Taguo's reputation as a *sanda* powerhouse and its rivalry with the Wushu Center, this coach should have been challenging either Coach Cheng or our team's best fighter, who was Baotong. Wanting to fight me was a cheap stunt. And as I looked at the softness of the Taguo coach's belly and the rings around his bloodshot eyes from too many nights of drinking, I could picture him last night with his buddies talking about how he was going to beat up the American. He thought of me as an easy way to recapture his glory days.

As I told Coach Cheng I would do it, I went cold inside. It was like all the emotion had drained out of my body. Usually before a match I felt a gut-wrenching mixture of fear, dread, and anxiety. But for the first time, I knew with absolute certainty that I wasn't merely going to win this fight. I was going to crush him.

After putting on gloves and a cup, we both walked into the center of the hall. Coach Cheng clapped his hands together and stepped back.

I had become used to my opponents calmly waiting for me to attack first. Instead, the Taguo coach charged me like a bull, opening with a roundhouse kick directed at my left thigh and followed by a series of left and right hooks. I backpedaled, bouncing and circling around to my right, keeping my head beyond his reach. Ferocity was one of the aspects of a kickboxer that Coach Cheng felt I lacked. I was too calculated, too cerebral. "Ferocity at the right moment can overwhelm your opponent," he had told me. "Turn his legs weak with fear."

The Taguo coach charged again, yelling and swinging for the fences, throwing everything he had into each punch. As I backpedaled again, jabbing and retreating, I felt like smiling. Chinese kickboxers rarely open with punches, preferring to kick first because of the greater range. But the legs are the first thing to go with age. At Shaolin, most kickboxers' careers were over by the age of twenty-five. The Taguo coach had to be at least thirty and his legs were shot. He had half the weapons I did, which was why he was trying so hard to end the fight as quickly as possible.

His punches came in combinations of five and then he had to rest for a second to catch his breath before launching into another flurry. By the fourth flurry, I was backpedaling and waiting for this pause. This time I reversed direction and feinted a left side kick to misdirect his attention. It worked, and his head and hands dropped to prepare a defense. Instead of attacking with the left, I planted and turned on it, coming around with a high right-roundhouse kick. Coach Cheng had taught us to work on the high and low planes, because it is mentally difficult to process attacks at different heights: fake high, attack low; fake low, attack high.

The Taguo coach didn't see it coming. This is the most dangerous type of attack because the body and mind don't have time to flinch and prepare for contact. The kick landed flush across the left side of his face. His eyes glazed and rolled back up into his head. His body stiffened with the onset of unconsciousness, and he fell like a tree in the forest, hitting the ground hard.

What does it feel like to hit another man so hard you knock him out? It feels like Christmastime. The joy was so pure, so primal I felt like I was glowing. Male violence isn't an aberration; we are hardwired to enjoy it.

The joy was diminished slightly as I watched the Taguo coach regain consciousness after his head hit the mat. The impact woke him up. Once he was back on his feet, he quickly charged me again, swinging with everything he had left. After two flurries, I reversed course, and the scene repeated itself. I faked with the left and followed up with a right roundhouse kick that caught him unaware and momentarily knocked him unconscious. He hit the ground and woke up again. He attacked. I feinted and kicked. The eyes rolled back in his head and he hit the ground a third time. A grudging respect filtered through my frozen veins. He was tough.

But the third time was enough. When he stood, his shoulders were slumped. He raised his arms and walked away.

I paced back and forth with the regret of unfinished business. My kicks were too weak. Had I landed one with real power, he should have stayed down. I wanted another shot at him.

But when I looked at him, I saw him sitting all alone on a chair near the exit. He hadn't brought an entourage, and no one would go near him, like he was infected with failure. The devastation of the loss was vivid in his face and posture. I felt a pang of pity for him. I went over to try to console him.

"You are very tough," I said.

"No, no, no, I am no good anymore."

"No, you are very strong. You kept standing back up."

"No, no, no, you are a great fighter," he said. "You kept knocking me down."

"It was just a lucky kick. It can happen to anyone."

After I said that he looked up at me with this unexpected expression, an odd combination of neediness and admiration that repelled me.

"You must be the greatest fighter in America," he said.

That's when I stuck the shiv into him.

"Oh no, I am not," I said. "There are many, many, many fighters in America who are better than me." The blade was long and my aim was true. The last little bit of self-respect drained from his face. I had stripped away the only face-saving excuse he could think of, and he sat there completely naked of any pride.

I was so shocked at what I had done that I literally backed away from him in horror. I hadn't actually felt any sympathy for him. I realized I had only tricked myself into thinking that so I could go over and soften him up for the final strike.

The difference between a man and a monster is demarcated by moral lines, and I'd drawn mine around the *leitai*. In that instant, I'd crossed over, becoming the thing I had hated most, a bully, looking for weakness and feeding on it. I was the villain. Most physical wounds heal, but those to the pride rarely do.

In his case, they didn't. Twice more over the next two months, I entered the performance hall to find him sitting there. He wanted a rematch, a shot at redemption. Each time I refused him, and he left. The first time I told myself it was an act of mercy. I knew as certainly as I had before the first fight what the outcome would be, and it was better to let the Taguo coach think that maybe I had just gotten lucky. By the second visit I knew that wasn't true. The truth was I couldn't stand to be near him. His physical presence brought back those vicious feelings, reminding me of what I had done, and letting me know just how much I wanted to do it again.

After the second refusal, he never came back, but I couldn't get him out of my mind. I dreamed about him at night, and it was the first time in my life that in my dreams I was the aggressor rather than the victim.

I tried to talk to Deqing and Cheng Hao about it, but they couldn't understand what was bothering me.

"But he came here wanting to make you lose face," Deqing said.

"Yes," I said. "But I still shouldn't have said that to him."

"But what you said was the truth."

"It was cruel."

"*Bao Mosi*, you should have seen yourself when you first came here," Deqing laughed, launching into an imitation of me. He hunched his shoulders over, drooped his head, and put on this frightened face. "You were just this college student, scared of everything. But now look at you."

It was a good caricature. It struck home.

Deqing asked Cheng Hao, "Did you see that look in his eyes when I said he was scared of everything?"

"Like he wanted to kill you," Cheng Hao said.

"Exactly. Six months ago, he did not have that look."

"No. He used to look like a strong wind would blow him over."

"*Bao Mosi*, now your eyes have fierceness," Deqing said. "This is good. You cannot be a good fighter if you are always afraid of what might happen."

I knew he was right. I had won the fight against the Taguo coach because I had reached a state of mind where I no longer cared about the consequences. What frightened me was how much I had enjoyed being there. And how hard it had been to come back. A good fighter must enjoy hurting his opponent. A good human being has to feel remorse about it. The only way for me to square the circle was to separate who I was and what I did inside the ring from how I acted outside it. What I had said to the Taguo coach happened outside the ring, and after several weeks of raking myself over the coals for it, I was desperate for some kind of extra penance so I could forgive myself. And because those seem to be the kinds of prayers God likes to answer first, He plagued me with dysentery.

Actually, I don't really believe God gave me dysentery—I'm not such a narcissist as to think that the Almighty took time out of his busy schedule to punish me personally. That's what the archangels are for. I'm not sure which of them handles fallen Catholics searching for enlightenment in Buddhist monasteries (Gabriel, perhaps?), but he had a wide selection of microbes at Shaolin to choose from. As a result, no Westerner spent much time in Shaolin before getting a severe case of diarrhea.

My first case during my first month at Shaolin lasted only a day, but during that day I wanted nothing else but my mommy. Despite drinking only Coke, I caught it so frequently—about twice a month—that I began to think of it as Mao's Revenge, a kind of viral guerrilla warfare bent on expelling the imperialists before we completely undermined his collectivist revolution. It was too late for the Chairman's rearguard action actually to win the war against the bourgeoisie—the number of capitalist running dogs and counter-revolutionaries was growing exponentially every day—but it was certainly demoralizing on a personal level.

Previously, Coach Cheng had come to my room to see why I

wasn't in class, and then give me some Chinese antidiarrheal medicine. The pills looked like licorice gumballs and were made of an unknown substance (and it was probably better that way). But they had always worked.

Not this time.

As the diarrhea worsened on the second day, it was joined by a fever and violent vomiting. My body was on fire, and the fluids inside me were charging for the exits. Fortunately, the sink was right next to the toilet.

I knew I had dysentery. As the fever became hallucinatory, I imagined my trips to the bathroom as mini–Bataan Death Marches. I became obsessed with the toilet paper, which in Shaolin was about as baby-soft as industrial sandpaper. In my fevered brain, it became a metaphor for the rise and fall of China. The Chinese invented toilet paper. They even invented perfumed toilet paper. And here they were after several centuries of bad luck, bad decisions, and bad neighbors, scraping their butts with a product that could remove wood varnish.

As my body weakened and my mind tripped out, I began to conflate my condition with the destiny of America. I became certain it had to avoid my mistake: a unilateral land invasion of Asia. I believe I hold the distinction of being the only person that dysentery ever turned into a foreign-policy realist. To this day the policies of the neoconservatives send me searching for the Imodium.

Coach Cheng took one look at me on the morning of the third day and left. When he returned he was pulling Comrade Fish by the arm.

"You see, he's sick nearly to the point of death," Coach Cheng said.

Comrade Fish looked everywhere but at me. He clearly did not want to be here. Coach Cheng was demanding that a decision be made, and Comrade Fish avoided making decisions with the same fervor with which he avoided work. He was the Bartleby the Scrivener of Shaolin. He had also gotten a good whiff of my restroom as he walked in, and he was starting to look as sick as I felt.

"How are you?" he asked.

"No problem," I said. This was what the monks always said when they were really hurt.

"He seems all right," said Comrade Fish.

"We must take him to the hospital."

"No problem," I repeated.

Comrade Fish left the room, followed closely by Coach Cheng.

My coach must have leaned hard on Comrade Fish because about three hours later, which was extremely fast decision-making by Chinese standards, I was being helped into Leader Liu's Toyota Santana. Leader Liu had even loaned me his driver, which really scared me. He would never have been that generous if he weren't seriously worried that a major revenue stream was about to dry up on him.

The several layers of clothing I was wearing could not stop my feverish shaking, so Coach Cheng loaned me his full-length People's Liberation Army winter coat. The driver took Comrade Fish, Coach Cheng, and me to Deng Feng.

Deng Feng's hospital was a one-story concrete bunker on the outskirts of town, which was particularly inconvenient because it had no ambulances. As we drove up, a man was dropping off an accident victim he had pushed to the hospital in a wheelbarrow. The parking lot, which was strewn with unevenly packed dirt and rubble, matched the hospital floor inside: The unevenly laid concrete had its own terrain, with hills and valleys where rainwater had collected into mini-lakes. And the dirt had been carefully swept into piles and left in mounds that had to be dodged as we tried to trace our way from the front door to the infirmary. The walls were painted Turkish prison green.

Coach Cheng talked to a nurse in the pharmacy about my symptoms. She was standing behind a window protected by metal bars, like a liquor store in the South Bronx. The nurse, after some intense haggling, handed Coach Cheng the same set of diarrhea pills he had given me when I first got sick and that I had been taking for the past three days to no effect.

"These do not work," I said.

"If those do not work, then there is nothing I can do," she replied and turned away from the window, but not before she sneered at me, like I was some homeless man begging for change.

Ah, socialized medicine.

"I need some tests," I insisted.

"That will take much time and money," Comrade Fish said.

Feeling as close as I did to death's door, I suddenly had an over-whelming urge to take someone else with me. This desire must have been evident on my face as I towered over Comrade Fish—eyes wide—and said, "I insist that I receive some sort of medical test," because he ran down the hall to grab one of the doctors, who pointed us toward another room.

I guessed that this room was the hospital's laboratory. The give-away clue was not the "scientists" sitting behind a series of desks, because they were wearing street clothes. It was the amazing dis-covery that these researchers had the exact same chemistry set my uncle had given me on my eighth birthday. There was the wooden rack to hold up half a dozen glass tubes. There was the same low-intensity microscope. And . . . well, that was it. That was all the equipment in the lab.

Comrade Fish told them that I needed to have some tests done, because I had a severe case of diarrhea. The researchers did not re-spond. This was not uncommon in government-run operations, where a request that someone do their job often induced a cata-tonic state that might last anywhere from a couple minutes to an hour. Comrade Fish waited a couple of minutes, and then repeated his request. One of the lab guys looked at me, then looked at his partner, then looked back at me. He lit up a cigarette while he con-sidered the situation some more.

Finally, he said, "Go to the pharmacy and buy some diarrhea medicine."

"It is not working," Coach Cheng said. "We don't know what is wrong with him. He needs a test."

"If you don't know what is wrong with him, how are we sup-posed to know?" the lab guy asked.

"This is a hospital, right?" I asked, feeling flush with fever and anger.

"Hey, the *laowai* speaks Chinese. Your Chinese is really good."

"Where? Where? Where?" I responded.

"Hey, the *laowai* is humble, too."

This minor miracle finally stirred the lab guy to action. He grabbed one of the long, thin glass tubes, dumped out whatever liq-uid was in it, and handed it to me. "Here," he said, "give us a sample."

"Where's the bathroom?" I asked.

"Go out the door at the end of the hallway."

In my weakened state, it took me a second to realize, as Comrade Fish, Coach Cheng, and I walked out the door at the end of the hallway, that it was in fact the exit to the building and we were standing at the south end of the parking lot.

"Am I supposed to do it in the dirt?" I asked.

"No, I think there is an outhouse over there," Comrade Fish said.

I looked at Coach Cheng, who, unlike Comrade Fish, had traveled to other countries—Italy, France, Thailand, Hong Kong, and Taiwan. He knew what this must have seemed like to me. He gave me an embarrassed, what-can-you-do smile and shrugged. I had always been fond of Coach Cheng. He was my kickboxing coach, after all, and a legitimately good guy. But at that moment I felt an intense love for him. That smile was the only recognizably human emotion I had encountered in this entire surreal trip. I clung to the memory of it as I walked across the uneven dirt, dodging the rubble, to the hospital's outhouse.

The state of the outhouse made the one in *Trainspotting* look like the Ritz-Carlton. I had expected that it would consist of a series of holes in the ground that you squatted over. I had even expected the stench from holes filled with excrement. What I did not expect was that every inch of the outhouse from the walls to the ceiling would be smeared in human filth.

In the kungfu movies, the adept has to go through a series of increasingly difficult tests, which are often quite bizarre. But I had never seen anything quite like this trial. I had been bedridden for three days. I was feverish and weak. My balance was off. I needed to pull down a pair of jogging pants, long johns, and tightie whities and then squat over one of the holes. There was nowhere to hang Coach Cheng's full-length jacket, so I had to cradle it in my left arm without letting it touch the floor. And with my right hand, I needed to place the glass tube underneath me and hit its thumbnail-size opening . . . without any splatter, because there was no toilet paper.

Somehow I managed to pass the test: My aim was true.

Standing up, I flipped the coat over my shoulder and used my left hand to pull up my underwear, long johns, and pants, while holding the test tube and its sample as far away from me as possible with my right.

The lab guy took the test tube from me with a smirk on his face. He directed us to sit on a bench outside the lab. We waited outside the lab for another hour as I dozed. Finally, the lab guy handed Comrade Fish a prescription before he went back into the lab and locked the door.

We walked over to the pharmacy.

The pharmacist handed me a set of pills.

They were the exact same licorice-ball diarrhea pills I had been taking before.

I just stood there in disbelief. This wasn't your average, every-day, say-five-Our-Fathers-and-call-back-at-Easter kind of penance. This was some serious old-school, Book of Job, wish-you-had-never-been-born retribution. At that moment, I gave up. I was too sick and too exhausted to fight anymore. I paid for the medicine, went back to Shaolin, and prepared for death.

But on the fifth day of my sojourn, God looked down, saw how bad it was, and finally relented.

I returned to training the next day.

7

ANOTHER AMERICAN

Ever my faithful spy, Little Tiger burst into my room one evening in June and delivered the words I'd been longing to hear. "*Bao Mosi*," he said. "There is an American here who has come to train for the summer."

As Little Tiger and I rushed to meet my fellow countryman, he gave me the new arrival's credentials, which was always the first information Chinese shared about strangers. His father was a wealthy businessman who owned several factories in China. The head of his father's China operations had delivered the son to the Wushu Center to smooth his path here. I was envious of his *guanxi*.

In one of the back offices in the main building, which doubled as an equipment room, I found a party in progress. There was a case of Tsingtao beer and a platter of food on the desk. The room was filled with young Chinese men—Coach Yan, Deqing, Cheng Hao, several other monks, and the American. He was ethnically Chinese, but he was a fully melted member of the American cultural stew: the baseball cap turned backward, the jeans slung low, the slouch hip-hop casual. Upon seeing me he called out in English.

"Yo, what's up? I heard there was another American up in this joint. It's good to meet you, bro. John Lee."

I introduced myself, grinning from ear to ear. The envy I felt in seeing he'd known before he'd even arrived what it had taken me months to figure out—that free booze and food is the key to the Chinese heart—was washed away in the sheer joy of having someone to exchange a hearty "Hey, bro" with. We clasped hands, and without thinking, completed the standard young American male handshake, shifting from hand to thumb to the tips of our fingers, which we snapped as we pulled our hands back. The monks stared at us.

"You want a brewski?" he asked.

"Sure, bro, absolutely."

The party went well into the night. And in between all of John and my *bro*ing and *man*ing and *dude*ing, the real show was the monks' curious, envious, prideful, resentful assessments of their Americanized cousin. It was like a display of "The Evolution of the Chinese Man" at the Museum of Natural History. To the left were the mainlanders, their bodies all sinew and bone and gristle, covered by a tight, stringy musculature. At the next stage was the Chinese-American, four inches taller with perfectly straight, white teeth and an easy, open expression. His weight-lifted, corn-fed, beef-eating muscles were thick and marbled, a filet mignon compared to the monks' rump steak. This was a flesh-and-blood demonstration of the prosperity effect. No wonder ambitious Chinese wanted to go to America. Who wouldn't want their children to be taller and stronger than they had been?

Of course, the body is one thing, the mind quite another. First-generation immigrants are cultural hybrids, and certain structural flaws are inevitable in the painful straddle between their parents' culture and that of their white friends. It didn't take many beers before John was telling me about his father.

By beer three, dad was still the great man who cast a long shadow. John said his family had been the second richest in Taiwan before the "Nationalist-Communist" Civil War cost them everything, which made me smile to myself because almost every single Taiwanese-American I had ever met had told me that their family used to be the second richest in Taiwan before the war. To rebuild the family's fortunes, John's father, an engineer by training, had come to America with nothing, built a successful company from scratch, and was now the patriarch of the Lee Manufacturing clan.

By beer six, the old man had morphed into a totalitarian somewhere between Stalin and Mao—an emotionally inaccessible man of unreasonable, impossible-to-fulfill standards. This made me smile to myself because it pretty much summed up the ideal Confucian father. John asked rhetorically if I could believe that his old man made his own flesh and blood fill out detailed monthly expense reports from college? Did I have any idea how hard it was to hide kegs of beer under school supplies month after month?

The truth was that John's father was like many successful Asian immigrants. He was educated, an engineer, so his move to America was a matter of choice, not desperation, and therefore represented the gamble of a lifetime, a bet that his and his family's life would be better in America than back in Taiwan. The problem for Taiwanese immigrants is that their birth-nation—perfectly positioned between huge consumer markets in the West, the technological savvy of Japan, and a huge pool of cheap labor in mainland China—refused to remain a backwater, which made keeping ahead of the Wangs that much more stressful. By the late eighties Taiwanese doctors, engineers, and businessmen were waking up across America to discover that their second-rate classmates who had never been smart or ambitious enough to emigrate were now extremely rich VPs of sales at Taiwanese microchip firms.

If John's father had been an economics professor from Bangladesh or a gastroenterologist from Zimbabwe, John's high school B- average, his preference for the weight room and the keg party to AP exams and SAT crash courses, and the easygoing second-child nature that had landed him at Rensselaer Polytechnic Institute (RPI) instead of Harvard or Yale might not have been such a family disgrace. It certainly didn't help that John had one of those nightmare older brothers, the kind all younger siblings of immigrants dread. Mark Lee was Harvard-squared: Crimson undergrad, Harvard Business School.

In such a family, John stuck out like a sore thumb, a sore thumb that was jammed into the eye of his father's American dream. So when his freshman grades at RPI had not improved from high school, he arrived home for summer break to find not a cushy job and plenty of free time to drink beer with friends and chase old flames, but a plane ticket to Beijing and a sentence of three months in Shaolin. His father had decided John needed discipline and believed the monks would give it to him. Shaolin also offered an excellent vantage point on the kind of poverty his family had been fleeing for generations.

After the party broke up, John and I went back to his room to finish off the rest of the beer. Drunk and furious at being banished to Shaolin, John was expressing his rage in a time-honored male fashion. He was punching holes in the closet door.

"Why am I treated like the bum of the family?" he said, punching his first hole in the wall.

"If I were white, my family would be proud of me!" he continued. Two holes.

"It's not like I'm a criminal or a drug addict!"
Three holes.

"What's so special about Harvard anyway?"
Four holes.

I felt I had to do something. We were both American expats in Shaolin, and he was younger than me and had arrived at Shaolin later, making him, by Shaolin's social-familial structure, my younger martial arts brother. It was my responsibility to look out for him, and he was like a big puppy. He didn't know his own strength. So I spent the rest of the evening showing him how to make the proper fist—wrist bent so you strike with the bottom three knuckles instead of the top two—to break plywood without injury.

Out of respect for John's family's wealth, Coach Yan decided to train his first *laowai* in several years. He started John with Shaolin's basic movements and Small Red Boxing. John did his best to go through the motions to keep his new master happy—Coach Yan was not someone you wanted to annoy—but his heart wasn't really in it. He didn't like forms. I sympathized. I had never liked them much either.

To keep John interested, I invited him to join my kickboxing teammates for an afternoon class. John was doing fine with the kicking and punching. The disaster arrived with the throws. We spent a great deal of time learning how to catch an opponent's kick and then throw or sweep him to the ground. Despite being only worth two points, the same as a kick to the chest, a successful throw has a disproportionate psychological affect on the judges. One fighter is standing and the other is flat on the canvas.

I showed John how to trap a side kick, telling him it was like catching a football. You lock it into your chest, hunch over, and clap your hands together. Next I picked out one of the less intense members of the team, so he would go easy on John. The first few catches went well. As a former football player, he already had the muscle memory for the motion. I watched him do it several times before turning away.

That's when I heard the snap of bone, followed by a guttural scream.

I turned to see John gripping his right hand, staring at an index finger suddenly pointing in a direction it was never intended to and alternating between hollering, "Fuck! Fuck! Fuck! My finger! Matt! My finger!" and "Fuck! My fucking finger! Fuck! My fucking finger! Fuck! Fuck! Fuck!"

John's fingers had been splayed and he'd misjudged the height of the kick—a common beginner's mistake. The kick had caught the top of his index finger and snapped it back.

Coach Yan rushed into the room. The nerve-rattling nature of John's cries—and the possible consequences of a permanently injured son of a powerful Chinese-American entrepreneur—helped Coach Yan and me secure Leader Liu's car in slightly less than thirty minutes of cajoling, needling, and negotiating. Warp-speed by Chinese Communist standards.

Coach Yan and I both had our arms around John in the backseat. Comrade Fish was riding shotgun and Leader Liu's driver was racing down the mountain road toward Deng Feng's hellhole of a hospital.

When we arrived, Comrade Fish pulled me aside.

"Tell him not to curse in English," he said.

"Why?"

"If they find out he's American, they will charge him more."

I turned to John. "Bro, could you try to curse in Chinese? Just repeat, *ta made*," I said. "His mother."

He complied.

The head nurse motioned us to sit down on some chairs and then walked away, leaving us there to wait. For what, I don't know. There were no other patients. As I'd discovered with my dysentery treatment, the Deng Feng hospital was a place you visited only if you didn't want life.

By the second hour of being ignored, John was getting desperate, begging me to do something. It was time for Crazy Foreigner Kungfu.

I have to give the nurse credit. She was a tougher nut to crack than the merchant had been. First, I physically blocked her passage, "My friend is in severe pain, but you do nothing. You must help him."

"I'm busy. Move out of my way."

Having failed to impress her, I decided to give my insanity a little local color, cursing her in Henan slang instead of Mandarin.

"*Nong sha le ni. Wo nosi ni,*" I snarled. "What the hell is the matter with you? I should strangle you to death."

"Who do you think you are?" she shot back.

I backed her into a corner and towered over her. "Who am I? Who are you? You listen to his cries and still do nothing. You're not even human."

"How dare you speak to me like that!"

I punched the wall. "In a second, I won't be using words, I'll be using my fists to talk to you."

I went over to the cage where the pharmacy was located. I grabbed the bars, jumped up like a monkey, and rattled the cage. "If you don't fix my little martial arts brother's hand, I'll tear down this shithole!"

Just as I was reaching the limits of my Crazy Foreigner Kungfu skills, she finally agreed to treat John.

I should have known it was a ploy. Along with paper and gunpowder, the Chinese invented passive-aggressive revenge.

In the X-ray room, she instructed me to hold John's hand open. She pulled the ceiling-mounted, potato-gun-looking X-ray machine back at a wide angle and started firing away. It was not until the moment before she snapped the first shot that John and I both realized at roughly the same moment that she had "forgotten" to give us a lead shield. "Protect the jewels," I cried. As we twisted our waists away, John and I each clasped our free hand over our groins in a futile attempt to protect our reproductive capabilities from a direct exposure of radiation.

Afterward, the nurse led us to the operating room, which looked like a primitive torture chamber. The operating table was a metal rack with leather straps, the scalpels and knives were dirty, and the floor was uneven concrete with puddles and piles of dirt just like in the lobby.

The nurse promised to deliver the X-rays promptly. Instead, she walked out of the hospital and went home for the day. I doubt there was even any film in the machine.

A Chinese man dressed like a taxi driver walked into the room. He had a scruffy white silk shirt, brown slacks, white silk socks, and brown leather shoes. There was peach fuzz on his face, his hair was unkempt, and there was dirt under his fingernails. I figured him for another patient who had gotten bored waiting. It didn't surprise me when he showed an interest in John's injury. The Chinese are a curious people, which is a polite way of saying they are a little hazy on the concepts of personal space and privacy.

I was surprised, however, that he was smoking. He nonchalantly puffed away on a Marlboro as he leaned over to get a closer look at John's injury. It was the sight of him blowing smoke directly into the wound that made me snap. I no longer had to pretend in order to be the Crazy Foreigner.

First I jerked him back by his collar. Then I knocked the cigarette out of his mouth. I followed this by grabbing him by the front of his shirt and jacking him up against a wall. And finally I asked him, "Who the hell do you think you are?"

"I think I am the doctor," he said.

"Oh right, sorry. So sorry. How embarrassing," I said, letting go of his shirt.

As I tried to smooth out the wrinkles, I said, "Would it be too much trouble to ask you not to smoke?"

I don't know if he was used to getting jacked up against a wall by patients' friends or if he was simply a man possessed of an incredibly even temperament, but he was not fazed in the slightest. He nodded with this slight smile on his face, went back over to John, pulled up a chair, and went to work.

It turned out that it wasn't a fracture but a compound dislocation. The bones had been separated at the second joint. The doctor grabbed each end, pulled them apart and put them back together. After one brief scream, John went quiet for the first time since the accident happened. Things were looking up, until the doctor went to sew up John's finger.

When you are the son of an orthopedic surgeon, you pick up a certain amount of medical knowledge as you are growing up, like the fact that needles should never be reused and if you have to reuse one it probably shouldn't be rusty. You also know how small they should be. So I was more than a little disturbed when the doctor reached into a glass filled with dirty water and pulled out a needle the size of a deep-sea fishing hook with rust marks visible from a distance of five feet. I was even more disturbed to see that the string he was going to use was as thick as twine. But what pushed me over the edge was that it appeared that he planned to sew up a wound that needed fifteen stitches minimum in five or less. This was going to be a hack job worthy of a Civil War–reenactment Oscar.

I broke out in a sweat. This was all my fault. I had invited John to spar with the team. As the self-recriminations clouded my mind, the room started spinning. The next thing I was aware of was Coach Yan's thumb digging into the space between my upper lip and my nose. (The Chinese believe there is a qi meridian—a nerve center, in Western medical terminology—at this point and that pressing against it can revive someone who has passed out.) This realization, along with the fact that I was staring up at the ceiling and the back of my shirt was soaked from one of the puddles on the floor, were my first clues that I had fainted.

"You need any help?" the hack doctor asked me, mid-stitch.

"Hey, buddy, I'm supposed to be the one hurt here," John said.

"Sorry," I said, as Coach Yan led me out of the room.

I wasn't able to save John from a permanent scar, but I was able to save his reputation. As soon as the monks heard I'd passed out when I wasn't even the one injured, they stopped talking about John's lack of stoicism in response to his injury and went on nonstop about me. They had never heard of anything like it. They were so inured to human suffering that the idea anyone could be so sensitive was incomprehensible. Afterward, anytime one of them complimented me by saying something like "the *laowai* is not afraid to eat bitter" or "his kickboxing is pretty good," a different monk would always add in response, "Yeah, but he fainted at the sight of someone else's blood."

BOOK FIVE

DISCIPLE

July–September 1993

酒色祸之媒。

"Wine and lust are the agents of disaster."

—TRADITIONAL CHINESE PROVERB

1

CHALLENGE MATCH

C oach Yan clapped his hands and stepped back.
I stared at Master Wu, my body tense with anticipation.
But Master Wu didn't move. As we both waited, the pressure mounted. It was a vacuum of action, and I felt myself sucked forward.

I attacked with a front left side kick—the kick I had practiced 10,000 times, or something close to it. But fear had pushed my mind into the rafters. My left foot fluttered out like a dying quail. My kick was more a toe-tickle than the thunderbolt I had intended.

Master Wu caught my foot easily. But instead of pulling my leg down and toward him, in order to spin me to the ground, he lifted my leg high above his head, intending to make me trip backward. But I had the height advantage and, through hours of extremely painful training, had become fairly flexible. He could not get my left leg up high enough to tip me over and, hopping on my right leg, I was able to pull free.

My brain was lost in a thick fog of fear and adrenaline. The front side kick was my best technique, and it had failed. After a dozen seconds bouncing on my toes, I scratched it off my mental list and went to my second most practiced technique: my right thrust kick.

If anything, this kick was even slower than the side kick and easier for Master Wu to catch. Luckily for me, he did not change his pattern. After he caught it, he tried to lift my leg above my head as he did before. And I was able, as before, to pull it free without falling down.

I was already running out of workable techniques. I felt as if I were about to give up. But then something remarkable happened. Time slowed. Or rather, my perception sped up. As I stood there, my previous two attacks looped in my mind's eye like instant replay. Both times as I had lifted my leg to kick, he had gazed down to my feet and lowered his hands in anticipation of trapping my leg. I suddenly saw the flaw in his defense and knew how to exploit it.

I took a jump step at Master Wu, initiating a side kick. I slid my right foot up to my front left foot. I raised my left foot into the air. Master Wu dropped his eyes and his hands. But instead of kicking again, I planted my left foot back on the ground, and then torqued my entire body off that single point, twisting around as I threw a wild overhead hook—a haymaker—with my right fist. In fact the entire motion must have looked less like a kungfu or boxing punch and more like a baseball pitcher winding up and then hurling a fastball.

Still focused on my left foot, Master Wu didn't see it coming.

As the punch connected, his eyes widened in surprise.

I hadn't practiced the motion 10,000 times. I'd never even thrown a punch like that before. I have no idea where it came from. And I doubt Master Wu had ever seen such an attack.

I danced back away from him.

When I had watched boxing bouts, I used to think that the sole reason for breaks between rounds was to allow fighters to rest their bodies. What I hadn't realized is that fighters need that time to reassess their strategies and refine their tactics. After the pain and punishment starts, the adrenaline pumps, emotion flares, and self-awareness is eliminated. In that state the mind freezes up, dooming a fighter to repeat the same mistake over and over again.

I jumped forward and lifted my left leg. Master Wu's gaze dropped down again. Once more I planted my left foot instead of attacking with it and pitched another haymaker, hitting his unprotected face with all the force I could muster.

I floated back, waited a moment, and then jumped forward again.

Wash, rinse, repeat.

Master Wu and I were locked into the same dance steps. I kept raising my leg and pitching that haymaker and he kept looking down at my left foot, each time forgetting that a punch was coming. The same sequence probably recurred six or seven times. I lost count. I lost myself. In my head the fight was happening in slow motion. As if a strobe light were flashing, I saw my fist busting his lip, then bloodying his nose, then sending his glasses sprawling across the room. I remember moving back and forth. I remember the shock through my body, the charge of electricity as my fist hit his face again and again, exactly the same technique with exactly the same result. After each blow he staggered back, bloodied. But he would not go down.

Coach Yan's directive broke through the fog.

Down to the ground!

As the blood ran down Master Wu's face I began to wonder why he wouldn't go down. As I moved in to hit him again, a word from my training repeated itself in my head. *Combinations.* Coach Cheng was always talking about combinations. Don't rely on one lucky punch or kick. Combine them. Pile them up. Stack one on top of the other until the weight of the collective blows brings your opponent down.

After another successful punch, I stayed inside his range instead of dancing back, negating my arm-length advantage and risking his greater strength and size. I hooked with a left to his gut, another right to the head. I roundhouse kicked him in the leg. I punched him in the head again with another right. We got tangled up. Out of my line of vision, the flat of his fist slammed against the right side of my head, pinballing my brain around the inside of my skull.

I took two halting steps back out of his reach.

We stood facing each other. My head ached, and my legs were wobbly. Blood was now streaming down Wu's face from his nose and mouth.

Master Wu raised both his hands.

He quit. He'd had enough. The Chinese kungfu master from Tianjin had surrendered to the *laowai* with the wild right.

I turned away. There was no elation. Instead I felt lost. I paced back and forth, trying to figure out where I was. Why was I surrounded by a bunch of Chinese peasants, their faces flush with emotion, shouting unintelligible words at me. Who were these people? What was I doing here?

Then I heard Master Wu arguing with Coach Yan.

"The *laowai* cheated. We agreed no punches to the face. I wear glasses. He's *pianzi*," Wu said. "A cheater."

Before China I had always bottled my rage. I'd been angry before but had almost always controlled it. But at that moment I snapped.

I began screaming at him. A string of curses flowed out of me involving what I had done to various members of his family, what I still intended to do to him, and what I was going to do after that to his corpse. It was a barrage.

It was also all in English.

"What did he say?" Master Wu asked Coach Yan in Chinese.

"Oh, you understand me, motherfucker!" I continued in English, unable to stop myself.

I then drew an imaginary line in front of me with my foot and dared him to step across it.

I was completely out of control. With each curse, I stepped closer to Master Wu, jabbing my finger in his direction. Before I was within attack range, he threw up his hands again and turned his back to me and walked over to his students.

I continued to follow him, taunting him to turn and fight so I could have another chance to put him down on the ground. Deqing grabbed me from behind.

"That's enough, *Bao Mosi*," he said. "It's over."

I just stared at Deqing, uncomprehending. He smiled and brought me back.

Deqing did not let me go until he'd steered me into the restaurant where he ordered a bottle of *baijiu* for the table of monks and expats who had followed us. The adrenaline letdown was so intense I couldn't force my hands to stop shaking. I spilled my first shot.

"To *Bao Mosi*," Deqing toasted. "The American who defended Shaolin's honor!"

One of the younger monks stood up, "To Lao Bao, bottoms up!"

"Lao Bao!" the monks repeated.

Lao means "old" or "elder" and is an honorific in China. Lao Bao is also a historical reference. It was the nickname of Bao Gong, a twelfth-century Chinese prime minister who was famous for being extremely brilliant and extremely ugly. Looking at myself from their perspective—big-nosed, ghost-eyed, college-educated—it was a pretty accurate allusion. After the challenge match, Lao Bao became my nickname with the monks, especially the younger ones.

There was one person who did not join the toast. Coach Yan came over to sit beside me.

"Why are you celebrating?" he demanded.

"What do you mean?" I asked, confused.

"I told you to beat him to the ground. At the end of the fight, was he not still standing? Next time, when I tell you to knock someone down, do it!"

Coach Yan finished my shot and walked away.

Deqing poured me another.

"Don't listen to him," he said. "Sometimes his disposition is not so good."

But even Coach Yan's disappointment could not temper my elation. For the rest of the night, I was the toast of Shaolin. I had fought a challenge match and defended Shaolin's honor. As far as anyone there knew, it was the first time a *laowai* had ever done that. And as far as I know, the last time as well.

The next day, I dragged my achy hungover body out of bed, washed out the abrasions on my right knuckles, and, having already missed breakfast, made my way to morning *sanda* class. My teammates were already in a line when I arrived. I slid in next to Baotong, head down.

"*Nong shale ni?*" Coach Cheng asked me in Henan slang. "What the hell are you doing?"

"Sorry, master. I'm late."

"You fought for Shaolin last night," Coach Cheng said, suddenly smiling. "Today you should take the day for yourself, Lao Bao."

My teammates slapped me on the back as I left class.

I spent the day in a restful, dreamless sleep.

That night I demonstrated to Pierre, the tightly wound French photojournalist, Deqing, and John the joys of my favorite computer strategy game, *Civilization II*. I had brought my Mac Powerbook to Shaolin after the winter break to try to do some writing, but instead found myself playing *Civilization* with most of my free time. The game is like crank for nerds with Napoleonic complexes. You start at the beginning of civilized history controlling one tribe and progress to the present day by mastering technological advances and conquering everyone else on the planet. After a night of extreme physical danger and a day of a severe hangover, there was great comfort in escaping into a virtual battle.

"This is nothing like a real war," Pierre said. "This is like your Gulf War, cruise missiles and video screens. Have I shown you my photos from Serbia? That was a real war."

"Yeah, you did," I lied. "But you haven't shown Deqing. Why don't you take him back to your room, so he can see them."

"Will you ask Deqing in Chinese for me?" Pierre asked.

"The French guy wants to show you some of his war photos in his room," I said to Deqing in Chinese. "Could you help me out and smile and be nice to him, so he doesn't want to come back?"

Thirty minutes later, I was in the process of transporting King Abraham Lincoln's cannons and knights across the Bering Strait (circa 800 A.D.) to launch my meticulously planned invasion of Asia, when Pierre came crashing into my room in a complete panic. It took him several moments before he could speak.

"What is it?" I asked.

"The monk, he is gay!" Pierre cried out.

"Who?" John asked. "Deqing?"

"Yes, Deqing, he wants to fuck me in my ass."

"No, no, no," John said, starting to laugh.

"Oh yes, yes, he is touching me, my back, rubbing. He wants my ass! What am I to do? A gay monk wants to fuck my ass. A kungfu master. How can I stop him? He has knowledge of ancient fighting arts."

"He was just being friendly," John answered.

"Yes, I'm sure he was just being friendly," I said, catching John's eye. "You're not his type."

"Not his type?"

"You're way too old. And too big, too broad in the shoulders," I continued, biting the inside of my cheek.

John caught on, "Yeah, Deqing likes them young and skinny. Like Matt."

He flashed a grin at me.

Turtle's egg.

"Like you?" Pierre asked.

"Well, it's all part of the martial tradition," I explained. "Young disciples and all. Like the Spartans. It didn't hurt nearly as much as I expected."

Pierre was edging his way to the door. "Everyone is crazy here. You are all assfuckers. I am flying this coop."

"Hey, hey, Pierre, where you gonna go at this hour?" I asked.

"Yeah," John said, "There's no buses at this time of night."

"No cabs either," I added.

"He could walk the highway."

"True," I said. "But that'd take three hours just to get to Deng Feng. And there are no streetlights. One false step. Splat! Right off the side of Song Mountain."

"Besides, Deqing has a motorcycle," John said. "Well, it's Coach Yan's, but I'm sure he'd let Deqing borrow it if one of his white boys was trying to get away."

"You see! You see!" Pierre cried. "He wants to fuck my ass."

"No, I doubt it," I said. "He was grabbing your shoulder, slapping your back, you said? See, that's just him being friendly. He didn't rub your head, did he?"

Pierre turned ashen, unable to speak.

"Oh, he did. Well, you are in trouble then. He's taken a liking to you."

"Ask Matt," John said. "He should know."

"I guess you could try hiding in one of the other rooms," I said.

"Yeah, but Deqing is friends with the key girl," John said. "It won't take him too much time to search twenty rooms."

"True, true. Well, Pierre, you can always stay with me, if you want. Deqing will leave you alone if he knows you've become *my* disciple."

"You dirty sick!"

"No, Pierre, please don't talk like that. That's hateful talk. I'm trying to do what's best for you. I'll be very gentle."

There might be a more enjoyable way to spend an evening than winding up a temperamental Frenchman in the middle of a gay panic attack, but I've never had one. Finally the fun was too much and it burst over the dam of our self-control in the form of paroxysms of laughter.

Pierre stood there trembling for a minute before he realized that we had been putting him on.

"He is not gay?" he asked, finally.

I explained it was customary for men in rural China to be physically friendly and that it didn't mean anything.

It took many more minutes of apologizing before he stopped cursing us, our mothers, and everyone in our families.

As if to mock my failure to end my celibate status, it took John less than a month to score himself a girlfriend. One Saturday, he was off to Zheng Zhou. By Sunday morning he was practically hitched.

"Her name is Yeli," John said. "She's a dancer."

"So you're saying she's hot."

"She's *so* hot."

"That's great, you bastard."

"I want to invite her to Shaolin, but she doesn't want to come alone. She has this friend . . ."

"John, Shaolin is very conservative. I could get arrested."

"We'll get them their own room. It's not prostitution until after midnight."

"It's not a good idea."

"Matt, she's a *dancer*," John said.

"I'll think about it."

I consulted with Deqing that night.

"John's new girlfriend is a dancer in Zheng Zhou," I told him.

"She must belong to Henan's dance *danwei*," he said.

The *danwei*, or work unit, was one of the basic organizational structures of Chinese society. It provided employment, free housing, schooling, and health care. In return it monitored for antiparty sentiment and controlled every other aspect of the workers' lives. If they wanted to change apartments or jobs or move to another city or travel abroad or marry or divorce, the leader of the *danwei* had to approve. The Chinese often called themselves *danwei* people.

"But what does the dance *danwei* do?" I asked.

"They perform traditional Chinese dances at festivals and public events."

"So they are like the monks."

He thought for a moment before saying, "You know Chinese VIPs, leaders, they like to dance, right? Sometimes, when they have a party, they need partners. So the dance *danwei* sends some of the pretty girls to dance with them. These men are old and powerful . . . you understand?"

I did. I went back to John and told him to invite the girls immediately.

Because John's date, Yeli, and mine, Miling, arrived in dresses that were a little too garish for the countryside and, unlike rural women, wearing makeup, it took only seconds for the waitresses at the Wushu Center restaurant to clock our guests as tarts and spread the rumor that a couple of prostitutes had landed at the Wushu Center to take care of the Americans. The manager of the hotel was snickering by the time John got around to arranging a "separate" room for them.

"Do you want the extra key?" he asked John.

The damage already done, there was nothing to do but go forward.

Besides, John and Yeli made a beeline for his room. As soon as Miling entered my room, she lay down on my bed without any preamble. I swallowed my surprise and awkwardly slid next to her for a smooth approach landing.

As I leaned in closer, she pulled back. There was something on her mind, a question.

"Is it true that Americans are very *kaifang*?" she asked. "Open."

"Some are," I said, knowing from her tone that she was referring to sexual, not political, openness. "Why do you ask?"

"Do you . . ." she paused. "Do you have AIDS?"

The Chinese government was terribly afraid of an AIDS outbreak at the time. News reports were filled with stories about the AIDS epidemic in America. Pools in big cities were segregated out of fear of contamination. To get a yearlong visa, Americans had to take AIDS tests to prove they were HIV-negative. For someone as paranoid as me, it was not a pleasant experience.

Being the only *laowai* within a thousand miles was never easy. This issue was just the most extreme way China made me feel less than fully human. I'd like to say that I understood it wasn't Miling's fault—her question a result of political propaganda, not personal prejudice. But the Beijing government was far away, and she was oh-so near. Plus, I was feeling pretty full of myself after the challenge match.

So I deadpanned, "Why, yes, as a matter of fact, I do."

She pulled back in terror, which offended me further.

She actually believed me!

So I continued, "But I only have a little bit of AIDS. It's not the kind that kills you, just makes you tired. But not to worry, you probably will not be infected."

Then, to my great regret, I laughed in her face.

As soon as Miling realized I was mocking her, her horror transformed into rage, and like a gunshot, she was up and off the bed, out of the room, and over to John's room where she stayed just long enough to tell Yeli what a damn turtle's egg I was. It was a sentiment shared by John, who had been interrupted in flagrante delicto. His mood was not improved by the fact that the dancers decided to return back to Zheng Zhou that night.

"Why did you have to be such an asshole?" John asked me after they left.

"That's easy for you to ask. You're Chinese," I said. "You try spending a year living in a country that treats you like a Ugandan street prostitute."

But John was right. I had been an asshole, and, worse, I had violated the first commandment of the wingman: Thou Shalt Not Mess Up Thy Main Man's Play. So I apologized. But it bothered me to do it. I was Lao Bao, defender of Shaolin's honor. Why did I still have to roll as wingman, damn it? I should have let it go, but I couldn't.

"Hell, we're probably better off," I said. "We might have gotten arrested, and those girls weren't worth it."

"Matt, I love her," John said with suddenly naked emotion.

"Shit, John, they're basically call girls!" I said, before thinking about it.

Seeing his hurt reaction, I immediately apologized. He didn't say anything. It took many apologies and many days before he finally forgave me.

Later, Coach Yan told me that one of the new coaches at the Wushu Center, a slimeball named Baoping, had wanted to call the police to have us fined, so he could collect a finder's fee. Coach Yan had stopped Baoping by yanking the phone out of his hand and threatening him with severe bodily harm.

"Don't invite them back to Shaolin," Coach Yan concluded.

2

MISTRESS MANAGEMENT

I met Yunfei one spring day while training. He was the son of two professors. His folks had been purged during the Cultural Revolution, which had turned Yunfei off to the idea of a university education. He'd decided to become a student of life and had left home to wander China after high school. He'd ended up at Shaolin and specialized in *sanda*, realizing as I did that it was the only martial arts discipline that someone starting so late in life could master in a reasonable amount of time. Soon after I joined the *sanda* team we became fast friends.

He was also that most dangerous and irresistible type of man for women: the commitment-phobic romantic. He was forever falling in love with another beautiful young woman, having a short torrid affair, and then breaking it off, because he did not "have the money to support a wife" due to his nomadic existence. I thought that was putting the cart before the horse. He led a nomadic life so he would have a good excuse to avoid settling down and marrying. But I didn't have the heart to tell him.

The day Yunfei met me it was the first week of his most recent return to the temple. He had been away from Shaolin for a year for reasons involving a woman as well as some vague business opportunities, returning when both turned sour. Within days he had scoped out the ten or so beautiful young women hidden around Shaolin. Living in a straw hut across the Shaolin stream were two sisters whose father, a kungfu fanatic, had sent them to Shaolin for two years of training. There was the diva-ish *wushu* instructor at

the Shaolin Kungfu Academy. Taguo had a tomboyish *sanda* practitioner who had started filling out her chest pads.

Yunfei was in the courtyard outside the gates of the Shaolin
Temple with a group of teenage girls from Deng Feng, and I, having
glued my wingman self to his side for the past month, was there as
well. The young women wanted a tour. Yunfei considered himself
Shaolin's official tour guide for attractive young women, so he
agreed to show them around. Of the group of five or so, one had
my attention—Jewel. She was the first young woman I'd met in
Shaolin who looked at me with even a flicker of genuine interest.

As we walked back to the bus that traveled between Shaolin and
the nearby city of Deng Feng, Jewel and I fell behind the rest of the
group. I screwed up my few slivers of courage and asked, "Would
you like to have dinner with me?"

Jewel was pleased but played coy.

"I don't know," she said. "What will people say?"

"I know the owner of a restaurant at the far end of the village,"
I said. "We can meet for a late dinner, say ten P.M., when the rest of
the village is asleep. Then no one will see us together."

She was relieved that I understood what was at stake for her.

"Next Friday," she said out of the corner of her mouth as she
turned to go.

That Friday I arrived at the restaurant early and ordered a half-
jar of *baijiu*. My conscience had been working on me all week—my
interest in Jewel was purely functional—and I knew I'd need some
Dutch courage to quell the internal debate. I had paid up-front and
extra for the meal to ensure the owner/cook avoided saying anything inappropriate. She arrived fifteen minutes late and extremely
nervous. After some furtive glances and attempts at small talk, she
hit me over the head with this question: "If a foreigner promised a
Chinese woman he would come back to see her again, would he?
Or was he lying?"

"It depends on the *laowai*," I said, playing for time. "Why do
you ask?"

"There was a German TV crew here filming the monks last year.
One of the cameramen promised he'd come back to see me."

As part of the peace settlement with my conscience, I had

promised myself I wouldn't make false promises or lie to Jewel to get her into bed. "A year ago?" I asked. "He's not coming back."

It was the right answer. She relaxed, deciding she could trust me.

"So you live in Deng Feng?" I asked.

"Yes, with my father."

"Ah, how is that?"

"It's difficult. He is a difficult man. He doesn't understand me." *Amituofo*.

I waved the chef over. This was going to take more *baijiu* than I had anticipated.

The streets were deserted and the lights off in most of the dorm rooms as we walked back to the Wushu Center, but we did not speak and she followed a step behind me as if we were strangers.

I led her around to the back of the hotel. When the manager went to sleep, he locked the front doors from the inside with a bike lock—fire safety wasn't a big priority—and closed all the windows except for the one to the indoor outhouse, which was such a foul, holes-in-the-ground job that it needed to be aired out constantly. I climbed inside and then helped Jewel through the window. I have to say that carrying her across the bathroom while holding my breath and carefully stepping to avoid falling into any of the holes took a great deal of the romance out of the illicit affair.

Once inside my room, she turned her back and undressed without saying a word. When she was done, she slipped under the covers. I followed.

I won't go into the graphic details here, but my first thought upon officially ending my self-imposed celibacy was: *No wonder she asked about the German coming back—that sneaky Hun got here first*. This was followed just moments later by a second thought: *Oh no, not yet!*

Without a word, she rolled over and immediately fell asleep, out of boredom, I presume. I knew I had to stay awake. She needed to be out of the hotel before dawn broke and the village roused itself, and I didn't want to take the risk of not hearing my alarm. I needed to think dark, irritating thoughts, the kind that keep a man awake at night. Fortunately, that was easy for me.

THINGS THAT ARE WRONG WITH MATT

1) Bad in Bed?

I had to see her again. It was a question of patriotic pride. I was very likely holding in my arms Henan Province's first G-8 groupie. (With Germany and America already under her precious belt, could Canada, England, France, Italy, Russia, and Japan be far behind?) It's bad enough that my fellow citizens rank last in international math and science testing, but now I had given evidence that we were rotten lovers as well. What if she told her friends and they told their friends? How long before Chinese women were saying to *laowai*, "Your Chinese might not be as good as the Canadian Dashan's, but your lovemaking skills are much better than the American Lao Bao's."

At 4:30 A.M., as I lifted her out of a first-floor window, I asked, "Will you see me again?"

"I don't know," she said. "It is risky."

"We can go to Zheng Zhou," I said. During the evening, I had developed the hypothesis that perhaps the danger of the situation had caused my premature excitement. Zheng Zhou was safer than Shaolin.

"Okay," she agreed.

"We can take separate buses and meet in front of the big department store in Zheng Zhou's shopping district."

"Next Sunday, two P.M."

As before, I was early, and Jewel was late. As I waited in front of the department store I thought about the story I had been told about the man who built it—Zheng Zhou's first millionaire. It was in the mid-eighties, and the amount of money he made was shocking to everyone. The province's envious political leaders instituted a kind of informal taxation policy on him. When the city needed a new airport, they went to his office and asked him to pay for it. They did the same when they needed a new highway to connect the city to the airport. Same for a new water tower. Now, this businessman was, as most successful businessmen are, a prideful man. He didn't like the way the politicos were bleeding him, acting like it was their money, not his. So finally one day, when they asked him to pay for one project too many, he not only refused, he threw them out of his office. His friends pleaded with him to change his mind, but he wouldn't budge.

Being good Maoists—"All political power comes from the barrel of a gun" is one of Mao's more famous sayings—the leaders sent in the police to arrest him, seized all his assets, and sold his department store to another businessman who was more accommodating. That is socialism with Chinese characteristics.

When Jewel finally arrived, we went up to the fourth floor so that I could buy a new suitcase I needed. The salesgirl was thrilled to help me, until she saw I had come with a Chinese date, whereupon she immediately disappeared with a look of disgust and did not return. In her place we acquired an audience of young male peasants. They gathered a respectful distance away to stare at the *laowai* and his Chinese date. They did not seem shocked or appalled or even particularly interested. In fact there was little sign of any sentience. They just stood there completely still and stared, every minute making me more and more self-conscious of the social transgression we represented.

I tried to console myself with bitter thoughts. *No wonder Chinese-Americans' average SAT scores are higher than white Americans. They left their stupid cousins behind.*

This didn't help. Soon I felt resentful and guilty.

When I couldn't take it anymore, I shooed them away. "What are you looking at? Go on, get out of here! Go on, look at someone else!"

They were like the oxen they used to work the land: They blinked at me several times as if they couldn't understand what I was saying, or why I was waving my hand at them. For a moment, I thought I'd have to slap them on the hindquarters to get them to leave us alone. Finally, they turned and left. I grabbed a manager and held on to his arm with a tight grip until the luggage purchase was complete.

"Are you ready to go?" I asked.

"I'd like to look around."

She led me over to the section where they sold the foreign purses: Gucci, Prada, etc. She examined several of them.

"What do you think?" she asked me.

Their prices ranged between $500 and $1,000.

"I think they're awfully expensive."

As she stared at them, I kept wondering how she had come up with the equivalent of a Chinese farmer's annual salary to spend on a purse. It did not occur to me—during the thirty minutes she spent staring longingly at those purses; nor when she reluctantly left the counter; nor when I asked her if she wanted to go to a hotel and she turned me down, saying that she needed to return home; nor during the three-hour bus ride to Deng Feng when she did not speak a word to me; nor when she did not respond to my request that she have dinner with me next weekend; nor during the next three weeks when I didn't hear from her; nor when she did finally find me on the street one afternoon and wanted to see me for lunch the next day and I suggested dinner instead but she insisted on lunch; nor when she sat down to lunch and I asked her what she wanted to eat and she told me that she needed to borrow 100RMB ($12); nor when I asked, moron that I am, if this was a loan or a gift—no, it did not occur to me until she put the money in her handmade cloth purse, stood up, and walked out the door of the restaurant that she had expected me to buy her one of those damn luxury purses. And because insights tend to arrive in bunches, this first revelation was quickly followed by the certainty that having proven myself so inadequate in the realm of mistress-management, I would never see her again.

I didn't.

Yunfei came to my room on a Sunday to ask if I wanted to visit Little Mei, the young woman he was courting at the moment.

"Isn't she training with her master up in the mountains?" I asked.

"It's not a very long walk."

"How long?"

"Couple hours."

"Yunfei, it's only a couple of weeks until the Zheng Zhou tournament, and you know Sunday is my only day to rest."

"I want to show you her master's style of kungfu. It is a fascinating mix of tai chi and Shaolin style."

"You want me to come along so your real reason for going is not as obvious."

Yunfei smiled. "You won't help out a friend? Friendship is very important. China has a proverb, 'One chopstick is easily broken, but a dozen can hardly be bent.'"

"The only thing you are going to break is that poor girl's heart."

"Lao Bao, how can you say that? I like this one."

"You like them all at first."

"Have you ever been up in the mountains?"

"No."

"Then you should come. It's beautiful."

"You're not going to leave me alone until I come with you, are you?"

"Probably not."

We walked west past the Shaolin Temple, past the Pagoda Forest. When we ran out of road, we turned onto a dirt path that led us up into the mountains. After a thousand-foot climb, the trail wound around the tops of the various peaks.

We had walked for about an hour when we turned a corner and ran smack dab into a mini-village. A dozen old women sat on stumps around an iron kettle over an open fire. Scattered around the women were twenty or so earthen huts with thatched roofs. A donkey was tied to a tree. The place took my breath away. It could have been a millennium ago. There wasn't a single sign of the twentieth century anywhere in the village. This was what rural China must have looked like to Marco Polo.

But the most amazing thing was that not one of the women turned to look at me. I had gotten pretty good at measuring how far into the boondocks I'd traveled by gauging the size of response I caused. The farther out I went the more people pointed and stared. But here I had finally found a place so isolated that the Chinese

were either incapable or too frightened to acknowledge my existence. Yunfei and I walked along the path barely twenty feet from
them, and I might as well have been a *yang guizi* (Western ghost).

When we were past the village, I said to Yunfei, "That was weird.
They didn't even look at me."

"It was strange," he agreed. "They didn't look at me, either."

"You're not their type."

"I'm every woman's type."

"At first."

Little Mei tried hard not to show how pleased she was to see Yunfei.
She was a delight—beautiful, sweet, and smart. Yunfei had impec-
cable taste in women. She was one of the sisters whose father had
sent her to Shaolin after she had finished high school to train. Ini-
tially, she had been at one of the schools in the village, but her father had heard about this old master in the mountain and sent her
here. She clearly was lonely in the mountains.

Yunfei hailed her coach, "Master Tung, I brought a *laowai* who
wants to examine your style of kungfu."

Master Tung, a rugged man with the physical vitality and size of
a Midwestern farmer, came out of his brick-and-tile house. It was
much larger than a typical one, and he looked prosperous. He must
have done something else for money besides farming, because
there wasn't much arable land in the mountains. He invited us inside.

After an unappetizing lunch of cooked Chinese Spam, Master
Tung had Little Mei give a demonstration of his style.

"I have developed a variation on Shaolin," he explained. "It re-
lies more on generating internal power than external strength,
making it useful for women."

Little Mei got into a horse stance, which made her look like she
was sitting on an invisible chair, and started punching. But the
punches were slow and not straight. She twisted her arms around
in a corkscrew motion. I tried to look interested, but I felt sorry for
her. Internal styles work, but they take years and years before they
are effective. I couldn't imagine her lasting that long.

Sensing I wasn't impressed, Master Tung asked, "Would you like me to demonstrate?"

"Oh no, master, please," I said. "That's not necessary. I can see the power in Little Mei's punches."

"Her technique is no good. You study kickboxing, right? Let me show you the power of the punch."

"Oh, no, no, please. It's okay," I said as I backpedaled across the yard.

It was a sufficient display of humility.

"Okay," he said. "But I do want to show you how I practice."

"All right."

He went to his shed and pulled out a hoe. We walked over to a garden about the size of a backyard swimming pool.

"I've planted sweet potatoes," he said.

He walked into the middle of the field and brought down his hoe three times. With the first he uncovered a potato. With the second he cut the root. With the third he pulled the potato out of the ground and flipped it to me.

Holding out his hoe, he said, "Here, you try."

I grabbed the hoe with confidence. How hard could this be? It took me five strokes to uncover a potato. I missed the root three times, slicing open the potato instead. It took three more strikes to sever the root and I had to bend over and pull the potato out of the ground with my hands, because my attempts to remove it with the hoe had further mashed it. By the time I'd finished, Master Tung and Yunfei were rolling with laughter.

"I just need practice," I said.

I was in the best shape of my life. I had trained seven hours a day for a year. I lasted five whole minutes before I was bent over panting for breath, the muscles in my back spasming.

"It's harder than it looks," Master Tung said, taking back the hoe and ending my lesson.

"You should pick a master and become a Shaolin disciple," Yunfei told me one day.

"Coach Cheng is my master," I replied.

"He's your coach. But he's not a monk anymore. You should pick a monk out of the temple and *bai tade weishi*," he said. "Become his disciple."

"How do I do that?"

"There is a formal ceremony."

"Who should I pick?"

"My master is Senior Monk Yongxin."

I hesitated. Monk Yongxin was the richest, most powerful, and best-connected monk at the temple, but he was therefore the most controversial. He had his own Mercedes-Benz with his own driver, a gift from a Beijing politician. He spent months at a time away from the temple cultivating his relationships inside the national army and the Beijing government. Whenever Beijing VIPs came to the temple, they were escorted by Yongxin. He was eventually made a deputy in the National People's Congress. He'd also set up a separate group of martial monks to compete with the Wushu Center's foreign-tour business.

"But I've never met him," I said. "He has never taught me any kungfu."

"He didn't teach me either. That's not the point," Yunfei said. "Picking a master is a political decision. Yongxin will be the next abbot. His *guanxi* with the Beijing generals is deep. I tell you, when Yongxin becomes abbot, he will use his *guanxi* to wrestle control of Shaolin from the provincial government."

That was interesting. It was well known and resented that the Henan tourism agency took all the revenue from ticket sales and then doled back only a small percentage to the temple. It was the main reason that life inside the temple was so moribund.

"Can you arrange it?" I asked.

"I wouldn't have suggested it if I couldn't."

On the agreed-upon day, Yunfei and I made our way to the temple. The policeman at the gate stopped us.

"Where are your tickets?"

"I'm a disciple of Yongxin," Yunfei said.

The guard waved us through.

Yongxin's quarters were in the back of the temple. Several younger disciples loitered around the entrance.

"Martial arts little brother," Yunfei said to the Tall One, the only monk in Shaolin taller than six feet. "Tell Master Yongxin his American disciple is here."

The Tall One knocked, opened the door, and ducked inside. After a moment, he waved us in.

Yongxin's residence had two rooms: an audience room to greet guests and, behind a curtain, his bedroom. We sat down in two chairs in the main room. There was a Buddhist shrine on a table against the far wall with a cushioned kneeling stool in front for prayer. In short order, Yongxin made his way into the room.

I had seen him at a distance, escorting PLA generals on tours of the temple and into Wushu Center performances. But this was as close as I'd ever been to him. He was plump with a well-padded, porcine face and an advanced Buddha belly.

I stood, pressed my hands together, and bowed.

"*Amituofo.*"

He urged me to sit. As Yunfei had instructed, I presented him with a *hongbao* (red envelope—a monetary gift is placed inside). In prepping me for the day, Yunfei had explained that new disciples give their new master a *hongbao*. The sum was somewhat optional, but given Chinese obsessions with numerology certain amounts were considered auspicious, particularly 888 and 1,111. He left dollars or RMB up to me. I was feeling pretty poor by this point, and I'd also lived in China long enough that I'd stopped dividing RMB by eight to get the dollar amount—1 RMB equaled $1 as far as I was concerned. I went with 1,111RMB ($140).

Yongxin took the *hongbao* but tossed it onto the table as if it were an unnecessary, unpleasant matter to be concluded as quickly as possible. Given how wealthy he was rumored to be, he'd discover how trivial it was when he opened the envelope.

As the fixer, Yunfei poured tea for all of us.

"I am honored you would agree to meet me," I said. "I am unworthy to be your disciple."

Yongxin spoke to me, but his regional accent was so thick I couldn't understand what he was saying. I turned to Yunfei.

Yunfei translated, "Master Yongxin says that he has heard many good things about you and that you are an interesting *laowai*."

"Where? Where? Where?" I said. "No need to be kind."

Yongxin spoke and again Yunfei translated: "And you are humble, too. That is very good. I hear you are a writer."

The monks had seen me typing into my laptop and word had gotten around that I was an aspiring writer.

"I'm not a writer. I'd like to be one. Hopefully with enough hard work and practice I might become one."

"I hear you are working on a movie script."

"I've just started on one," I said. "It is my first. It is very poorly written."

"Perhaps you can write a movie about Shaolin for Hollywood. Tell what you have seen. What life is like here in modern times. It would help spread the fame of Shaolin to America. You come from a great country. I enjoyed my visit. The Americans were very kind to us."

"Master, I want to ask you a question. Have you heard about the fate of two monks who remained in America after Shaolin's first tour?" I said, referring to Yanming and Guolin, the two monks who had defected.

"It is still not easy for them. But their lives are improving."

"But was it not embarrassing to have them leave in the way they did?" I asked.

He smiled at the delicacy with which I'd phrased the question. One of the defecting monks, Guolin, had been his disciple.

"For some. For me, I think of it as planting Shaolin flowers around the world. A seed drops in this country. A seed drops in that country. Soon Shaolin is everywhere."

"I see."

"Shall we begin the ceremony?"

Yongxin instructed me to kneel before the altar. He opened an ancient text and placed it onto a bookstand. He lit incense candles. He picked up a tiny bell with his right hand.

Yongxin read for about fifteen minutes, interspersing the chanting with rings of the bell. I could pick out only a few words. The text was in classical Chinese, which is to modern Chinese what Latin is to Italian. Most of the words were Chinese transliterations of Sanskrit Buddhist terms. And then there was his impenetrable accent.

What I heard was: "Buddha [something, something, something]

Buddhist monks [something, something] Buddha [something] Buddhism [something, something, something] Buddha . . ."

Toward the end, it became clearer.

"Do you vow to devote yourself to the Buddha?" he asked.

"I vow," I said.

And then I kowtowed. Yunfei had taught me the proper way. First you place your right hand down on the floor, then your left, then your right again, then you turn your left palm up, then your right, then you close both into a fist, then you touch your head to the floor.

Yongxin rang the bell.

"Do you vow to devote yourself to the Shaolin Temple?"

"I vow," I said, kowtowing again.

Yongxin rang the bell.

"Do you vow to devote yourself to your new master?"

"I vow," I said, kowtowing a final time.

Yongxing went on, "[Something, something, something] Buddha [something, something] Buddhism."

Yongxin rang the bell three times, and the ceremony was over.

I stood up, "*Amituofo*, master."

"*Amituofo*," he said.

And with that I was a disciple of the Shaolin Temple, the first *laowai* ever, as far as anyone there knew.

3

TOURNAMENT

We filled a minivan for the trip to the Zhengzhou tournament. There was Deqing, Coach Cheng, Cheng Hao, my teammate and sparring partner Baotong, Monk Xingming, and Little Tiger, along with various hangers-on. All we needed were some cheerleaders and it would have been like a high school football game.

With their spirit of hospitality and sense that I was the frailest member of the troop, everyone tried to cheer me up with their advice on how to beat Wuhan Sports University's champion, the best 70 kg. *sanda* fighter in China.

"You want to charge while punching to his head," Baotong said. "And as he defends, duck low, pick him up by the waist and throw him."

"Make sure you turn your hips into each kick," Coach Cheng offered. "Given how fast he is, you won't get many chances, and you want to make each one count."

Cheng Hao, having heard the story of the crazy Finn Mikael, smiled and said, "Step on his lead foot and jab. It's Bruce Lee's technique and it's impossible to stop."

"You could try begging for mercy," Deqing suggested. "'Please, stop hitting me. I can't take it anymore.'"

I turned to Monk Xingming. "What would the Buddha suggest?"

"He taught us the principle of universal love," Monk Xingming replied. "You could try loving him. But the Buddha had lousy kungfu."

At this point, our driver narrowly avoided a multiple car pileup, giving me something more urgent to fear than the Champ. The suggestions continued for the rest of the journey, but I had too firm a grip on the luggage rack above me to really hear them.

After a restless night in the Zheng Zhou International Hotel, we joined the parade that kicked off the Zheng Zhou International Wushu Festival. Teams of martial artists from twenty-six countries walked the main avenues of Henan's capital between floats filled with young women waving at the crowds lining the sides of the streets and kungfu stylists in feudal Chinese garb pretending to fight each other. While it had all the earmarks of a homecoming parade, there was something forced about it, like a Soviet May Day ceremony with MIGs and ICBMs. It was as if Henan Province were saying: "Look at our kungfu power."

Each team had a sign girl, an attractive teenager in a short dress who carried a sign bearing the name of the team in Chinese and misspelled English. The largest team was, of course, the Chinese National team, but it was not as large as it could have been. If this had been an international competition they would have flooded each category in order to sweep the medals, but this was a festival, an event to promote "friendship and tourism" as the posters said, so the Chinese were entering just one martial artist for each *wushu* (forms) competition and each *sanda* (kickboxing) weight division. The catch was that every member of the Chinese team was the national champion in his form or weight class and almost all were world champions as well. The Chinese wanted to be gracious hosts and were happy for the foreigners to leave with silver and bronze medals, but gold was out of the question.

At the last minute, I was told by Coach Yan, who was acting as intermediary between the leaders and me, that I could not, as a foreigner, represent either the Shaolin Temple or the Wushu Center. I was rather angry about this, arguing that if I was good enough to fight a challenge match for Shaolin I should be good enough to represent my school in this tournament. Coach Yan hemmed and hawed and came up with enough reasonable excuses that I could not determine which was the real one and so could not undermine it. At the tournament's registration I invented my team: Princeton University Wushu Team. At the parade, I walked behind my sign girl, who was wearing a pink dress and carrying the sign PUWT, U.S.A. Coach Cheng and Deqing had ducked out to meet old friends.

I was a little annoyed that Deqing had left me to walk the parade alone, but all was forgiven when I returned to my room to discover that Deqing had spent that time looking up two very attractive Zheng Zhou women. The one who was sitting proprietarily near him was clearly one of his many fans and the other, looking at me somewhat nervously, her friend. They wanted to make us dumplings after my weigh-in to celebrate the breaking of my fast. I'd dropped six pounds in the last two weeks to arrive at an anorexic 149 pounds on my six-foot-three frame. Surveying the scene, this could have been a double date if it weren't for the fact that one of us was a celibate Buddhist monk and the other a potentially AIDS-infected scarecrow who was condemned by law to turn nice young Chinese women into prostitutes at the stroke of midnight. Still, all in all, it beat fasting in a mountainous monastery where my friends pounded on me six hours a day to prepare me for a fight against a national champion. We made arrangements to meet at the fan's house at five P.M.

Because all the foreigners were staying in the Zheng Zhou International Hotel, my weigh-in took place there. I stepped off the elevator to a hallway full of men from various parts of the world standing around in their underwear. It was like a Benetton ad come to life.

We were arranged by weight class. There were only five 70 kg. (154 lb.) fighters, fewer than the other classes. There was a short, pudgy Korean in his mid-thirties, a wiry Japanese fighter in his late teens, a tough-looking Russian in his mid-twenties, the Chinese Champ, and scrawny, lanky me.

There are not many sports where opponents stand around with each other half naked before the competition begins. It makes for a rather awkward social situation. I could see why pro boxers always come to weigh-ins with their posses. The weigh-in really is the first round of the fight where the psychological warfare begins. I urgently wished I had asked Deqing or Coach Cheng to come with me. Alone, I wasn't sure how to act.

Neither did the Champ, who clearly felt out of place—he was used to fighting real rivals, not a bunch of overpaying foreigners. But then the coach of the Chinese team came over and gave me something to react to, my strong suit as a fighter and a person. He introduced himself and said that he was a coach at Taguo and that he had heard that I was very good, worked hard, and was able to eat bitter.

"Oh no, no, no, no need to be polite," I said, offering the usual Chinese response.

"So, do you think you are going to win?" he asked with an ingratiating smile. "Are you going to beat my fighter?"

But his cynical eyes didn't match his grin and I immediately took a dislike to him. He was too *jiaohua*, a slick-talker, and he was trying to psych me out. The coach either wanted to get me to say something arrogant, which would anger and motivate his fighter, or he wanted me to be excessively humble, which would help the confidence of the Champ.

"How could I ever hope to beat your fighter?" I said, smiling back.

Without thinking about it, I had apparently decided to do my best imitation of extreme Chinese humility. I lowered my head, lifted my arms as if in supplication, and raised my voice an octave.

"I am but a small man," I said. "A lowly *laowai*. We are terrible at kungfu. How could I ever even think I could beat a Chinese fighter, let alone a national champion?"

This was not the reaction the coach had expected. His smile vanished and he took a step back. The Champ looked extremely uncomfortable. So I continued to lay it on thick.

"Besides, you are both Taguo-trained fighters, while I studied at the Wushu Center. We are soft; you are hard. We train indoors on carpet. You train outdoors on the dirt. Look at how dark your fighter's skin is from the sun. Look out how white I am. He will certainly be the victor. I am simply honored to have the chance to be defeated by him."

I finished with a deep bow and rose smiling like an idiot. Rattled, the coach walked away. I knew I stood little to no chance against the Champ, but I had clearly won the first round.

Over dumplings with the girls that night, I recounted this story to Deqing. Toward the end, my nominal date's expression changed from indifference to intense interest. A young warrior was about to go off into battle, and it was her biological duty to the species to pass his DNA information on to the next generation before it was too late.

It is no wonder that young men have always been willing to risk themselves in stupid, potentially fatal adventures. It's such an aphrodisiac.

I don't remember the rest of the meal. Her look had fired my libido straight into the stratosphere. I pretended to pay attention, but my mind was racing through the logistical difficulties and my various tactical options. I had to get the women to walk back with us to the hotel. But Deqing was rooming with me. Somehow I had to drop Deqing and his fan off in Coach Cheng's room and then find a reason to excuse myself and my date—whose name I'm embarrassed to say I never actually caught—to my room without anyone else following. And then somehow execute a quick seduction (not so easy, despite that look of hers) with a quick conclusion (very easy, unfortunately) before Coach Cheng or Deqing became suspicious and came knocking at the door. And all this had to be done before midnight, because the key girl on our hallway would be taking note and probably calling the police if the young woman was not out of my room by then.

The first part of the campaign went off without a hitch. I said I wanted to drop in on Coach Cheng. We all sat down and chatted for a bit. After a few minutes I turned to my date and asked if she wanted to see "the thing" she had asked me about. She looked confused but nodded. We went off to my room. I pulled out some photos I had of the monks and myself at Shaolin in various kungfu poses. While she was still slightly confused, I leaned in closer to point out aspects of the photos, while slipping an arm around her back. Our heads tilted toward each other.

But right before contact, there was a knock at the door. I held my date to me. Since neither Coach Cheng nor Deqing had a key to the room, I decided to pretend we weren't there and hope they went away.

As the lock turned we scrambled apart. Deqing, Deqing's fan,

Coach Cheng, and his girlfriend, Shou Ting, stood behind the key girl, who opened the door. I cursed myself for forgetting about the key girl.

After a few awkward moments, I tried to hint that Coach Cheng would be doing me a big favor if he made himself scarce with some head nods and eye rolls in the direction of the door. At a certain point a sheepish smile flittered across Coach Cheng's face. The rotten turtle's egg had staged an intervention. He held out until the prostitution hour neared and Deqing's fan and my date had to go. We walked them to the elevator. When I returned to the room, Coach Cheng was waiting outside his door for me.

"Why did you do that?" I asked in a tone of voice kungfu students do not use with their masters.

"After the tournament do what you want but not before."

"Why?"

"It makes your legs weak."

And then I suddenly realized who I was talking to and how I was talking to him and what he could and ought to do to me for acting that way. I immediately apologized. He waved me off.

The Zheng Zhou sports arena was the biggest indoor stadium I had ever been inside. It seemed like there were 50,000 Chinese packed in there. Actually, it couldn't have been more than 10,000, but that was still ten times bigger than anything in Topeka. It was an intimidating space. The floor was covered with multiple mats for *wushu* forms competitions and three *leitais* for the *sanda* fights.

There was a large room off the arena floor where the fighters congregated and changed. The brackets for each weight class were posted. Because there were five fighters in 70 kg., two had to fight a wild-card round. The play-in was between the Korean and the Japanese fighter. The winner would fight me in the semifinals. The Champ and the Russian would fight in the other bracket. The winner of those two fights would face each other for the championship. The wild-card match was to be held in the morning, the semifinals in the afternoon, and the finals the next day.

No matter when each one of us was scheduled to fight, we all got suited up that morning. Everyone stripped down to loose kickboxing shorts and a T-shirt. As for pads, we all had two sets—black and red—of the same equipment. I was red for my first match. My date from the night before was there, having apparently promoted herself to my corner after enduring the previous night, and was helping me put on the pads. There was a padded cup that went over the outside of the shorts; two thin shin guards to limit bruising, which could balloon a man's leg; two thin foot guards to protect the tops of the feet from the same; a thin chest guard; light eight-ounce boxing gloves; a mouthpiece; and amateur boxing headgear.

As my date laced up the chest gear in the back, I felt this boyish grin spreading across my face. I'd been dreaming of this tournament every night for nine months. I couldn't wait to get started.

From the fighter's room, a large hallway between the stands opened up onto the main hall. I found myself at the end of the hallway standing next to the Champ when the fight between the Korean and the Japanese fighters started. We were both looking for weaknesses.

The Japanese fighter slid forward on his left foot and raised his right foot, bringing it around in a right roundhouse. At that exact instant, the Korean fighter dropped into a crouch and executed a right front sweep. His right instep hooked the Japanese fighter's left standing leg, his only point of contact with the earth, causing him to tip precariously for a second before finally falling over.

The Champ and I looked at each other with disbelief. The right front sweep was almost never used. To perform it you drop into a crouch over a bent left leg, placing both hands on the ground for balance. The right leg is kept straight and swept counterclockwise along the ground like a broom. The point is to topple your opponent, but since the kick is weak it will work only if you catch him with one of his legs up in the air. Obviously, timing is crucial. But that's not why the kick is avoided. The problem is, while crouched over your knee with both hands on the ground, you leave your face completely exposed at waist height, teed up like a pumpkin on a short fence post. If your opponent is aiming at where your head was while standing he will miss high. But if he is aiming at where your waist was, he will smash your unprotected face.

Fortunately for the Korean, the Japanese fighter had been

aiming at his head, so he missed. The Korean's sweep connected with the Japanese fighter's standing leg, causing him to topple to the ground. It was a very risky opening gambit, only justifiable because it was such a surprise, like running a flea-flicker on the first play of a football game.

But then on the very next exchange, the Korean tried it again. This time the Japanese fighter managed to keep his balance.

The Champ asked me, "Are you seeing this?"

"Yes."

"What a stupid egg!" he said, patting me on the shoulder. "Your luck is good."

The front forward sweep was the Korean fighter's lone decent attack. His only other technique was to charge forward with his head ducked as he punched wildly with both hands. From a distance, he looked like a snot-nosed ten-year-old forced to fight on the playground.

The one thing more amazing than watching this Korean fight with only two techniques, one of which was extremely risky and the other juvenile, was that they were working. Three or four times he knocked over the Japanese fighter with his front sweep. And his wild charge kept his opponent back on his heels. I kept waiting for the Japanese fighter to adjust and level the Korean, but it never happened. The Korean won the first two rounds and the fight.

That afternoon I was ready. Despite it being my first time on a *leitai* (there had never been one at Shaolin), I stepped onto it completely focused. The Korean fighter and I stood at opposite ends and started to stretch. From the corner of my eye I studied the Korean's flexibility. His splits left a couple inches of space at the crotch, while mine was flush to the platform. I tried not to smile at the advantage. He would have difficulty kicking high enough to reach my face.

The referee blew his whistle to call us to the center of the ring. The traditional *sanda* introduction was to put your gloves together and bow and then come together for a brief hug to show mutual respect. The Korean was at best five-foot-six in shoes. I had eight or nine inches on him. He was chubby. I was skinny as a rail. We looked like a multiethnic Abbott and Costello. When I embraced him I purposively bent my back at an exaggerated angle, stuck my ass out, and threw my elbow out wide, as if I were reaching down to pick up a child. A big roar of laughter emanated from the crowd. I had succeeded in my goal to intimidate and embarrass him. He hung his head as he stepped back. (The next day the wits at Zheng Zhou's newspaper would write, "It was as if a lamppost had squeezed a stuffed bear.")

The whistle blew.

My initial strategy was based on my experience that fighters almost always rely on their strongest technique first—the kick they had practiced 10,000 times. For the Korean fighter, it was his front sweep.

I stepped forward to plant my left foot and raised my right knee up high as if aiming at his head. As expected, the Korean dropped to a crouch over his left knee and swept his right foot around at my standing leg. At this moment, I lowered my knee and brought it around at waist height, aiming at his unprotected head. Mentally practicing it before the fight, I knew it was a matter of timing. My foot had to reach his face before his foot struck my left standing leg. But I hadn't anticipated being nervous. I swung my leg hard but I didn't turn my hips into it, which is what generates the extra force.

Just before his foot reached my left leg, my right connected flush against the side of his face. I watched his eyes roll into the back of his head as he was knocked flat onto the platform. But there was no joy. I could here the voice in the back of my head scream, *You leg kicked him. You're supposed to turn your hips.*

I turned around to look at Coach Cheng. He was shouting the same thing as he twisted his body, "Use your hips!"

Turning back around, I could see the Korean struggling to his knees as the referee counted over him, ". . . four, five, six . . ." It had only been a leg kick but it had been hard, especially with his head planted at waist height, unprotected. As he stood up, I felt a grudging respect. He had an iron jaw. That kick would have ended most fights.

Tournament fighting is different from, say, championship boxing, where a boxer fights for ten or twelve rounds once every six months or so. In those situations, you are supposed to leave everything you have in the ring, because you have many months to recover. In a tournament, you want to expend as little energy with as little risk as possible in the early rounds. You want to give just enough to win. Other than losing, the biggest danger is that you will be injured or exhaust yourself, making victory in the later stages of the tournament difficult or impossible.

The perfect result would have been a knockout from that roundhouse in the first five seconds, but it hadn't worked out. I fell back to reconsider. The Korean was wobbly, and he was scared to try that front sweep again, which eliminated his best technique. I might have been able to finish him, but I didn't want to chance it. So for the next two rounds I used my superior height and range to score points and keep him at bay. Whenever he tried charging with his head down and swinging wildly, I would dance back, jabbing over his hooks or front thrust kicking him in the chest to knock him back. I kept my kicks at chest level or lower; my punches were all straight jabs to his head. It wasn't a rousing, crowd-pleasing strategy, but it was effective on the scorecards. I won both rounds and the match.

Afterward Coach Cheng kept at me about turning my hips on my roundhouse.

"You would have knocked him out," he said.

The Champ's fight with the Russian was scheduled after mine. I stayed to watch. It was frightening. The Champ beat the Russian like a drum. He knocked him from one side of the *leitai* to the other, several times blasting him off the platform, which was about a yard off the ground and surrounded by the kind of thick foam padding used in stunt falls. It was a rout.

In the first thirty seconds of round two, the Champ kicked the Russian with a low left roundhouse. It landed on the side of the Russian's right knee, which buckled momentarily, causing him to drop down six inches and lower his guard. The Champ followed the left with a high right roundhouse, but the Russian's collapse had brought them too close. Instead of landing with his left foot as was the Champ's intention, he blasted the Russian in the face with his knee, which is illegal (knee and elbow attacks are legal in Thai kick-boxing, but not in *sanda*). The referee ruled it an unintentional knee attack, so there was no penalty. But it didn't matter. The knee had broken the Russian's nose. He was lying flat on his back, cough-ing up blood. Medics rushed in and carted him off on a stretcher.

"Damn!" I said to Deqing.

"Don't worry," he said. "They won't carry you out on a stretcher."

"No?"

"You are too tall for Chinese stretchers. They will leave you on the platform instead."

"Thank you."

"No problem."

After a big dinner (there would be no more weigh-ins), Coach Cheng, Shou Ting, my date, and I went back to my room to relax. Deqing had left early to meet someone. After about an hour, he en-tered the room accompanied by an elderly man and a younger man in his late teens. From the way Deqing was ducking his head, he looked like he had been roped into doing something he didn't want to do. He leaned over Coach Cheng and whispered in his ear.

"Absolutely not," Coach Cheng replied.

Deqing stood up and shrugged his shoulders at the old man.

"It's just a challenge match," the old man said. "It won't take much time."

I walked over and asked Deqing what was happening.

"This is a martial arts instructor. He was one my master's class-mates," Deqing said. "This is his disciple. They saw you fight today. The master wants his disciple to gain experience. He wants him to challenge you."

I must have looked horrified, because Coach Cheng jumped in.

"What were you thinking? Lao Bao has to fight in the champi-onship tomorrow."

Deqing shrugged. What could he do? A classmate of one of his instructors had made a request. He was honor-bound to try to fulfill it.

I felt like a marked man. All I had done was beat a second-rate Korean. If I somehow found a way to beat the Champ tomorrow, they'd be standing in line for me. The absurdity of the situation set me back on my heels. I already was feeling tired and achy from my earlier fight. The top of my right foot was swelling from that first kick. I knew I needed to ice it down. I had absolutely no interest in a challenge match.

Thankfully, Coach Cheng repeated definitively, "Lao Bao will not fight him."

Silence descended. This was frequent in Chinese negotiations. Someone made a ridiculous request, but the various webs of obligation required that some sort of satisfactory solution be found.

It was up to the old master to plead his case. "My student needs the experience. He needs a challenge match to test his skills."

"My student has to fight tomorrow," Coach Cheng replied. "What if he gets hurt? Can your disciple fight in his place in the tournament?"

More silence.

The old master leaned forward, "Maybe someone else can fight?"

Coach Cheng thought about it for a moment.

"Okay," he said finally. "I'll fight him in Lao Bao's place."

And with that, the relaxing, contemplative evening before my big fight ended. Never very stable in the best of circumstances, Shou Ting exploded.

"You can't! Don't do it! What if the police come?"

She came at Coach Cheng, who was about to be in a real fight, swinging. He grabbed her wrists and smiled that painful smile all men use when trying to calm hysterical women in front of friends.

"No problem, no problem, no problem," Coach Cheng said while looking over at me and raising his eyebrow apologetically. His face said, *What can I do with a woman like this?*

"I will leave you!" Shou Ting yelped, her voice starting to crack, indicating to every male in the room that a flow of tears was soon to follow.

Coach Cheng stepped back, and Deqing, right on cue, stepped in between them.

"Don't worry," he said. "This is very common. No police will come."

Our room emptied into the hallway of the twelfth floor of the Zheng Zhou International Hotel, a narrow affair—standing in the middle I could touch both walls with my fingertips. In the process of arranging ourselves, the disciple, his master, and Deqing found themselves facing us with their backs to where the elevators were located. Coach Cheng, Shou Ting, my date, and I had our backs to the window at the far end of the hallway. Somehow while exiting the room, Deqing had deftly exchanged places with me, and it was now my responsibility to physically restrain Shou Ting. Fortunately, she was no longer trying to attack Coach Cheng. She was content merely to shout invectives and threats about the future of their relationship at him. I felt like a police officer standing in front of a protestor. My date looked shell-shocked.

Not a single door opened—were the *laowai* cowering next to their peepholes?—but it did bring the twelfth-floor key girl running from her desk in front of the elevators.

"What are you doing?" she demanded.

Deqing, who was nearest, intercepted her.

"It's nothing. Just play," Deqing said, beaming and laughing in his most charming way.

She tried to get closer, but Deqing gently stood in her way.

"Are they fighting?" she asked.

"No, it is not a fight. It is just a challenge match."

The fine distinction between *dajia* (fighting) and *qie cuo* (a challenge match) was lost on her.

"You can't do this here. We have guests."

"No problem. They are all martial artists. They love challenge matches."

"I will call the police."

At this point, Deqing gently but firmly grabbed her arm while still laughing and pleading. "No need, no need, no need. It will be over soon. You have foreign guests here, right? You don't want the police to disturb them. Your boss would be very angry with you."

That quieted her down.

The disciple was now ready. So was Coach Cheng.

There was an electrified moment's pause before the disciple

attacked. It was a traditional kungfu attack, but I didn't recognize the style. He slid forward very quickly along a right angle and then switched quickly to a left-angle approach before he was in kicking range, rotating his arms for defense. At that moment, Coach Cheng, who had remained completely still, let fly his supersonic right roundhouse kick to the head. The disciple pulled back his head just in time to save himself. The kick caught the tip of his nose instead of the side of his head, which would have been the end of him. Unlike me, Coach Cheng had remembered to turn his hips into the kick.

The disciple retreated. There was a fine line of blood where the disciple's nose attached to his face. He had pulled back just far enough to keep his nose from being ripped off. I thought that would be it, but his master pulled out some medical tape from his pocket and secured his student's nose in place.

Facing each other again, the disciple approached the same way as before but with even more speed than the first time, sliding to his right and then to his left. As he came into range, Coach Cheng used his patented forward left side kick to the chest. He meant it to stop the disciple's forward motion, and then he could follow up with punches.

But the disciple was traveling too fast. Coach Cheng's kick crumpled against the disciple's body as his forward motion carried him into punching range. The disciple fired a reverse palm strike, which is like backhanding someone across the face. Coach Cheng responded with the classic *sanda* counter. He ducked the punch and grabbed the disciple around the waist. The next move in the counter was to lift your opponent off the ground and throw him. But the disciple's forward momentum pushed Coach Cheng backward. The disciple was wearing a jogging suit and rubber-soled *wushu* shoes; Coach Cheng, unfortunately, was in his best outfit—a button-front shirt, black slacks, and black leather shoes with hard plastic soles. They didn't have any traction. As the disciple's momentum pushed Coach Cheng backward, the shoes slid along the carpet and then slipped out from under him. As Coach Cheng fell to his knees with his arms locked around the disciple's waist, he dragged the disciple to his knees as well.

The disciple's upper body was above Coach Cheng, who had his head tucked against his opponent's right hip. His arms, wrapped as they were around the disciple's waist, were no longer free. Coach Cheng's back was exposed, and he was unable to defend himself. In a red-eyed panic the disciple started to wail away at Coach Cheng's kidneys with his fists.

In a proper *sanda* or challenge match, the two fighters would break apart and stand up to fight again. Coach Cheng's knees had hit the ground first, so he had lost this exchange. The point is to see who has the better technique while standing.

But the adrenaline-pumped disciple did not stop. He continued pounding away at Coach Cheng's back, a definite no-no. Coach Cheng squeezed his arms trying to unbalance the disciple, so he could flip him over onto his back. But he only managed to move the disciple further down his back so that the disciple's blows started landing on Coach Cheng's backside.

It had happened in a matter of seconds. But the sight of Coach Cheng being spanked set everyone watching into motion. First, of course, was Shou Ting. She broke past me and jumped onto the disciple, slapping at his head.

"You hit his ass! Fuck your mother! You hit his ass?" she screamed.

I moved to grab Shou Ting around the waist and pull her off the pile. After that, Deqing and the master grabbed the stunned disciple to pull him off of Coach Cheng.

Coach Cheng stood up. He looked at me, a little shaken and also slightly embarrassed, "My shoes slipped. I should have taken them off. They are dress shoes. They slipped on the carpet."

I said, "Yes, I know. It doesn't matter."

Shou Ting continued to scream, "What kind of challenge match is this? Fuck your mother. You pound his ass. You like to hit asses? I'll fight you. You can hit my ass. Do you know who he is? This is Coach Cheng. He was the 1988 national *sanda* champion."

At this the master visibly blanched.

"Oh, Coach Cheng. I did not realize it was you. We will go."

He grabbed his disciple by the arm and yanked him back down the hallway past the stunned key girl.

Coach Cheng, who was still embarrassed and unhappy he had lost the previous round, didn't want them to leave yet. In the most reasonable of voices, he smiled and said, "No, no, don't go yet. Let's try once more. No problem. No need to go. Let's try once more."

The master continued to pull his disciple down the hall while apologizing over his shoulder. Shou Ting, who'd broken my grip, continued to curse and challenge the disciple. All the while, Coach Cheng was cajoling them to stay and fight just one more time.

"You like to hit asses? I'll fight you!" Shou Ting yelled. "Do you know who Coach Cheng is? Hit my ass and see what happens!"

"No, stay," Coach Cheng coaxed in his calm voice. "Just one more round."

"I'm so sorry. I didn't know it was you, Coach Cheng," the master said. "We will leave. Please."

"You like to hit asses? Fight me!"

"Don't go."

"Hit my ass!"

"Sorry, sorry, sorry."

"Don't go."

"I am sorry, Coach Cheng."

This scene repeated itself over and over again, until we reached the elevator bank.

As the doors slid open, the master and his disciple slipped inside. Coach Cheng had by this point put his hand on the master's arm.

"We can go outside," he said. "Just once more. No problem."

The master was pushing on Coach Cheng's chest to keep him from getting on the elevator with his left hand while he frantically pushed the button for the lobby with his right. As the doors started to close, my date, having decided with good reason we were all completely insane and wanting to escape from the asylum, darted inside the elevator.

She shrugged an apology as the doors closed.

Walking back to our rooms, Coach Cheng patted me on the shoulder.

"At least you won't have weak legs for tomorrow," he said.

———

Standing in the fighter's room thirty minutes before my fight, I could hear the rumbling of the crowd in the stadium as it watched the final matches of the lower weight classes. After a long internal debate, I finally couldn't stand it anymore. I tiptoed down the hallway into the stadium to furtively glance at the crowds. There they were: 10,000 Chinese waiting for the Champ to send me packing on a too-short stretcher.

The Fear, which had been gently feeling around my guts in order to get a better grip, finally squeezed as I knew it would. A victim of fairly severe stage fright, I was experienced with the sensation. Everything inside of me had to come out immediately, one way or another. I made a dash to the bathroom, which was a typical holes-in-the-ground job, but a good deal cleaner than the one in the Deng Feng hospital. Still, it was a trick to avoid tipping over while fully ensconced in kickboxing pads.

When I returned to the fighter's room, fifteen minutes remained. Coach Cheng and Deqing looked worried. I was perspiring heavily and pale with panic. Coach asked me if I was okay. But as soon as I said I was, the Fear gripped me again. It hadn't quite cleaned me out the first time. I raised a finger to indicate that this would just take a minute, turned tail, and ran back to the bathroom.

As I squatted this second time, the minutes ticked past as the Fear squeezed and then let up and then squeezed again. I felt tears streaming down my face. I wanted to go home. I wanted to stay in that bathroom forever. I wanted to do anything but get on top of a platform and face the Champ in front of 10,000 screaming Chinese. I schemed over the various possibilities for flight. But there weren't any good ones. It was a matter of face. Mine didn't matter to me at the moment, but Deqing's and Coach Cheng's did. And then it occurred to me on a complete tangent, as my jagged brain zoomed around for something else to occupy it, that this was why armies are always organized in small platoons: Men can rationalize away personal cowardice when alone but can't stand to shame themselves in front of their buddies. We're pack animals.

Right after that bathroom epiphany, it dawned on me with a certain gallows humor that I was literally scared shitless. This made me chuckle, and as soon as I started laughing my moment of crisis was over. Having passed through the crucible, my spirits lifted dramatically.

On my return, I found Coach Cheng and a referee arguing. Coach Cheng had a strong grip on the ref's arm, which he released when he saw me. Coach Cheng was furious, but trying not to show it.

"Are you okay now?" he asked.

"*Mei shi, mei shi, mei shi*," I said. "No problem."

"If you need to use the bathroom again," he said, "do it in your pants."

I was laughing. I was buoyant. I was literally bouncing down the hallway. What was this? Nothing. A kickboxing match? Nothing. Where was the challenge in this? Send me into a real battle. A reckless courage pumped my veins. I was ready to defend the Ardennes, charge the Turkish lines at Gallipoli, hold the pass at Thermopylae. My heart grappled with my brain to see which was bigger as my ego shouted encouragement from the sidelines. Coach Cheng, who'd seen this fever in other fighers before, gripped my shoulder to make certain I didn't crack.

I went up and stood next to the Champ, who was waiting at the edge of the arena.

"You fought well yesterday," I said.

"So did you."

We fell into silence. I felt awkward, but not because we were about to climb onto a platform and start fighting. I felt awkward because I liked him and we were about to climb onto a platform and start fighting. In all my previous matches, there was something that irritated me or that I didn't respect about my opponent, but I liked the Champ. He was *laoshi*. There was no bullshit about him. He was just one of those solid, straightforward peasant kids who came to Shaolin from his parents' farm and had trained really hard for the last decade and was now the best in the world at what he did. And while there was no way for me to know for certain, I was pretty sure he liked me, too.

"*Wo ju ni chenggong*," I said. "I wish you success."

It is what everyone says to a fighter before a match, everyone but his opponent, of course, because he'd be wishing for his own defeat.

It took the Champ a moment, his brow furrowed, before he got the joke and smiled.

"No, no, no," he replied, "I wish you success."

"No, no, no, I wish you success," I replied in the repetitive custom of Chinese self-effacement.

"No, no, no, no, I wish you success."

We were both grinning when the head referee waved for us to enter the arena. In *sanda* tradition, fighters were expected to run out together to show their enthusiasm and mutual respect. As we started running, the Champ grabbed my hand, which was an extremely unusual show of solidarity—I'd never seen it done before, let alone experienced it. The crowd roared its approval. Looking back it strikes me that if only we'd started skipping, it would have been the gayest fighter's entrance in the history of combat sports.

On top of the platform we went to opposite sides to stretch. The Champ's splits were perfect, so despite my six-inch height advantage he'd be able to kick me in the head. I stopped glancing over at him.

As we approached the center of the ring, the noise of the crowd rose and the disparate shouts joined into a singular distinct voice crying two phrases over and over again in a steady drumlike beat:

Shale ta! (Kill him!)

Da si laowai! (Beat the foreigner to death!)

I shot a look over at Coach Cheng.

Once again my only anchor, he shrugged apologetically.

Amituofo.

To be fair, the crowd had no way of knowing I spoke Chinese. I'm certain if they had, they wouldn't have been chanting for my death. They would have been too self-conscious. But ignorant that I understood them, they kept at: *Beat the foreigner to death! Kill him!*

The referee explained the rules. The Champ and I bowed to each other and hugged. This time I kept my back straight.

When the bell rang, I could no longer hear the crowd.

We stood deathly still in the middle of the ring, neither one of us wanting to bounce or show any signs of anxiety. The pressure built. I felt compelled to move. I hopped forward and back, feinting to see if he would react. He didn't. I feinted again and then took a bigger step forward with my left to close within kicking range, and launched a right roundhouse.

This is what the Champ was waiting for. He had correctly antic-ipated a kick. Without any wasted motion or doubt, he trapped my leg, ducking his head down, so I couldn't punch him in the face. And with a speed I'd never experienced before, the Champ dropped his left leg back and lowered his body, which pressed my leg away and downward. Before I knew it I was flat on my back with him standing over me.

2-0.

The catch and throw was so perfectly executed it intimidated me. I decided to switch from an offensive to defensive strategy and try to catch one of his kicks.

He shuffle-stepped forward and launched a left side kick aimed at my chest, which was about the level of his neck. I saw the kick coming, but it was too fast for me to trap it. I felt the impact before my mind was able to register the kick had landed.

4-0.

I was rocked back a step. No one, not even Baotong, had ever kicked me that hard. I remember thinking with astonishment, *That really hurt*, as I watched him repeat the attack. I tried to trap his foot again, and again I was too late. My breath blew out of my mouth as the force of his side kick pounded my sternum.

6-0.

We were in the dance now, and I was on the losing end of it. I knew I had to attack. I tried a side kick, but he blocked it down-ward with his right forearm, sending a jolt of pain up my leg as he stepped back and out of the kicking range.

Combinations!

I immediately followed the failed side kick with a right round-house. He hooked it to the side of his body, allowing the kick to connect with his left arm. My body tensed, preparing to be thrown to the ground. We were standing face-to-face. He placed his right hand on my chest, and then he started running forward. With only one leg to stand on, I was forced to hop backward to keep my bal-ance. He was running me, like a wheelbarrow, off the platform.

As I reached the edge of the *leitai*, he let go of my leg and pushed with his hand against my chest. Flying through the air, the thought that flickered through my mind was: *That's not fair*. To prevent a wrestling match, the referee is supposed to stop any throw that takes longer than two seconds to execute. *That took longer than two seconds, hometown ref!*

The air left my body as I landed on the foam padding below. I was staring up at the hundred-foot-high rafters. It felt like it took forever to stand up.

10-0.

I knew with a sagging dread that this round was over. The psychological impact on the judges of throwing your opponent off the platform was worth much more than the official four points. Unless I was able to knock him off the *leitai* in the next minute and a half, I'd have to win the next two rounds.

As I stepped onto the platform, the realization that he'd dropped me to the canvas, kicked me twice, and tossed me off the *leitai* in less than thirty seconds settled over me like a heavy weight. With absolute certainty I knew he was too good for me. There was no way I was going to win. As we faced each other again, I could hear these words bouncing around inside my skull: *Pride. Too good. Face. Coach Cheng. Pride. Deqing. He's too good. Pride. You're fighting for pride now.*

So I started to dance. I shuffled. I backpedaled. I circled around the ring using my longer arms and legs to keep him out of range. It wasn't Ali, but I was dancing. Shuffle. Punch. Backpedal. Shuffle. Kick. I had generalship of the ring, if only for a brief moment. In my head I was moving faster than in fact I was, but still I held the Champ off for the rest of the round. I'd closed the scoring gap but not enough: 20–10 was my best guess.

The five referees lifted their cards. They were all black for my opponent.

I'd lost the round but salvaged my pride.

But I wasn't thinking about that when I returned to my metal chair where Coach Cheng and Deqing were waiting for me between rounds. As I sat down, I didn't believe I would ever be able to stand up again.

Coach Cheng had my legs up on his knees, rubbing them. Deqing was pouring water into my mouth.

"Keep moving, you must keep moving," Coach Cheng shouted at me.

I could barely hear him over the screaming crowd and buzzing in my ears.

"My legs," I whispered.

"What?"

"My legs. They feel like cement."

"*Mei shi*. Keep moving. Punch, kick, move."

"I can't. My legs, they are so heavy."

"*Mei shi*," Coach Cheng kept saying. "No problem."

It angered me. I wanted him to say it was okay. I'd done enough. I could quit now.

"I am so tired," I said. "I have never been this tired."

Deqing grabbed my face. "Remember what I told you before, 'It takes real courage to fight when all hope is gone.'"

I nodded. But I didn't believe him.

It took both Deqing and Coach Cheng to pull me off the chair. I hated them for doing it. Couldn't they see how tired I was?

The walk to the *leitai* was the longest of my life. It felt like I was underwater. I slunk the ten feet to the platform with my head down. I had to brace my leg to step onto the platform.

I wasn't going to dance anymore. I didn't have the strength. And where's the pride in running? When the referee blew his whistle I charged. My side kick landed. I followed with a right haymaker. The Champ ducked it. We rammed each other in the center of the platform. He had his hands around my waist. I grabbed him around his head. He lifted. I focused my *qi* toward the ground, imagining my feet rooted to the center of the earth, as Coach Cheng had taught us. I couldn't let him break my contact with the *leitai*. He heaved. I held firm. The referee blew his whistle and separated us.

I attacked immediately. I felt wild, the last thrashings of a wounded beast. Left roundhouse to his leg. Right roundhouse aimed at his head. I needed to end this now.

He caught my right leg above his shoulder. My foot had connected with his face—two points—but it was trapped. He was carrying my leg like a log over his shoulder. He placed his right fist in my chest and started running forward. The endless, repetitive loop of a nightmare. I hopped backward until he launched me into the air.

That was longer than two seconds!

I was furious. I wasn't angry that the fight was for all practical purposes now over. I was in a rage that he had embarrassed me. Wounded my pride. All I could see was red. I was going to knock him off the damn *leitai* if that was the last thing I did.

At the first opportunity, I ducked my head and charged him like a linebacker, tackling him around the waist and driving forward with my legs.

He reached down and grabbed me around the waist as I drove him backward. It was the classic defense. You score four points if you throw your opponent off the platform while remaining on it, but if both fighters go over together, no points are awarded, no matter who hits the ground first. I knew he was going to pull me off the *leitai* with him. I didn't care. He was going off and I was going to land on top of him.

I drove to the edge with a shout. He went backward dragging me with him. In vain, I tried to remain on the platform. As I tipped over I decided to jump, so when he hit the foam, I could ram into him with as much force as possible. I even tucked my right shoulder so I'd strike with a sharper point.

I didn't see any visible signs of pain on his face. He was as placid as ever. The referee blew his whistle. No points. But the Champ was on his back, off the platform, and I was on top of him. That was victory enough for me.

For the last thirty seconds of the round, we danced around each other. He scored a few more blows than I did, but it was a formality. The fight was already over on the judges' card and in my mind.

The front cover photo of the special Wushu Festival edition of the Zheng Zhou newspaper showed me shaking hands and grinning with delight at the Champ from the silver-medal position on the top of the platform. The clear subtext was: "Look at how happy the *laowai* is to have had the chance to be defeated by a Chinese champion."

In fact, at that moment, the list had popped up in my head.

THINGS THAT ARE WRONG WITH MATT

1. ~~Cowardly~~
2. Boy/Not a Man

Getting back up on that platform and fighting a hopeless round was the bravest thing I'd ever done. I'd won by losing and in so doing accomplished the goal I'd set out to achieve at Shaolin. I was grinning at the Champ, because I'd finally found my courage.

4

NO PROBLEMS

After the tournament, John Lee followed my bad example and dropped out of college for a year. His cover story for his father was that he wanted to improve his Mandarin Chinese at Tsinghua University in Beijing, a reasonable enough excuse for a Taiwanese manufacturing family. His cover story for me was that he wanted to start a new business and make millions. China was the Wild West for entrepreneurs, he repeatedly told me. This was our moment to strike while the iron was hot. The real reason was that Yeli, the Zheng Zhou dancer, had lassoed his heart, tied it up into a little bow, and attached it to her ring finger.

With the summer over, John had moved to Tsinghua for the fall semester of classes. I had stayed in Shaolin to continue with my training. I wanted to learn how to do backflips.

Early one Sunday morning, Comrade Fish woke me up from a deep sleep to tell me I had a phone call. It was my first phone call in over a year. The village's only international phone worked so infrequently I hadn't given anyone I knew the number, but for a moment I thought I was back in Kansas. For the life of me I couldn't figure out why a Chinese man with brown stained teeth was in my bedroom. Comrade Fish repeated himself several times before I remembered where I was and felt the irritation of having had my personal space violated again.

"What are you doing opening my door?"

"Very sorry, you have a phone call."

"Really? Who?"

"John."

He pronounced it *Jah Ni*. John had a Chinese name, but the locals never used it, preferring to use his English name because, I think, it was a way to separate him from them. Mainland Chinese had mixed feelings about *huaqiao* (overseas Chinese).

Comrade Fish didn't know what John wanted at that hour, only that there was a problem and it was important that he talk to me. It had been over a month since he'd left for Beijing.

"John, what's up?"

"Matt," he whispered. "Is that you?"

"John, I can barely hear you."

"Matt, I'm in trouble, bro," he continued to whisper.

"What is it, bro?"

"Yeli is staying with me."

"With you? I didn't know that." I said. Yeli and I were not on speaking terms, because being young and stupid I had felt it was my duty to tell John that she wasn't right for him (I believe the adjective I used was "gold digger"), and John being young, stupid, and in love felt duty-bound to tell Yeli what I had said.

"Yeah, sorry."

"So what's wrong?" I asked.

"Her ex-boyfriend."

"She has an ex-boyfriend?" I asked.

Yeli was eighteen, about the age good Chinese girls started dating. I had assumed John was her first boyfriend.

"John, I told you not to date a dancer."

"Matt, listen to me. Her ex-boyfriend is here."

"He's a Beijinger?"

"No, he's from Zheng Zhou. When he heard Yeli had moved in with me he came with his crew to bring her back."

"His crew?"

"Matt, you gotta listen to me. Her ex is *hei shehui*," he said. "Black society."

It was slang for "Chinese mafia" or "Triads."

"Mafia? John, this isn't Hong Kong. This is northern China. The rackets are run by army officers. It's the beauty of living in a police state."

"I don't know. Yeli said he had relationships with *hei shehui*. He called the room three days ago. He was outside the building on a cell phone. He told Yeli she had to return with him to Zheng Zhou. When she said no he called her a whore. Said she was only with me for my money."

I came very close to saying, *Well, he was her boyfriend. Maybe he knows something you don't.* But I refrained myself.

"I lost my cool, you know?" John continued.

"Yeah, John, I know."

"I went outside to hit this fucker, but out of nowhere there were like ten of his guys all around me. What was I supposed to do? I barely got away from them and back inside. They've got the building surrounded and keep calling."

"Why don't the officials who run the foreign students' dorm call the cops?"

"They don't want to get involved. Matt, I'm scared."

He said it again in a whisper. I imagined him hunkered beneath the window with the curtain closed and the lights off.

"Don't worry, John. I'll be there," I said without any hesitation or any thought otherwise.

"Thanks, Matt."

"I'll take the overnight train from Zheng Zhou tomorrow. Can you hold out that long?"

"Yeah, I've made friends with some of the African students here. They are keeping us well supplied."

"Good, I'll see you in about twenty-four hours."

Later that morning I went to Deqing and Cheng Hao's room for advice. What did I know about dealing with Chinese mafia members who are insane with jealousy? The sum total of my knowledge about the Triads came from Hong Kong movies starring Chow Yun-Fat. Based on those, I'd need two handguns that I'd have to fire simultaneously while diving horizontally in slow motion through dozens of white doves.

When I finished recounting the situation, Deqing and Cheng Hao looked at each other.

"*Guai guai,*" Cheng Hao said. "Very strange."

He ground out his cigarette and lit another as he contemplated the situation in his cool, silent way.

Deqing turned to me, "Lao Bao, China has a saying, 'Reduce big problems into small ones, small problems into no problems.'"

"Okay."

"But I have a saying," he continued, "'If no problems become small ones, and small problems become big problems, then sword, staff, spear.'"

Deqing jumped off his bed and dug beneath it. He pulled out one of the samurai swords they sell to tourists on the street: The blade was dull but heavy. He told Cheng Hao to get a nine-section whip. Cheng Hao grabbed a heavy version and handed to me. I folded it up and put it in my pocket. Deqing gave me a dagger with a sharp blade.

"You can tuck this into the back of your pants," he said.

The weapons and words of wisdom were nice, but I actually had come to their room looking for a posse. I sat in their room for another hour discussing the problem, waiting for them to volunteer. If I asked for help, they'd be duty-bound to do so, but I couldn't bring myself to put them in a potentially face-losing situation. So I waited until it was obvious to me they weren't going to offer. I'd seen them in too many potential fight situations to think it was fear that held them back. They must have felt I was able to handle this situation on my own. It was a compliment I'd rather not have received at that particular moment.

I spent the next four hours in a cab from Shaolin to Zheng Zhou, the following six inside the Zheng Zhou train station, ten more sleepless hours on the overnight from Zheng Zhou to Beijing in the hard-seat section (the only tickets available) and two more after that stuck in Beijing traffic working myself into a frothing rage about Yeli. It was much, much easier to blame her. This trampy gold digger trades in her psycho Triad boyfriend for a flush Taiwanese-American, and now I have to confront the psycho and his crew armed only with a sword, dagger, and nine-section whip. I told John she was no good. I told him not to fall in love with a dancer. And now this.

So it didn't help when I finally arrived at John's room and Yeli didn't turn around to look at me. It also didn't help that she refused to say anything or in any way acknowledge my presence. It was incredibly rude by any standard. For a Chinese person, it was like spitting in my face.

"What's wrong with her?" I said to John in English.

John shrugged and tried to appease me. "She's upset."

"She's upset? John, I spent the last twenty-two hours traveling to deal with her fucking Triad ex-boyfriend, and she can't say 'hello'?"

"Matt, I'm sorry. She's upset. I'm sorry. Thanks for coming, bro. It's good to see you."

"You too. So where are they? I didn't see anyone outside."

"They left last night. He called and said he'd be waiting for her at the Sunshine Hotel."

"Did he leave a room number?"

"813."

"Does this goombah have a name?"

"Li Hetai."

"Okay," I said, looking around the room at the green carpets and unmade mattresses on the floor. I focused on the closet doors. John had already marked his territory. There were several fist-size holes in the plywood. "John . . ."

"Yeah?"

"You could always send her to him. End this right now before someone gets hurt."

John's gaze dropped. In my anger, I'd put him into an impossible bind: the love of his girl or the safety of his boy. Without being able to look at me, he finally said, "I can't do that, Matt." His voice cracked. "I love her."

That decided it. Love is love, even when it's for the wrong woman. I remembered what that helpless grip felt like.

"Okay then, we'll just have to handle it," I said, standing up. "Better get this over with."

"Yeah," John said, looking down again, letting me know he didn't intend to join me. I knew it was a bad idea for him to come along. Putting John with his uncontrollable temper in the same room with his girl's jealous mafia ex-boyfriend would have been a disaster. But still I wanted him to offer to help. I was starting to feel like Gary Cooper in *High Noon*.

I looked in the mirror to make certain the dagger hidden in the back of my pants couldn't be seen while I was wearing a coat. I refolded the nine-section whip in my right pocket. I thought about taking the sword in my hiker's backpack, but taking the backpack would seem suspicious and there was nowhere else to hide a three-foot samurai sword. Briefly I toyed with the idea of just carrying it, but that seemed an unlikely method to turn big problems into no problems. Still, it would be dramatic: a stunt from the Crazy Foreigner Kungfu School of International Diplomacy. In the end, I decided to leave it.

John and I hugged silently before I left. Yeli did not say good-bye. I returned the courtesy.

The foreign students' dorm at Tsinghua was a two-story building located on a sprawling campus. There was a cobblestone parking lot in front where cabs waited for foreigners in need of rides (Tsinghua was located on the outskirts of Beijing). I told my cabdriver to take me to the Sunshine Hotel.

"Where are you from?" he asked.

"America."

"America is a powerful nation, very rich."

"How long until China catches up?"

"China is inadequate," he said. "It'll take at least fifty years."

I smiled.

"Before we get there, please stop at a shop where I can buy cigarettes."

I fired up a Marlboro as I stood outside the Sunshine Hotel, a run-down ten-story building in a decrepit area of Beijing. I didn't want a cigarette, but to make my threat credible I needed to demonstrate I was a *Zhongguo tong*, China expert. Offering him a cigarette would establish my intention to negotiate a peaceful, face-saving solution, but I needed to make certain I could light one up without my hands shaking.

As I inhaled, my brain went to work trying to figure out how I

had ended up at this moment. I had been interested in kungfu and
Zen Buddhism. I had moved to Shaolin to study them both. I'd become friends with a Taiwanese-American. He fell in love with a local girl. She had a past. A led to B, B led to C, and so on until one
afternoon I found myself in Beijing with a dagger tucked into the
back of my pants about to confront an enraged Triad member who
wanted his girlfriend back.

It took me a minute of smoking and deep breathing before I was
able to reduce the tremors to the point where they were no longer
visible. I put out the cigarette, squared my shoulders, tipped my
chin up, focused my breathing into my stomach, waited for the fear
to let go of my guts, and then walked into the hotel.

A young man in his early twenties wearing thick, black-rimmed
glasses opened the door to 813 when I knocked.

"Is Mr. Li here?" I asked in as polite a tone of voice as I could
manage.

Glasses was startled. It was not every day that a tall, skinny
white boy knocked on his door.

"Who are you?" Glasses asked.

"So sorry to bother you, I have a matter to discuss with Mr. Li."

"He's not here."

"When will he be back?"

"Please, come in. Maybe you can discuss the matter with me."

"Oh, no, no, no, I don't want to waste your time," I said, as I let
him pull me into the room by the arm, an insistent form of Chinese
politeness.

Inside the drab hotel room with its two single beds were two
desks with old IBM knockoff computers on them. Sitting at one of
the desks was a twentyish young woman who was also wearing
thick, black-rimmed glasses. Both the guy and the girl had smooth
faces with a bit of baby fat. They looked completely harmless, nothing hard about them, like a pair of graduate students working on a
special project. Office space was scarce in Beijing, and many hotel
rooms were being rented out to tiny companies.

"You do business here?"

"Yes. Mr. Li is a business associate."

I pulled out my Marlboros.

"Here, here, here, have a cigarette," I said.

"No, no, no."

"Please, please, please. They are good. They are American."

Glasses took a cigarette. The young woman came over to pour us tea as we sat down.

"Where is Mr. Li?" I asked.

"He returned to Zheng Zhou this morning. What did you need to discuss with him?"

A side door connected to the next room. I wondered if the mafia crew was in there.

"It seems he has a problem with my friend, who is dating his old girlfriend."

Glasses nodded. He knew what I was talking about.

"Her current boyfriend is my martial arts little brother," I continued.

The young woman spoke up, "Your martial arts little brother?"

Glasses shot a glance at her to shut her up.

"Yes, I am a disciple of the Shaolin Temple. My martial arts little brother called me in Shaolin to tell me he had a problem in Beijing."

"You came here all the way from Shaolin? Are you *pian* us?" the woman asked. "Tricking us?"

"Why would I want to *pian* you?" I snapped back.

Glassed stared hard at the woman until she dropped her gaze. Turning to me, he said, "I'm very sorry. Please continue."

I tried my best to keep my voice soft and friendly. "Yes, I've just come from the Shaolin Temple where we are both disciples. He is my martial arts little brother. If Mr. Li has a problem with him, he has a problem with me. But my master has a saying, 'Turn big problems into small problems. Turn small problems into no problems.' I want you to tell Mr. Li to leave my martial arts little brother alone. If I have to come back to Beijing, I won't come alone"—I hoped—"and then small problems will turn into big problems."

I leaned forward and lowered my voice, "Do you understand my meaning?"

"I understand."

I stubbed out my cigarette and as I looked at Glasses I suddenly had this vivid image of how I could kill him. With its thin layer of subcutaneous fat, his neck looked plump and weak. I could drive the dagger up underneath his chin into his brain. His female partner was sitting behind a couch. I'd have to leap the couch to grab her before she got to the door. Her neck looked fragile and easy to snap. The temperature of the room seemed to drop. Time slowed. I noticed for the first time the mole on the side of his nose.

"This situation is now part of the past," I said. "There is no need to discuss it again."

Glasses had started to shake. It took me a second to realize what had happened. He had seen the monster behind my eyes. In all the excitement, I had left the cage unguarded and it had wandered dangerously close to the surface. Now I was scared, too.

Trying to quietly backtrack my way out of this situation before the monster did something everyone in the room would regret (them more than me), I said, "You have been very polite. I am sorry I had to discuss this with you. Please let Mr. Li know I was here."

I stood up.

"You don't need to leave," Glasses said out of reflex. There was no conviction in his voice.

"Thank you, but I should go."

When I walked out of the Sunshine Hotel, I was a different man from the one who had walked in there. This time when I lit a cigarette I couldn't get my hands to stop shaking.

Mr. Li never bothered John again, but he did call Yeli to complain about her having sent a *laowai* after him. So he got the message.

5

THE WESTERN SPEAR

As thanks, John invited me to dinner at his favorite restaurant in Beijing: the Pauline Brewhouse in the German-backed Lufthansa shopping mall. (As an added bonus, Yeli refused to join us.) The food was fantastic—hot pretzels served with pâté and butter, fried pig's leg with new potatoes—but I lost my heart to the stunning hostess, Wenqing.

I was gobsmacked the moment I saw her. The porcelain face, the wisp of a body, the jet black, straight hair down to the small of her back (oh, the small of her back!), the sly smile, the dancing eyes. I would do anything to have her: sell national secrets, lead the Mongol horde down from the northern steppes, sack Troy. The one thing I didn't seem to be able to do was speak to her. I just stuttered whenever I tried. John, feeling the helpful pity only a man securely in love can feel for his single buddy, decided he would hook us up. For five nights in a row, he insisted we go to dinner at the German restaurant. By the third night, Wenqing found this immensely funny, "You again?"

"We like the food," John said.

She treated me the way beautiful women treat their more interesting suitors. She smiled while looking away, flipped her long hair, and pretended not to know what I was really there for.

The table conversation between John and me devolved into:

"Talk to her."

"I can't."

"Show some guts."

"She doesn't like me."

"She does."

"Do you think so?"

"Ask her out."

"I can't."

It is painful to realize that courage in the ring does not necessarily translate into courage in romance.

By the fifth night, I was getting desperate. Wenqing was losing interest. Shyness is cute for only so long before it becomes pathetic. John was losing faith. And even the fried pig's legs were losing their luster. I had noticed one of her jobs when walking around the restaurant was to relight any candles that had gone out. So in desperation, I blew out the candle on our table. She lit it and walked away. I snuffed it out again. She was smiling on her next pass around the restaurant.

"What is wrong with your candle?" she asked.

"It seems to be broken, miss," I said, finally finding my voice.

On the third pass, she was laughing, "You are a naughty boy."

"It is not me. It is the candle. Is it German? Their workmanship is inferior."

"No, it is superior."

"For cars, maybe, but not candles."

By the fourth pass, she was mock-angry. "I will not light it again, naughty boy."

"Is it not your job?"

"You will just blow it out."

"I will not."

"You promise?"

"Yes, but only if you promise me one thing."

"What?"

"To give me your telephone number."

She tried to hide her smile by turning around. Through desperation and dumb luck, I had apparently hit on a strategy just dorky enough to seem charming.

She came back to our table with her number on a piece of paper. She held it above the candle and lowered it as if she intended to set it on fire. At the last moment, I blew out the candle.

"You lied to me. I will not give this to you, then," she said and walked away.

But on her next pass she lit the candle and dropped her number on the table.

I called her the next day. After stumbling through some Chinese circumlocutions, she agreed to see me the next night.

The date went well. It was a wonder to actually be able to walk around with a Chinese woman in the open without drawing a crowd, only the occasional dirty look from young Chinese men.

Wenqing had worn her best dress and put on extra red lipstick. She gripped my arm the entire time and kept her face looking at mine, perhaps to avoid noticing the disapproving looks. Feeling confident, I invited her back to Tsinghua's foreign-student dorm.

Tsinghua was fifty minutes by car from the center of town where we'd had dinner. Halfway through the drive she realized how late it was and how far away from her home I was taking her.

"You have to take me back," she said.

"Why?"

"It is too far."

"I had not thought of that."

She laughed, "Naughty boy."

Tsinghua's foreign dorm had its own doorman, who served as a watchman to prevent just the sort of fraternization with the local population I had in mind. But he'd had the job long enough to know there was no way to stop it. Still, there were matters of face to consider, as there always were in China. I'd learned from talking to several members of Tsinghua's large population of African graduate students—they faced far greater prejudice on the dating front than Western foreigners; race riots had broken out in Nanjing, Shanghai, and Beijing in 1988 over the issue, which in a strange twist of fate became one of the undercurrents that led to the Tiananmen Square protests four months later—that the key was to send the girl in first and then follow her, so the doorman did not actually see the two of you entering at the same time. By Henan standards, this was almost libertine.

John had secured a dorm room for us. Wenqing and I sat on the edge of the bed. I offered her a glass of Johnnie Walker Red, which she sipped once before handing it back with a shake of her head.

"Too harsh," she said.

I sat next to her. Her eyes darted around the room. I placed my hand on the small of her back. She pulled away like I'd burned her.

"Okay, okay, okay," I said, removing my hand.

She stood up suddenly, "I need to go home. Get me a taxi."

I stood up. "Okay, okay, okay, I will."

As I stepped closer to her, her knees buckled. She fell into my arms.

"Here, sit down for a second," I said.

We didn't get back up for a long, long time.

How long? I don't trust myself to answer that honestly.

Sometime around brunch, when physical hunger replaced our seemingly insatiable sexual appetite, she stared at me intently as if trying to reassure herself that I was real and what had happened had actually happened. Finally she spoke.

"Do you know what the Chinese saying is for having sex with a *laowai*?"

"No, they didn't teach us that in college."

"*Bei kai yang chiang*," Wenqing said. "To be opened by the Western spear."

I looked down at her, her sweaty hair fanned across the pillow, her face the picture of conjugal bliss, her eyes awed, the most beautiful transformation in a woman's set of expressions, the sunset of lust, and thought to myself that at that moment I had never loved anything more than I loved Chinese culture.

The Western spear! No wonder Marco Polo hadn't wanted to leave.

6

ENDINGS

After the tournament, I spent less time training and more time meditating in the mountains. From the top of Song Mountain, the hectic pace and unsightly aspects of Shaolin village were diminished. From that height, I could see the plots of farmland dotting the valley. It was very contemplative, a great place for epiphanies.

One day I was looking inside myself and discovered that the revenge fantasies I'd been quietly nursing for years against my playground tormentors had magically disappeared. Once you know you can beat someone up, it takes most of the fun out of dreaming about it. Besides, I figured there should be a statute of limitations on childhood bullying. Still, it may be the first time in history that an Irish-Catholic ever voluntarily let go of a grudge.

As far as my kungfu training went, I realized I'd reached the point of diminishing returns. It is easy to be tougher than most, impossible to be tougher than all. And there were limited (legal) career options for that particular skill set. I wasn't the baddest mofo on the planet, but I was bad enough. It was clear to me that I had accomplished almost all of what I'd come to Shaolin to achieve, except one.

THINGS THAT ARE WRONG WITH MATT

1. ~~Cowardly~~
2. ~~Spiritually confused~~
3. ~~Unattractive to the opposite sex~~
4. Still a boy/not a man

One day, as I was working on my unified field theory of religion, I had an insight, which was all the stronger for its obviousness. All the religions disagreed about where the soul went after death. The Western religions (Judaism, Christianity, and Islam) believed that it went to another spiritual dimension permanently (Heaven, Hell, Purgatory, or Sheol). The Eastern religions (Hinduism and Buddhism) believed the soul was reincarnated in another physical body unless enlightenment had been achieved, in which case it was released from the cycle of birth and death. But the point they all agreed on was that we get only one chance with this soul and this body. Even in reincarnation, there is no memory of past lives (unless you're Shirley MacLaine). So even if the soul survives, your current self does not. Life is a one-shot deal. It was like my head opened up and a light was shining down upon it. I would get to be Matt only once.

The next week, as I was meditating on the mountain, the list flashed in my head.

THINGS THAT ARE WRONG WITH MATT

1. Still a boy/not a man
2. No money/career
3. No wife/family

I laughed at myself. I finally realized that while I could eliminate items on the list, there'd always be more to replace them.

While I understood why men choose a religious life, I now knew

I didn't want to spend my life in a monastery. I was a bourgeois boy from a bourgeois society. I wanted a wife, children, and a place in society. If I knew at that time how hard it would be for me to accomplish these goals, I might have reconsidered.

With my to-do list's new marching orders, I started to spend more time in Beijing. China's capitalist fever had fully infected John. He was certain we could leverage our Shaolin *guanxi* into a successful business. After debating various schemes, we finally settled on the idea of a Shaolin Summer Camp. We would set up a travel company to bring American martial artists over to Shaolin to train.

Certainly Wenqing's fiery presence in Beijing made a life of eating bitter in a remote mountain monastery with 10,000 Chinese boys less and less attractive as my time in China came to a close. But after the initial euphoria, it quickly turned into a tumultuous relationship with a lot of crying and a lot of making up. The basic problem was that she was convinced I would change my mind about not wanting to get married, while I was certain I wouldn't. After about six months, when she finally accepted I wouldn't, she left me for an Australian friend, or, as I thought of him, "The Backstabbing Spear from Down Under."

The last time I saw the monks before I returned home was in Beijing. They had a two-day layover before they went on tour in Europe. At their request, John and I took them to Kunlun Hotel, which had the most popular discotheque in town. As the foreign diplomats and Beijing entrepreneurs with their mistresses formed a circle, Deqing, Cheng Hao, Coach Cheng and the rest of the team put on a kungfu/dance extravaganza filled with backflips, flying kicks, and break-dance moves. At the end of the evening, we exchanged addresses and promised to stay in touch.

I was relieved when I first landed on American soil. But the country had changed on me. I found a nation enthralled with the O. J. Simpson case, all-protein diets, and email. It took me several months to stop missing life in a village with only one international phone, a diet with all the carbohydrates you could eat, and political show trials with a 100 percent conviction rate. I returned to Princeton that fall with plenty of material for my senior thesis, but with all of my friends graduated and moving on in their lives, I felt terribly alone, caught between two worlds.

That Christmas in Kansas, my mother threw a party to celebrate her prodigal son's return. She invited all the people in Topeka with any connection to China. Unlike when I'd left, China was now hot. The news media had done a 180-degree about-face. Japan Inc. was moribund. The Asian Tigers—Singapore, Taiwan, Thailand—were small potatoes. By late 1994, the future was with the Rising Dragon. *Newsweek* and *Time* put China on their covers. Hacks across the country were unearthing Napoleon's famous quote: "China is a sleeping giant. Let her sleep, for when she wakes the world will tremble."

A VP from Payless Shoes cornered me. He'd been in China recently to open a factory. He was concerned because he didn't drink alcohol, which seemed to offend his hosts. I told him he needed to bring a designated drinker to cover for him.

"They won't mind if you don't," I said. "But you need an underling to toast in your place."

He said, "Your skill in Chinese gives you a real advantage in the job market. When you graduate, you should send me your résumé."

As the party unfolded, it was clear that my prior faults had become the family's future hopes. My mother was finally pleased I had gone to China.

After the guests had left, I bear-hugged my father. It had been a ritual between us since I was an adolescent. I'd grab him around the waist and try to lift him into the air. As a counter, he'd press his palms against my forehead and push. With forearms that had labored on farms as a youth and had yanked broken bones into place as an orthopedic surgeon, he'd always been able to bend my thin neck back, leaving me staring at the ceiling, overpowered and helpless. But that night, after two years at Shaolin, the muscles in my neck held. Like Hercules, I picked Antaeus off the ground and danced him in the air like a rag doll before setting him down.

My father turned to my mother and said with an awkward chuckle that was both regretful and proud, "My son is too strong for me. I can't beat him anymore. He's a man now."

The list flashed in my head. There was one less item on it.

Amituofo.

EPILOGUE

SHAOLIN REUNION

November 2003

有朋自远方来，不亦乐乎。

"Is it not a joy to have friends visit from distant lands?"

—*CONFUCIUS*, THE ANALECTS

"**D**ude, you have to go back," John told me over the phone. "Everything has changed,"

We hadn't seen each other in a couple of years. I was just telling him that I was finally writing my Shaolin book. Since I'd last seen him, John had done one better than become like his father. He'd become his father. He was married with a kid on the way, and he had replaced the old man as the head of the family company. He was moving to Beijing to oversee operations from up close.

The mainland Chinese call the overseas Chinese who were returning home to exploit their Western-educated skills in China's explosive economy "turtles," because turtles return home to raise their young. John knew a trend when he saw one. After college he had started as a consultant, then a part-time day trader, then head of a dot-com start-up, then unemployed, and had now gone turtle. Chinese-Americans, Taiwanese-Americans, mainland Chinese foreign-exchange students were all returning to the motherland. They were voting with their feet, vivid testimony to China's continued success.

November 2003 was exactly ten years since I had fought in the Zheng Zhou tournament. I decided it was time for my reunion. I was determined to see what was totally new and what had remained the same.

———

The flights to Beijing from the U.S. were now, blessedly, nonstop: no eight-hour layover in the price-gouging Tokyo Narita Airport. But a look at the newspaper gave me a certain chill of déjà vu. As in my first journey in 1992, a Bush was president, and he was presiding over a troubled economy with a massive deficit and a serious unemployment problem. The Asian country that the current President Bush blamed for our troubles was no longer Japan, however; it was now China. It was exporting too many goods (textiles, electronics, bras) too cheaply. One category he left out was female babies, which, from a look at the passengers on the plane, were also a major export. There were a number of white couples with very young Chinese daughters who were going back for another. They spent the flight giving advice to the young white couples who were going to China for their first.

SARS had displaced AIDS as the major concern of the Health and Quarantine Declaration Form on Entry Into China. "Fever, cough, and difficulty breathing" had been added to the "Please check the box before the items of the following symptoms or illnesses if you have any now" inventory. But I was amused to see that "psychosis" was still on the list. It made me think of the Finn Mikael and his sixth race, the French photojournalist Pierre and his boots, the Spanish kungfu instructor Carlos and his nocturnal visit from Jesus, and me and my self-conscious quest for manhood. Extended stays at Shaolin required a bit of psychosis.

Beijing's airport was my first big shock. Mental exclamation marks started firing off in my skull. ATM machines! Sound-dampening panels! Sit-down toilets! Moving sidewalks! Efficient and almost-friendly customs agents! With its recent renovation, the Beijing airport was a good deal spiffier than LaGuardia or JFK.

But I was most excited about the chance to speak with a Beijing cabbie. Conversations with them always started with the same formula. He'd compliment my Chinese. I'd say it wasn't very good. He'd ask where I was from. I'd say America. He'd say America was a great (or powerful or rich) nation—the greatest in the world. I'd say not really. He'd say, oh yes. I'd say, well, China is certainly advancing rapidly. He'd say with a certain degree of frustration, oh no, China's advancement is too slow (or inadequate). I'd say it is getting better every day. He'd say with a certain degree of doubt that it would take fifty (or sixty or a hundred) years for China to be adequate.

I wanted to see if the pattern had changed.

I plunked myself into the cab and asked to go to the Great Wall Sheraton.

"Hey, your Chinese is very good," my cabbie said.

"Oh no, please, there is no need to be polite."

"No, it is very good. Do you live in Beijing?"

"No, I'm just visiting," I said. "I haven't been in China for nearly ten years."

"What do you think?"

"It has changed a lot. China has advanced rapidly."

And this is where he completely ignored the old formula.

"Yes," he said. "China has changed a great deal."

I was momentarily at a loss for words.

Doesn't he want to know what country I am from?

"Ah, yes, just look at the airport," I said, to change the subject. "It is so much better."

"No, it is still inadequate," he said, dismissing my compliment. "They are going to build a much better one down the road in time for the 2008 Olympics."

"Oh right, the Olympics. I remember when I was here in 1992, everyone was disappointed that the 2000 Olympics went to Sydney, not Beijing," I said, with a little bit of concern. The Chinese still held America, who switched its vote at the last minute from China to Australia, responsible for that loss.

"True, we were not happy," my cabbie said. "But it is better this way. Eight more years of preparation. Now the conditions are much better. When we are introduced to the world, the world will respect us."

"The world will give China face," I said, and he laughed.

"Where are you from?" he asked me.

Finally.

"America."

"America is a very rich country."

"Not these last few years. It has been tough."

"Yes, I have read that," he said. "But look at it this way:

America is at the top of the mountain. It is very hard for her to keep going up."

I was stunned. Was that pity?

After a moment of silence, he continued. "But America's economic report for the last quarter was very strong, so maybe things will start to improve."

This made me smile. They were still watching us as closely as ever.

"How long before China is America's equal?" I asked.

"Never happen," he laughed like he didn't mean it.

"Come on."

"Fifty years," he continued still laughing.

The Chinese dream was still the same: to catch up with America. And it was still a multigenerational marathon. But there was a confidence now that wasn't there before. Look at the mile markers they had already passed: membership in the WTO, manned space flights, and soon the Olympics. Catching up with us didn't seem so impossible anymore.

The Green Hotel, where I first stayed in Zheng Zhou, was gone, replaced by a supermarket. The International Hotel was being renovated.

"Its time has passed," my cabdriver, Chang, told me while taking me to the new four-star Sofitel.

He pointed out what is new about Zheng Zhou. But truthfully, it was not much. China's transformation was trickle-down. Huge buckets of foreign capital had flooded the coasts, totally remaking cities like Shanghai and Beijing. By the time this cash flow dripped into the interior its impact was less obvious. There were more cars, fewer bikes on the road, and no oxen, but it was still the same city I remembered.

Chang, who had served in the army for four years, was in his mid-thirties with a paunch and spiky black hair. When he was discharged, he went to work for a state-run *danwei*, or work unit. It went bankrupt—the government had stopped propping up failing state industries. The leader of the *danwei* had absconded with what was left of the general funds to America, where rumor had it he bought an entire street. Now Chang drove a taxi to support his wife and son.

Chang had insisted on driving me everywhere I needed to go. When I asked the price to go to Shaolin, he said it didn't matter, we were friends, my Chinese was so good, it was a pleasure simply to drive me around, I could pay whatever I wanted, I didn't even have to pay.

All of which meant that he intended to squeeze every RMB he could out of me.

I didn't mind. After six years of living in New York City, it had been a long time since anyone thought I was rich enough to waste time trying to rip me off.

Chang was a font of illicit information. *Can guns be bought on the black market?* Yes, for $500 he could get me a German handgun. *Really, it used to be only zip guns.* That was ten years ago. *What about the legal system? Can you still pay a fine instead of serving jail time for murder?* Sure, if you know the right people. *How much does knowing the right people cost?* $15,000 to $20,000. *That's ten times what it was ten years ago.* That was ten years ago.

But it was his military service that interested me the most.

I waited until we had almost reached Shaolin before asking him, "So when you were in the army, who were the enemies you were taught to train against?"

At first he didn't take the bait.

"Oh, no enemies," he said. "We just trained. You know— marching, drills. It was the army."

I didn't say anything in response, letting the silence linger. After fifteen minutes, he finally bit.

"Do you think, and I do not mean to be rude, but do you think America could beat China in a war?" he asked.

"That is not an easy question to answer."

"Oh yes, of course. It doesn't matter," he said. "War is between governments. Not us common folk."

It was the standard preamble for any politically sensitive discussion.

"The common folks always suffer in war," he continued. "We are just talking, two friends, common folk."

"Yes, yes, we are just two friends talking, common folk," I said. "I guess it depends on what you mean by win. On the ocean, probably. On the land, in China, I doubt it."

"Yes, well, America has the most advanced weapons on earth. But America could never take over China."

"I agree. There are too many Chinese."

My last comment revved him up.

"This is just talk, two friends talking," he said. "But that is exactly it. China has five people for every one American. Any Chinese city America might capture, we'd still have you surrounded."

"Yes. And there is the small problem that both countries have nuclear weapons."

"But it will never happen. This is just talk. America and China should be friends."

I agreed with him. But what I was thinking about as he was talking was that before 9/11, many prominent neoconservatives—speaking of nerds with Napoleonic complexes—were shopping around for America's next enemy, and China had been a leading candidate. When an American spy plane was downed on Chinese territory in April 2001 and the Chinese government was tardy in returning our boys, the *Weekly Standard* editor William Kristol went on *Meet the Press* on April 15, 2001, and said, "Well, I think we're engaged in a kind of Cold War with China. I think the right combination of pressure, and some inducements, could work to help topple, ultimately, the dictatorship in China. That should be the goal of U.S. policy, not to get along with dictators who are brutalizing their own people and who are aggressive abroad."

I found myself standing in my apartment and screaming at the TV. "Are you insane? Even the gay Buddhist monks would fight us!"

John Lee had told me what to expect, but the new Shaolin was still a shock. As driver Chang veered off the highway into the half-mile, one-road cul-de-sac of the Shaolin village, my breath caught. This was how I imagined Shaolin would be the first time around, how it was portrayed in countless kungfu movies: a lonely monastery tucked into a valley surrounded by five mountain peaks.

Almost everything was gone except for the temple: all the lean-to restaurants to feed the tourists, all the corrugated-tin-roof shacks selling kungfu tchotchkes, almost all the private schools. Even the sublimely absurd attractions had been removed: the World War II cargo plane with a sign claiming it was Mao's first plane, the ski lift that took tourists up to the top of one of the mountain peaks where they could fire machine guns, and even the 2,000-year-old mummy, which turned out to be an ape skeleton wrapped in cloth.

Kungfu World was no more.

In 1999, Suxi, the legendary acting abbot, had finally succumbed to ill health. He was replaced, as everyone anticipated, by my master, Yongxin. Abbot Yongxin recognized what everyone who lived there did: Shaolin's reputation (not to mention its spiritual life) was seriously undermined by all the tourist trappiness. Capitalism had certainly been better for Shaolin than communism, but it was awfully tacky. But unlike the rest of us, Yongxin had the connections and the authoritarian determination to make the necessary changes. Over the last couple of years, he called in his markers (rumored to have been very expensively purchased) inside the army and police force, and they came into the village and physically removed all the local merchants and knocked down their property—the Maoist version of eminent domain.

As I walked down the street, it was like visiting a ghost town. Over to the left was a movie theater. And next to it was the outdoor stadium. And wasn't that where the Shaolin Kungfu University was? Where were all the people?

Since I had left, the population had dropped from around 10,000 to below a thousand. Where there once was building after building, there was now one big wide-open space with a few cinderblocks lying on open dirt. When the grass grows back, it will be very contemplative. At the moment it looked like it was about to be turned into a huge parking lot. This was what we all had wanted, talked about constantly, but once I saw it, I missed the old tacky village. It had life, vitality. This place felt like coming home to an empty house.

The only significant structures remaining were those that existed prior to the 1980s tourism revival—the temple itself and the

Pagoda Forest—and the few institutions that had enough *guanxi* of their own to resist Abbot Yongxin's iron will: the Shaolin Wushu Center (my former home); Taguo, the kickboxing machine; and the ticket center (you still have to buy a ticket to enter the village, and another to enter the temple).

I stopped for lunch at the Shaolin Wushu Center's restaurant. The place I ate breakfast at every day for two years was one of only three restaurants left in town. Aside from new curtains and a new floor, it was the same: big and awkward. The only person I recognized was the hotel manager, who was wearing the same outfit (black slacks, gray shirt, green leisure jacket) that he had ten years earlier. He sat with me and caught me up on the goings on at the Wushu Center.

Leader Liu had been assigned to another top government post. "He really wasn't Shaolin," the hotel manager said. Deputy Leader Jiao had replaced him in the top spot, as I always suspected he would. He was too devious not to grab control. He was at this moment in Japan negotiating another tour. Coach Yan, my Playing Hands master, was head coach of one of the four martial monk performance teams.

"Four?" I asked.

"They compete with each other," the hotel manager said. "They rotate daily performances. But only one team gets to go on the foreign tours."

It was Machiavellian—just what I should have expected from Deputy Leader Jiao. On the old team, the best performers—Deqing, Lipeng, Cheng Hao, and others—refused to be the quiet puppets the leaders wanted and expected. They also emigrated at inconvenient times.

Cheng Hao had moved to Houston, where he had opened his own studio. So did two other less prominent members of the former team. With three Shaolin monks, Houston now rivals New York City for Shaolin representatives. The two monks who defected in 1992, Yan Ming and Guolin, have schools in downtown Manhattan and Flushing, Queens, respectively. Lipeng also teaches in New York. He originally moved to Holland, where he built up a large school, but came to America when he married a Brooklyn woman.

"She's much older than him, right?" the manager asks.

"Yes," I said. The Shaolin rumor mill was still very effective.

"An older American woman . . . *guai, guai.*" he said, shaking his head. "Too strange."

"They had a child together," I told him.

Deqing's story was the most unique. Due to the vagaries of visa regulations, the best he could do was Hungary, where he was working as kungfu instructor for their military's special forces. I had met up with him two years before—in Las Vegas of all places. A PBS documentary crew doing a feature on overseas Shaolin monks paid for him and two guests to come. He showed up with his mother and a deadly looking Slavic commando who was a blackjack fanatic. Deqing may not have been able to build his mother a new house with all the Hong Kong movie money he dreamed of making, but a free week in Las Vegas was not a bad consolation gift.

As for everyone else, a few have gone to Beijing to try their hand at becoming mainland kungfu movie stars. One was trying his luck in Hong Kong. Several had opened kungfu schools in Deng Feng. The number of kungfu students in that town had jumped from a few thousand to 40,000. The net result was that I knew almost no one at Shaolin anymore.

China was so busy replacing old buildings with new ones that there was little energy for renovations. The Wushu Center was the first place I'd been to that had kept the same exterior structure but received a complete makeover. The courtyard, which had been filled with traditional kungfu training equipment, now had marble pathways that led to stone stools around stone tables that had Chinese checkerboards carved into their surface. It was darling. And inside the main building, I had to stop for a moment. Marble had replaced the cracked linoleum floors and the concrete pillars. The staircases had wooden (*wooden!*) banisters. I walked over to the staircase underneath which Lipeng's father, Doc, and mother used to live. It was a storage closet with walls and a proper door, like something you'd find in a Park Avenue duplex.

The biggest change was the performance hall. Before, it was basically a training studio: one big red mat, surrounded by rows of wooden chairs. Now it had gone Broadway. Stadium seating, a raised stage, and set backdrop, which was a life-size version of the Shaolin Temple's gate.

I slipped in on an afternoon performance. I didn't recognize any of the martial monks. But they were as good as they used to be, perhaps even a bit more professional. No doubt the surround-sound music timed to sophisticated stage lighting helped. The old team, my team, thought of themselves as martial monks first, performers a necessary second. Like actors waiting tables, they were doing it to support their art. The group performing now seemed to take their dramatic job much more seriously. They were breaking bricks over their heads and wooden staffs over their arms with precision and a dearth of emotion. They whipped through their forms (drunken sword, monkey, Shaolin Small Red Boxing) with brio. Shaolin was always unique in having two types of monks: the cultural or Buddhist monks (*wen seng*) and the martial monks (*wu seng*). It seems they now had a third type: the performance monks (*biaoyan seng*).

Afterward, I wandered back to the training hall where I had spilled sweat and blood for two years. It was exactly the same: the same tattered green mat, the same cracked wall of mirrors, the same hand- and footprint-stained white walls (we used to punch and kick them to harden our feet and hands).

One of the teams of martial monks was beginning practice. Their coach was sitting, his foot in a cast. I introduced myself, somewhat wishfully thinking he'd recognize the name, Lao Bao, my legend having lived on (the challenge matches, the tournaments), but it hadn't. Soon I found myself telling him these stories, about how I trained here from 1992–94 and fought in this international tournament, where I placed second. Did I mention there was this big challenge match I fought with a Tianjin master? The coach nodded politely, trying his best to look interested.

A voice in my head said, *You are now officially the sad, old alumnus back on campus to bore the current class with stories of your glory years.*

It took a minute or so of internal wrestling, but I finally managed to stop my ego trip down nostalgia lane and asked him some questions about him and his team.

It was as I had suspected. This new breed had very little connection to the temple. They were extraordinarily skilled martial artists who had basically tried out and won parts in the long-running hit musical *Shaolin's Martial Monks*.

At the back of the Wushu Center, where there were apartments for employees, I ran into two of the martial monks who used to be on my team, Little Wang and Tiwei. They were married with children and running their own kungfu schools in Deng Feng, the nearby town where all the schools displaced from Shaolin had set up shop.

"Are you married?" Little Wang asked.

"No," I said. The still-current list flashed in my head:

THINGS THAT ARE WRONG WITH MATT

1. No wife/family
2. Not enough money

"I had to get married and have kids," Little Wang smiled. "Otherwise, my mother would have killed me."

I asked about my kickboxing instructor, Coach Cheng. We had lost contact with each other, and I was hoping to find him. Little Wang told me that Coach Cheng was working for his older brother, Big Wang (the man who went on the lam when he beat up the nephew of a Guangdong party official), at his new school in Deng Feng. The town was hosting a traditional forms competition tomorrow. I could find Coach Cheng there.

The Shaolin Temple's gate still gave me a thrill of excitement. I could never stand in the courtyard and not think I was in the middle of a kungfu movie. As for the rest of the temple, it was still fairly modest, despite some recent renovations. Shaolin still didn't make the cut in most package tours.

I bumped into the Tall One, Abbot Yongxin's top disciple, in the courtyard in front of the temple. I asked him if our master was there.

"The abbot is in Beijing," he said.

We talked about the changes to Shaolin as we wandered through the temple. It was near dinnertime, so the day-tripping tourists were mostly gone. Inside, I discovered a group of Buddhist monks gathered for evening prayers. Many of them were from other monasteries, because Shaolin was hosting a Buddhism conference. According to the Tall One, Abbot Yongxin had invested a great deal of time and money to rebuild a community of Buddhist monks, a welcome change. It was now even legal for foreigners to study with a monk inside the temple instead of only at the Wushu Center. Currently, at the temple, there was an African-American who had stayed for a year and a German who had crushed my record, having trained for nearly eight years. I tried to be Zen about it when the Tall One told me but failed miserably.

The Tall One teasingly asked if I wanted to run up to Damo's cave for old time's sake. I didn't. It was a steep haul up the mountain behind the temple. The coaches assigned runs to Damo's cave as punishment. We used to joke that Damo stayed meditating in the cave for nine years because he was so exhausted from getting there.

I returned to the Wushu Center's motel. They were planning to replace it next year. They needed to. It hadn't been cleaned since I left.

As darkness descended, the memory of just how lonely and isolated I felt when I first arrived here in 1992 thumped me in the chest. *How did I manage to stay for so long?* And then I remembered. It was the kungfu, the glorious kungfu. Ten thousand of us practicing together in a narrow valley in the mountains of the Middle Kingdom. It was like being wrapped in a cocoon of common purpose. The key was to stay healthy. As long as I was practicing, everything was good. It was only when I was hurt and unable to practice that I felt like I was living on the opposite end of the earth.

As luck would have it, I could not practice with the monks in Shaolin, because I had injured myself before my trip in the most non-bad-motherfucker way possible. I had been engaging in my first ever *Men's Health* "six weeks to perfect abs" program because I was worried that the first thing Coach Cheng would say to me when I saw him was, "Lao Bao, you have gotten fat." (The Chinese are extraordinarily polite about almost everything except physical appearance. "Old fatty" is considered an affectionate nickname.)

And I had managed to pull something in the back of my knee on the treadmill during a workout. Or at least I think that is what happened. I half-suspect the injury was psychosomatic: My subconscious knew my ego would try to prove I still had it in Shaolin, so it took out my knee to prevent a more serious injury.

Whatever the cause, when I found Coach Cheng the next day in Deng Feng, the first thing he said to me was: "Lao Bao, you have gotten fat."

"Yes, master, you know you told me I was too thin before," I said. "Not enough power in my attacks."

"I said gain some weight, not get fat. I almost didn't recognize you. Are you still practicing?"

"Some, not enough."

"Obviously. To practice kungfu you must not fear to eat bitter. You look like you have learned to love to eat sweet."

God, I missed him.

He still had the same sorry excuse for a mustache, still walked with the same hunched shoulders, and still had the same ham hocks for hands that dropped so many of his opponents back when he was a national kickboxing champion.

Coach Cheng showed me Big Wang's school, the Special Shaolin Wushu College. It was one of the five massive kungfu schools that had been built on the highway leading to Shaolin. They each had thousands of young boys studying kungfu and had been built in a phony European-style complete with domes and pillars. It was the Las Vegas aesthetic, faux-coco.

But it was a dramatic improvement.

The kungfu students actually did classroom work in the mornings, math and literature. They used to talk about that at Shaolin, kept promising it, but there never seemed the time, money, space, or will. I always worried about the consequences of training a large number of illiterate boys to be very good with a stick, because so many eventually went on to serve in the army and police force. (When your only tool is a hammer, everyone starts to look like a nail.)

Wandering around town, I mentally apologized to the city of Deng Feng, which a decade ago I considered to be the irredeemable armpit of China, a justification for mass suicide. But when the kungfu schools moved from Shaolin to Deng Feng, the government declared the city a special tourism and economic zone, and just like that it was completely transformed. They even tore down the old, hateful hospital that had tried so hard to kill me and replaced it with a five-story structure with clean, level floors and an efficient staff who wore white smocks and didn't smoke indoors. The difference was so dramatic, it bordered on the miraculous. I started snapping pictures with my camera, much to the surprise of everyone inside.

Big Wang and Coach Cheng threw a banquet to celebrate the prodigal son's return. And being a banquet, there was a great deal of toasting and Playing Hands. I was rusty and lost frequently.

"I can see your patterns," Coach Cheng said.

"Are you married?" I asked him.

"Yes. I have a six-year-old daughter."

"Did you marry—"

But before I could say Shou Ting's real name he shook his head as if mentioning it was bad luck.

"Someone else," he said.

I dropped the topic.

As the *baijiu* took hold, Coach Cheng softened. We reminisced about the time he knocked out the Japanese challenger with one kick, and the time I knocked out the Taguo instructor with several kicks. He reminded me of the time I passed out in the Deng Feng hospital, so I told the story about the time he slipped during the challenge match in the International Hotel. We even tossed in a few stories involving Big Wang so he wouldn't feel like he wasn't the most important man at the table.

After the banquet, we all went to watch the traditional forms competition. The participants were mostly the young students, but there was a seniors category, which in the kungfu world is anyone over the age of forty. Most of the seniors were kungfu instructors from the various schools. They were heartily cheered by their students. The man who impressed me the most, however, was a peasant in his seventies, his gray hair peppered with a few black strands.

He did not wear the flowing silk garb of kungfu forms competitions. He wore what he wore to work every day: a thick blue cotton jacket, gray cotton pants, and traditional black kungfu shoes. His weapon was the *pudao*, a large staff with a thick blade at one end and a spear point at the other. It was not a light performance *pudao*, which was made out of hollow wood with a tin blade for increased ease of movement; it was the traditional version with thick wood and a rusted steel blade, the kind of heirloom handed down from father to son.

His technique was not great—clearly he would not win one of the top three prizes—but he moved with a certain grace. As he slowly maneuvered the *pudao* around his body, pacing up and down the mat, his back bent, it occured to me that he had been practicing this form for at least the last sixty years, which meant he was practicing it during the Japanese invasion, during the Civil War, during the ban on kungfu, during the Cultural Revolution, and during this capitalist explosion in wealth. From the roughness of his hands and the deep wrinkled tan of his face, he had been either a farmer or a manual laborer his entire life, a tough, dusk-to-dawn, backbreaking life. But somehow he had found the time to keep at this form.

All this rolled over me in a wave of unexpected emotion. And as I took his picture, I found myself having to keep the camera against my face to hide the flow of tears, which, loosened by the *baijiu* and mixed with the feelings about seeing Coach Cheng again, wouldn't stop.

When I was twenty-one what I admired most was the tremendous skill of the monks. I wanted to be that good at something, anything. But as I watched this old man, what most impressed me was the devotion. It was what had allowed this culture to survive—and now thrive—despite the traumas. As he finished his form, what I wanted was to love something, anything, as fiercely as he so obviously loved Shaolin kungfu.

Amituofo.

AUTHOR'S NOTE

This book recounts the experiences of the author while he lived at the Shaolin Temple as accurately as his aging, *baijiu*-damaged brain would allow. A few names, however, were intentionally changed to protect the innocent. And as long as he is in a confessional mood, he would like to admit to an occasional reorganization of events for the sake of the narrative. He also wants to fess up to being far less charming and clever in real life than how he has portrayed himself in the book.

ACKNOWLEDGMENTS

吃水不忘掘井人。

"When drinking water, don't forget who dug the well."

—*TRADITIONAL CHINESE PROVERB*

It was about the hundredth time I started a sentence with the phrase, "This one time, at the Shaolin Temple," like I was talking about band camp that my friend and editor Brendan Cahill, hoping to shut me up, first brought up the idea of a book. It took him only five years to convince me to start it and another two for him to cajole me into finishing. Actually, it was more like three years to finish—okay, four, but the point is my life would be very different without Brendan's encouragement, and, frankly, I'll never forgive him for it.

A number of friends and colleagues provided crucial help to strengthen the structure, improve the prose, and reduce the number of errors. Tim Mohr helped me unpack the story and rethink the ending. Elana Zeide offered some keen fashion advice. (Orange is the new black.) Drew Hansen brushed up my prose and provided a great deal of moral support in the early stages. Andrea Fessler helped to rescue several lost chapters and to reign in some of my excessive tendencies as a writer.

Gene Ching, who has taken up Shaolin's cause in America, filled me in on the palace intrigue of recent years and in the process helped me to avoid several grievous mistakes. Jingjing Chen answered countless questions, fixed my horrid *pinyin* spelling, and made crucial suggestions as to how to avoid offending a billion Chinese people. Unfortunately, it was advice I ignored. Marla Geha gently told me when it was time to let go and sat on my chest while

Patrick Mulligan and William Shinker at Gotham Books pried the manuscript from my cold, dead hands.

My unflappable agent, Joe Veltre, was as good on the editorial end as he was on the business side. My creditors owe him a great debt (as in mine) of gratitude. They should also consider sending a thank-you note to Howie Sanders at UTA who deftly made all the movie arrangements with Elizabeth Gabler, Carla Hacken, Drew Reed, and the rest of the wonderful people at Fox 2000. I have final cut, right?

After reading an early draft my mother taught me a new kungfu move: Angry Tigress Washes Cub's Potty Mouth Out with Soap. The book possesses hundreds of fewer curse words thanks to her relentless scrubbing. My sister Shannon's edits were excellent. My father kindly bit his tongue and didn't mention law school once the entire time I was writing.

Finally, I must thank my teachers and friends at the Shaolin Temple who shared not only their knowledge but also their lives with me. I hope this book does their generosity justice.